Mandatory Housing Finance Programs

Morris L. Sweet
S. George Walters

The Praeger Special Studies program—utilizing the most modern and efficient book production techniques and a selective worldwide distribution network—makes available to the academic, government, and business communities significant, timely research in U.S. and international economic, social, and political development.

Mandatory Housing Finance Programs

A Comparative International Analysis

Praeger Publishers   New York   Washington   London

PRAEGER SPECIAL STUDIES IN U.S. ECONOMIC, SOCIAL, AND POLITICAL ISSUES

Library of Congress Cataloging in Publication Data

Sweet, Morris L
    Mandatory housing finance programs.

    (Praeger special studies in U.S. economic, social, and
political issues)
    Bibliography: p.
    Includes index.
    1. Industrial housing--Finance. 2. Housing--Finance.
I. Walters, Sherwood George.   II. Title.
HD7289.5.A2S94   301.5'4   75-19826
ISBN 0-275-09290-9

PRAEGER PUBLISHERS
111 Fourth Avenue, New York, N.Y. 10003, U.S.A.

Published in the United States of America in 1975
by Praeger Publishers, Inc.

Printed in the United States of America

To Our Wives
Sally
and
Sandra

The completion of a book of this character could not be accomplished without drawing upon the work and assistance of others. Among the many who have materially aided us, we particularly want to acknowledge the contribution of the following individuals: Ethienne Baillon, Hill-Fantus Corporation, Paris; Jean Paul Bardin, Union Nationale Interprofessionnelle du Logement, Paris; Paul Brace, formerly Urban Affairs Officer, U.S. Embassy, Paris, presently with Office of Policy Development and Research, U.S. Department of Housing and Urban Development, Washington, D.C.; Raymond C. Ewing, formerly First Secretary and A. Tavecchia, U.S. Embassy, Rome; Susan Ripley, Centro di Documentazione, Milan; Juan Antonio Menendez-Pidal and Francisco Summers, Ministerio de la Vivienda, Madrid; Enriqe Labarca Ricci, Ministeri de la Vivienda y Urbanismo, Chile; M. Popovich, M. Poulton and M. Soic, Yugoslav Information Center, New York; the president, vice-president, and faculty of the Academy of Economic Studies, Bucharest; Michio Noma, Planning Bureau, Ministry of Construction and Yoichi Uchida, Housing Bureau, Ministry of Construction, Japanese government; Heinz Umrath, International Housing Committee, International Confederation of Free Trade Unions-International Federation of Building and Woodworkers, Amsterdam; Dr. Draha Bill, Regional Librarian, U.S. Department of Housing and Urban Development, New York; Edward Schwartzman, New York State Office of Planning Services; Concetta G. Capoen, Chief, Documentation and Publication Branch, Office of International Affairs, U.S. Department of Housing and Urban Development, Washington, D.C.; C. R. Wynn Roberts, International Labour Office, Geneva; Raymond Rabenold, UN Industrial Development Organization, Vienna; Guy Coriden, Bureau of Educational and Cultural Affairs, U.S. Department of State, Washington, D.C.; and Oliver Vesey-Holt, Graduate Business Center, City University, London.

In addition we are deeply indebted to a number of officials and executives in government, commerce, industry, and labor in our field research in Eastern and Western Europe, Latin America, and Japan. These overseas resources should be absolved of any responsibility for any misinterpretation resulting from the translation and incorporation of their remarks into this manuscript.

The contents and conclusions are the responsibility of the authors and should not be attributed to any organizations to which the authors are or have been affiliated or served as consultants.

CONTENTS

LIST OF TABLES AND FIGURE

LIST OF ABBREVIATIONS

AEC	Atomic Energy Commission
AFL–CIO	American Federation of Labor–Congress of Industrial Organizations
AP	Accession a la Propriete
BMIR	Below Market Interest Rate
BNH	Banco Nacional de Habitacao
CCN	Comite Confederal National
CER	Committee on Residential Construction
CESES	Center for Economic and Social Studies
CFDT	Confederation Francaise Democratique du Travail
CGT	Confederation Generale du Travail
CIL	Comite Interprofessional du Logement
CIPE	Interministerial Committee for Economic Planning
CITC	Industrial Centrale of Electronics and Automation
CORVI	Corporacion de la Vivienda
EEC	European Economic Community
EPPC	Employment Promotions Projects Corporation
ERP	European Recovery Program
FHA	Federal Housing Administration
FHLB	Federal Home Loan Bank
FHLMC	Federal Home Loan Mortgage Corporation
FNMA	Federal National Mortgage Association
FO	Force Ouvriere
FTGS	Funda de Garantia de Tempo do Servico (Guarantee Fund for Time of Supervision)
GDP	Gross domestic product
GESCAL	Gestione Case Ai Lavoratori
GNMA	Government National Mortgage Association
GNP	Gross national product
HAP	Housing Assistance Payments
HBM	Habitation a Bon Marche
HLC	Housing Loan Corporation
HLM	Habitations a Loyer Modere
HLM/O	Habitations a Loyer Modere-Ordinaire
HOPE	Home Ownership Promotion Enterprises
HUD	Department of Housing and Urban Development
IACP	Istituti Autonomi Case Popolari
ICFTU/IFBWW	International Confederation of Free Trade Unions/ International Federation of Building and Woodworkers
ILM	Immeuble a Loyer Moyer
ILN	Immeuble a Loyer Normal
ILO	International Labor Office

IM	Interfunctional Management
INA	Istituto Nazionale Assicurazioni
INFONAVIT	Instituto del Fondo Nacional de la Vivienda para los Trabajadores
IRI	Istituto per la Ricostruzione Industrialie
JHC	Japan Housing Corporation
LHA	Local Housing Authority
NASA	National Aeronautics and Space Administration
OECD	Organization for Economic Development and Cooperation
PEP	Political and Economic Planning
PLR	Programme de Loyer Reduit
PSR	Programme Social de Relogement
SMSA	Standard Metropolitan Statistical Area
SVEI	Industrialized Building Development Company
UDC	Urban Development Corporation
UNIL	Union Nationale Interprofessionnelle du Logement
VA	Veterans' Administration

INTERNATIONAL CURRENCY
EXCHANGE RATES

New York City, July 1975

Country	Currency Unit	U.S. Dollars per Unit
Brazil	Cruzeiro	.1260
Chile	Escudo	.000180
France	Franc	.2418
Italy	Lira	.001564
Japan	Yen	.003386
Mexico	Peso	.08006
Romania	Lei	.085*
Yugoslavia	Dinar	.0606

*Tourist dollar; commercial rate is .2012; customs valuation rate is .05.

Sources: Wall Street Journal, July 8, 1975, p. 32; Yugoslav Information Center, New York; First National City Bank, New York; Romanian Trade Office, New York.

Mandatory Housing Finance Programs

1

INTRODUCTION:
A STUDY OF
HOUSING FINANCE

A comparative study of housing programs can have significant value in policy and legislative formulation for housing in the United States and other countries. The continuing search for solutions to the critical housing situation mandates study of any innovation that could possibly have applicability outside the country of origin.

> It is recognized that international comparisons must be of limited scope because of the great diversity of institutional framework among countries. Nevertheless, because all governments wish to accomplish their policy objectives with the most efficient allocation of resources possible, and because experience within a given country may be insufficient to draw firm conclusions as to the most effective means of stimulating housing production, it behooves individual countries to draw on the pool of experience shared with other countries.[1]

The purpose of this study is not to offer the reader exotica or interesting case histories, which lack continuing effectiveness or pertinence on a broad scale, but rather to examine in depth, and separately, the body of experience from various housing programs that have been operational for a good number of years in Western Europe, Eastern Europe, Latin America, and the Far East; to extract from this experience an understanding of the policy and operational problems to a point where a course of action becomes clear; and, finally, to determine the suitability of adoption or adaptation elsewhere.

UNDERLYING CONCEPT

The concept with which this study is concerned has been put into effect in both developed and developing nations. Although industrialized countries, such as France and Italy, are more comparable to the United States than the other countries examined, the experience of less industrialized countries should not be overlooked as potential catalysts of housing policy.

The concept that is explored in depth in terms of history, content, and functions is based on the employment relationship: a mandatory financial contribution based on wages and salaries, either contributed unilaterally by the employer or bilaterally by both employer and employees. The concept has received little attention in housing literature, other than UN reports. To date, we know of no full-scale analysis. In view of the shortage of capital for housing and the failure of so many housing programs, a Seminar on Housing Finance, conducted by the UN Economic Commission on Europe, called attention to the potential importance of this concept and the value to be gained from a careful examination.

> Direct investment by institutional investors and the obligation by employers to invest a certain percentage of the total wage in residential property seem to be of such a size that further investigations are recommended.
> On the whole this source seems to be of a size which would make further information desirable.
> Is housing by employers an efficient and desirable instrument of housing policies?[2]

IMPORTANCE OF HOUSING

In order to justify consideration of a substantive program with a powerful and far-reaching impact on the economy, the need to assist the housing sector has to be demonstrated. Thus:

> Whatever the level of economic development, construction (not only housing) accounts for more than half the gross domestic fixed capital formation of which housing represents 20 to 50 percent and higher percentages can be found in the less developed countries. Thus, construction in economic terms is second only to agriculture in developing countries and to manufacturing in the industrialized countries. Per

capita annual expenditures are estimated to be at
least \$104. Construction in industrialized countries
utilizes as much as 10 to 15 percent of the total labor force. Housing, its infrastructure and related
community facilities account for 10 to 35 percent of
total national investments in fixed capital.[3]

The primary consideration is to ensure that there is adequate
shelter for the populace as contrasted to the use of residential construction as a contracyclical measure. In the United States, there
still are many households in physically inadequate or overcrowded
housing or with excessive rent burdens. Nor has the United States devoted so large a share of gross national product (GNP) to housing as
have other major industrialized nations. Housing has not been a high
priority goal in the United States. As this book is being completed,
the outlook for housing production is gloomy. Inflation, high interest
rates, and lack of mortgage funds are affecting housing. The public
attitude toward growth and environment works against housing. The
national administration follows a policy of downgrading new residential construction in its housing policy.

A higher level of employment and incomes comes from stabiliz-
ing the construction industry and stimulating the national economy in
periods of recession or depression. The allocation of resources to
housing can be antiinflationary, in contrast to the purchase of alternative goods and services. "There is ample evidence that people building a home at all income levels save more, and thus reduce their
other consumption calls on resources."[4] Another consideration often
overlooked is the contribution to national wealth from the housing
stock.

The necessity for housing legislation in the United States to ease
the heavy burden (financial and nonfinancial) of sharp fluctuations in
housing starts is highlighted by the number of short-term cycles
housing starts have periodically undergone since World War II in response to changes in general credit conditions. The stop-and-go rate
of housing activity leads to severe economic dislocations and ineffi-
ciencies. It is costly to construction firms, occupants, and government when building booms, and labor and capital must be attracted,
and there is subsequently a downturn, at which point there is no need
for these resources until the next upturn commences. Construction
teams, composed of skilled craftsmen, are disbanded and then must
be reconstituted. The skilled artisan looks favorably upon opportunities to move to other industries that can also utilize his skills, while
providing him with the employment stability lacking in construction.
The rise in construction costs are borne by the occupant, either in
purchase price or rents.

ECONOMIC ROLE OF HOUSING

In recent years, the economic role of housing has been reevaluated and raised.

> There has been a tendency to minimize the contribution of housing to national output and welfare because of its high capital to output ratio. Such a simplistic approach, however, may considerably underestimate the importance of housing partly because both "capital" and "output" are ambiguous in this context.[5]

Housing may be viewed as a prerequisite for economic growth in developing countries:

> Of comparatively recent origin is the idea that housing and other social overhead investments generate benefits which may be regarded as either necessary conditions for economic growth or, in a more positive way, as instruments contributing to economic growth through the generation of indirect benefits. The essence of this difference is more than subtle. The necessary condition (or "precondition") for development involved providing the tangible equipment —railroads, ports, shelter—necessary to provide for the basics of life for the labor force and the means by which physical resources could be moved. Viewed somewhat differently, special overhead investment increased the pay-off of direct investment in the means of production. In this sense, good housing, as the immediate example, would contribute to improving the quality of labor, thereby increasing productive efficiency.[6]

NEW HOUSING PROGRAMS

What is the best approach to follow in devising a new housing program? Should major political and economic decisions be made because an experiment, model, or simulation technique provided an answer? Much is to be gained from the use of models; however, there is no substitute for full-scale operational results, when available. Logically, a concept has to be developed before it can be made opera-

tional. The actual results of proposed systems can go far afield from
what was anticipated.*

The value of models for housing analysis purposes could be considerably enhanced if improved data were at hand. For example, it
is only recently that the federal government's published input-output
data, a key analytical measurement, have separated construction into
residential and nonresidential categories. The United States is not
alone in neglecting the requisite analysis of the housing sector:

> The output from provision of dwellings stands in ur-
> gent need of a deeper analysis of direct and indirect
> impact on available national resources and foreign
> exchange. With the exception of one study in Japan
> which tends to confirm the much higher rating to be
> given house construction if the linkages are taken
> into account, and a more general analysis in the
> case of Colombia, the overall impact of housing does
> not appear to have been carefully investigated. [8]

All too often, legislation is the result of political factors, a
need to meet the demands of pressure groups or an administration
that wishes to present a housing program identified as its own. A
succeeding administration may later decide to disassociate itself from
the program. It is too simplistic to attribute enactment of new housing
legislation to one such factor. Regardless of how initiated, a most
serious deficiency in the process of enacting housing legislation is the
all too frequent tendency to arrive hastily at a decision without sufficient prior research and analysis.

Congress has neither the time, the temper, nor the staff for
careful inquiry and detached reflection. Nor are the results of for-

---

*In formulating the new and extremely complex maximum base
rent system of rent control for New York City, which subsequently developed serious defects, there was apparently no utilization of the
many years of rent control experience in other countries by such
prominent consulting firms as the Rand Institute and McKinsey and
Company. They were engaged by New York City to devise a replacement for the existing rent control system. An example of the serious
weaknesses that arose is the estimate by McKinsey from sample data
that forms, and error correction requests, for 14,000 housing units
would have to be completed by landlords. But in fact more than
500,000, almost half the number of rent controlled units, were rejected
on the basis of data errors. [7] After the expenditure of millions of dollars in attempting to get the system to work properly, a new city administration decided to either drop or radically revise this system.

eign experience adequately drawn upon as guidelines. To illustrate,
the much discussed housing allowance program is the subject of controlled experiments, which, despite their value, cannot replace the
knowledge that can be gained from a full operational system. There
appears to have been no thorough examination of the ongoing housing
allowance programs that were enacted in other countries many years
ago.[9]

COMPARATIVE STUDIES

Despite intercountry differences in ideology or tradition, there
is often a commonality of experience and problems in the financing of
housing, which should be mined in depth. One viewpoint is that public
problem solving is probably more an adaptive than an inventive art; as
the way nations cope with problems is surveyed, it is surprising how
seldom a really original or revolutionary approach can be found, and,
whether communist, socialist, or capitalist, finally, most problems are
handled by prosaic means.[10]

Studying foreign experience may give more ideas than answers
and could lead to the exploration of new paths. A value to be derived
from comparative studies is that they can help free us from the paraly-
sis of the unquestioned assumption. Premises that are frequently re-
peated become self evident, and that which is customary is accepted as
inherent.[11] To illustrate, prior to commencing this study, the authors
had serious reservations about the feasibility of direct employer involvement in housing for employees; but, as will be seen, an examination of Japanese experience casts doubt on any summary dismissal of
policies by employers of providing housing or housing assistance:

> The value in learning that others follow different
> premises to different conclusions is not to prove that
> ours are wrong, but to compel us to confront the ques-
> tions whether ours are right. New and better solutions
> to our old and difficult problems are more likely to be
> found by a healthy scepticism of what has been taken
> for granted than by spinning new logic from worn prem-
> ises. At the very least we are encouraged to think
> the impossible and to consider the possibility of that
> which has been assumed impossible.
> The value in studying solutions developed by other
> countries, however, is not that they can provide mod-
> els which we can imitate, but rather that they can open
> our minds to fresh ways of looking at our problems and
> suggest new kinds of solutions which we can tailor to

meet our special needs. Looking at foreign law may
teach us nothing we could not otherwise know; we begin to question assumptions which detached reflection would have told us were creatures of habit and
not of reason; we gain a new perspective of particular
legal rules and the problems involved, but the perspective is new only because traditional teachings
have blinded us to the obvious; and the different solutions may be nothing more than we, with a little in-
genuity, should have long ago invented. [12]

Perhaps, on a less ambitious scale, there is value to be derived
from a detailed review of foreign activities; although sweeping innovations might not ensue, policies and techniques that were previously unknown or overlooked could emerge. For example, a management technique or tool may be utilized, while the overall program, of which it
is a part, may not be transferable.

Though the thrust of this study is dependent on comparative analysis, there should also be an awareness of the caveats. Merely because a program has worked well in another country does not assure
that it will work as well everywhere. As has been observed:

All political scientists and economists suspect the
transference of institutions between cultures. It is
a process fraught with pitfalls. The postwar experience of political and economic development has
taught, if it has taught anything, that institutions and
processes are apt to act in rather unpredictable ways
when transplanted to cultures other than those from
which they emerged. [13]

Direct borrowing or transplanting without thorough analysis and
an understanding of the indigenous and interfunctional factors can lead
to failure. Also, the purpose or objective of the study has to be kept
in mind or the end result can be costly and the benefits add up to a
bag of miscellaneous, interesting, and indigestible data.

Work in comparative law is constantly in danger of
becoming little more than the collecting of legal rules
as souvenirs for scholarly display and intellectual
one-upmanship. Elaborate and finely drawn comparisons may have little more meaning and less excuse
than the travelling schoolgirl's collection of foreign
dolls in native dress. This danger is greatest when
the emphasis is on comparing how the law solves

common social problems. Beyond the rootless question of how the law of another country compares with
ours is the practical question of what we can learn
from foreign experience which will enable us to better understand and deal with our own problems.[14]

A lack of success in the application of a concept in the initiating
country should not be a deterrent to a full-scale analysis; the actual
experience with a program's operations can be more potentially significant as a guide to policy formulation than can reliance upon debate,
theoretical discussion without empirical data, or being unduly influenced by the mystique of models and related and "trendy" techniques.[15]
Close scrutiny, the analysis of the actual functioning of a program, and
the isolation of the purely indigenous factors can provide the foundation for serious consideration of the introduction of new housing policies and legislation with which this study is concerned.

NOTES

1. United Nations, Economic Commission for Europe, Committee on Housing, Building and Planning, Financing of Housing (HBP/
SEM.2/2), November 15, 1973, p. 5.
    2. Ibid., pp. 10, 73, 77.
    3. United Nations, Committee on Housing, Building and Plan-
ning, World Housing Survey: Report of the Secretary General
(E/C.6/CRP/1), January 31, 1974, pp. 13-14.
    4. World Bank, Sector Working Paper, Urbanization (Washing-
ton, D.C., June 1972), p. 45.
    5. Ibid.
    6. Leland S. Burns et al., International Housing Productivity
Study, Housing: Symbol and Shelter (Los Angeles: University of
California Graduate School of Business Administration, 1970), p. 2.
    7. New York State, Temporary State Commission to Make a
Study of the Governmental Operation of the City of New York, The
Management of the Maximum Base Rent (MBR) Program by the Housing and Development Administration of New York City—from June
1970 to October 1972 (November 10, 1972), pp. 46-47. Country monographs covering rent control are in International Confederation of
Free Trade Unions/International Federation of Building and Woodworkers, ICFTU/IFBWW International Housing Committee, Problems
of Rent Policy (Brussels, 1967).
    8. World Bank, op. cit., p. 46, fn. 1.
    9. Country monographs covering housing allowances are in In-
ternational Confederation of Free Trade Unions/International Federa-

tion of Building and Woodworkers, ICFTU/IFBWW International Housing Committee, The Housing Situation of Low Income Groups (Brussels, 1970). On allowance experiments, see U.S. General Accounting Office, Observations on Housing Allowances and the Experimental Housing Allowance Program, B171630 (Washington, D.C., March 28, 1974); and Linda E. Demkovich, "Housing Report/Administration Weighing Plans for Low Income Allowances," National Journal Reports 7 (February 15, 1975): 243.

 10. Charles W. Anderson, The Political Economy of Modern Spain (Madison: University of Wisconsin Press, 1970), p. 9.

 11. Clyde Summers, "American and European Labor Law: The Use and Usefulness of Foreign Experience," Buffalo Law Review 16 (Fall 1966): 221, copyright © 1966 Buffalo Law Review.

 12. Ibid., pp. 223, 228.

 13. Andersen, op. cit., p. 164.

 14. Summers, op. cit., p. 227.

 15. Ida R. Hoos, "Systems Techniques for Managing Society: A Critique," Public Administration Review 33 (March/April 1973): 157.

Instituting a mandatory financing program for housing raises the question of whether the housing sector merits special consideration or coequal status with other social and economic needs. If sufficient funds are not forthcoming from private sources, should public policy be directed toward filling this gap? Can a preference for housing investment in terms of resource allocation be warranted in the face of the national requirements for health, education, transportation, and new plants and equipment.

There already exist mandatory provisions in various forms and degrees for the financing of health, transportation, and education. Health care is reimbursed from Medicare contributions, and some form of health insurance tied to a payroll tax is probable. The gasoline tax is a source of funds for transportation. Various state constitutions mandate free public education. Revenues for education at the local level, for the most part, come from an override on property taxes, but this system faces an overhaul, as court decisions have demanded that expenditures for education be equitably allocated statewide. Thus, the concept of mandatory financing in the United States is not revolutionary.

HOUSING NEEDS

Any discussion of housing priorities has to explore the extent of housing needs before considering comparative priorities. Despite the questions that are raised about measurement, there is no gainsaying the existence of a severe housing shortage. A full-scale discussion of the subject of measurement could preempt any examination of the theme of this book; needless to say, it is a reflection of inadequate expenditures and time lags for censuses and information-processing systems that there still remain serious inadequacies in the measurement of the condition of the housing stock. Yet, there has been progress in the determination of housing needs; the approach has become more sophisticated in recognizing that an aggregate figure, specifying x number of units as the total needs, is no longer sufficient. This changed emphasis is reflected in two 1973 studies: America's Housing Needs: 1970 to 1980 and World Housing Survey.[1]

The 1967 Kaiser Committee report[2] resulted in the formulation of the housing goals of 26-million units needed between 1968 and 1978. The 1973 Joint Center for Urban Studies report, American's Housing Needs: 1970 to 1980,[3] was critical of the Kaiser Committee's approach to measuring housing needs; it contended that the Kaiser report seriously underestimated the degree and dimensions of housing deprivation in the United States as being between 6 million to 8 million households.

In turn, the Joint Center, on the basis of a behavioral approach and eschewing simple aggregates, estimated that 13.1 million households in 1970 were suffering from some form of housing deprivation and that there would still be 5 million substandard units in the 1980 inventory. The housing deprivation figures consist of 6.9 million households living in physically inadequate housing, 700,000 in overcrowded conditions, and 5.5 million with an excessive rent burden; there was no double counting. The 13.1 million households represent a sizable proportion, 21.4 percent, of the total number of households (63.4 million) in the United States. The Joint Center could underestimate the number of deprived households in limiting them to households with incomes no greater than $10,000; $10,000 is not an adequate income for all households, for example those residing in New York City. If the income constraints were relaxed, the number of housing-deprived households would rise to 15 million.[4] Another weakness, not of the authors' doing, is the measure of physically inadequate units. The 1970 Census lacked even the subjective standards of the 1960 Census in measuring the condition of housing and housing needs.

The study points out that there remain serious housing deficiencies for many Americans and makes no attempt to draw public policy implications, even though the study was intended to make the methods and data developed by the project directly useful to policy makers in government and industry for their assessment of the likely effectiveness of housing programs. A Federal Home Loan Bank (FHLB) working paper found that the forecasts have too high a degree of error to be the basis for housing policy recommendations.[5]

In viewing housing demand in broader terms than housing deprivation, demand is projected by three studies as averaging between

2.3 million and 2.9 million units annually for the 1970–80 decade, or a total of 22.9 million to 29.1 million units (see Table 2.1).

Since this study is not only concerned with housing in the United States, worldwide housing needs are also investigated. The UN World Housing Survey[6] reaffirmed the conclusions of previous UN studies that housing conditions in general continue to deteriorate at an alarming rate. It concluded that numbers drawn from a comparison of statistical units could be misleading, since they measure the potential process of development in relatively developed countries. The number of dwelling units does not adequately express the different housing needs of the inhabitants of countries in regions with different climatic, social, and economic characteristics, where varied solutions are feasible in terms of housing construction. The implication is that simple quantitative terms are no longer sufficient and that a new entity of measurement has been devised without presenting any aggregate figure of need. This entity is the "useful housing solution" needed to take care of a household under differing standards, for example, a house, a mobile housing unit, a natural shelter, or a tent. They could be comparably calculated but have variable basic physical characteristics.[7]

The need for increased housing investment in the United States is pointed out by the 41 percent of occupied units built prior to 1939.[8] Also the United States is devoting a relatively smaller share of its GNP to housing than the major Western European countries. Despite the high rate of new construction in 1971, the U.S. investment as a percentage of GNP was 4.0, a rate below those countries, except for the United Kingdom; the rate for the Federal Republic of Germany was 5.9 percent and for France, 6.9 percent. An index, with 1960 or 1961 as 100, of the investment in housing as a percentage of GNP reveals that the United States dropped to 87 in 1971, whereas the United Kingdom showed no change, with a rise to 104 in Germany and a sharper rise to 147 for France in 1970.[9]

Putting aside the comparisons with the Western European countries, housing in the United States has been a low-priority goal. From 1962 to 1969, while GNP rose 37.5 percent, expenditures for housing fell 5.5 percent (see Table 2.2). Looking ahead, based on National Planning Association economic projections, the estimated cost of attaining the goal standards in 1980 for housing is $83.1 billion (in 1969 dollars), and the 1980 expenditures are estimated at 67.5 percent of goal requirements.[10]

In and of themselves, dollar figures or percentage allocations may be a symbol of national commitment, but they tell little of the extent to which goals are being achieved or the efficacy of the expenditures. Not to gainsay the importance of dollars as a prerequisite to progress, allocations within existing programs are not always the

TABLE 2.1

Projections of Housing Demand, United States, 1970–2020
(thousands of units)

Years	Number				Percentages			
	Total Demand	Net Increase in Households	Replacement	Net Increase in Vacancies	Total Demand	Net Increase in Households	Replacement	Net Increase in Vacancies
1970–80								
Marcin[a]	25,594	12,764	8,994	3,836	100.0	49.9	35.1	15.0
MIT-Harvard[b]	22,850	14,660	6,660	1,530	100.0	64.2	29.1	6.7
Kokus[c]	29,108	14,480	12,225	2,403	100.0	49.4	41.9	8.6
1980–90								
Marcin	27,570	12,646	11,694	3,230	100.0	45.9	42.4	11.7
Kokus	30,110	10,880	15,015	4,215	100.0	36.2	49.9	13.9
1990–2000								
Marcin	27,277	10,262	13,461	3,554	100.0	37.6	49.3	13.1
2000–10								
Marcin	32,381	12,553	15,463	4,365	100.0	38.8	47.8	13.4
2010–20								
Marcin	34,726	12,666	17,751	4,309	100.0	36.5	51.1	12.4

[a]Thomas C. Marcin, Projections of Demand for Housing by Type of Unit and Region (Washington, D.C.: Forest Service, U.S. Department of Agriculture, Government Printing Office, May 1972).

[b]Joint Center for Urban Studies, Massachusetts Institute of Technology and Harvard University, Toward Housing Goals for the United States: Concepts, Methods and Measures, commissioned by Department of Housing and Urban Development (Cambridge: The Joint Center for Urban Studies, MIT and Harvard, August 15, 1973), p. 5.

[c]John Kokus (for the National Association of Homebuilders' Financial and Economic Studies Task Force), Projection of Future National Housing Demand 1970–1990 (Washington, D.C.: National Association of Homebuilders, 1974).

Source: "Strong Long Term Housing Demand Forecast," Economic News Notes for the Building Industry, National Association of Homebuilders, 19 (December 1973): 3–4.

TABLE 2.2

Expenditures for National Goals, United States, 1962 and 1969
(billions of 1969 dollars)

Goal Area	1962	1969	Percent Change 1962-69
GNP	678.0	931.4	37.5
Urban development	84.0	94.7	11.0
Housing	37.5	35.4	-5.5
Other urban facilities	46.5	59.3	13.0

Source: National Planning Association, Changes in National Priorities During the 1960's: Their Implications for 1980, prepared by Leonard A. Lecht, Report no. 132 (Washington, D.C.: National Planning Association, September 1972), p. 13.

best course for achieving objectives. In many instances, policy, programmatic, or institutional changes should be given equal or higher priority than increased dollar allotments.

The low priority accorded to housing, combined with an aging inventory, indicate that there is a lack of replacement housing and inadequate maintenance of the existing stock. However, housing makes up an important share of national wealth and has to be replenished:

> If there is anything which chiefly characterizes a modern industrial society, it is the possession of a large stock of capital assets of houses, factories, warehouses, office buildings, dams, machinery and other facilities designed not to be consumed but to be a means, and together with labour, of producing goods and services. The importance of such a stock to the achievement of a high standard of living is well enough illustrated by the eagerness with which so called underdeveloped countries seek to increase the amount and variety of their capital equipment. Different endowments of natural resources have of course a most significant bearing on differences in national wealth, but natural resources without the capital equipment to exploit them are only potential riches, and by and

large countries with high standards of living are also
countries with relatively large stocks of capital equipment per head. [11]

The low priority given to housing raises the issue as to whether
the housing inventory will continue to deteriorate to a point similar to
the position of railroads and utilities, where the obsolescent plant and
equipment demand massive expenditures for replacement. Housing
built in recent years lacks the durability of older housing, and there
could be a more immediate need for replacement housing. [12]

THE INTERFUNCTIONAL CONCEPT

Too often, the housing issue is regarded merely as one of
economics. But it is far from that: it is both interfunctional and interdisciplinary. It is interfunctional in that it involves more than
one department or function of government, for example, not merely a
housing or development agency but also planning, finance, public
works, education, police, fire, and sanitation. A housing program
is inadequate unless it also encompasses neighborhood and community
improvement.* It is interdisciplinary in that it not only cuts across
more than one discipline of economics but across other disciplines as
well, such as psychology, sociology, and anthropology. Whatever the
function or discipline, there are many gaps within and among them as
they pertain to housing. A caveat should be expressed in respect to
the interdisciplinary approach, that is, the ease with which the interdisciplinary can deteriorate into the undisciplined. [13]
Using the interfunctional management concept, that is linking
diverse functional areas in business and government, could lead to

---

*A differing viewpoint is expressed by the results of the 1971
Quality of Life in America Survey by the University of Michigan Institute of Social Research, namely, that the most important reason for
moving concerns the house itself, not the neighborhood or larger community. These findings challenge the conventional belief that it is
the negative environmental factors that cause people, especially in
urban centers, to seek new homes. For those who have lived in one
place for less than 11 years, the implication is a "need for 'adaptable'
housing or replacement of obsolete structures quickly and efficiently
with minimal disturbance to the encompassing neighborhood, or a
combination of the two." ("Desire to Move Is Tied to Housing Rather
Than Poor Community Services," Institute for Social Research, University of Michigan Newsletter 1 [Winter 1974]: 7.)

the formulation of housing programs that interrelate increases in productivity, wages, and profits with the availability of funds for housing.

The need for an understanding of interfunctional and interdisciplinary theory does not only apply to housing:

> Interfunctional management and analysis concerns
> those problems which cut across more than one busi-
> ness or government function. They are problems,
> the solution of which call for theories, concepts and
> analytical tools drawn from more than one business
> function and in many cases from more than one dis-
> cipline.
>
> In a sense, it is unfortunate that organizational
> behavior was invented one hundred years or more
> after economics. Economics focuses on specializa-
> tion. For the most part, we have organized our
> business schools and schools of administration on
> the basis of specialization by function. The concepts
> of Interfunctional and Interdisciplinary are hard to
> come by in that sort of environment. [14]

Returning to the gaps in knowledge, it is all too often at the national level—where key decisions are made—that there is a lack of
realization of the necessity for research, as witnessed by the decision of the federal government to forego the continued construction of
input-output tables for the national economy. The tables show product
flows from one industry to another and are invaluable in perceiving
how the economy functions and the various interrelationships.

The first officially compiled input-output table for the U.S.
economy was for the year 1947. After the release of the 1947 table,
practically all work was discontinued until 1962, putting the United
States far behind France and somewhat behind West Germany. [15] The
1958 and 1963 tables were not released until some six years later
"As the nation reconsiders its priorities, such improvements of the
statistical system as this must be seriously reconsidered, both for
their scientific value and for their potential contributions to wiser decisions in areas of national policy." [16]

There is a need for expediting the publication of input-output
data and for an immediate special housing census to be followed by
more frequent censuses than decennially. This would provide a sound
basis for setting housing goals, developing programs, and determining national, state, and local appropriations for housing. The HUD
Annual Housing Sample Survey, started in 1973, is an intermediate
but not final step in this direction.

A more recent illustration of the failure to understand the importance of housing in the economy is the response by a Department

of Housing and Urban Development (HUD) official to the chairman of the House of Representatives Appropriations Subcommittee for HUD, Representative Edward P. Boland, who asked: "Have any economic analyses been taken by the Department to determine the short and the long-term consequences of this curtailment? What has been the effect on jobs, housing production, gross national product and that sort of thing? If you don't have the answers to it, you may supply that for the record." Deputy Assistant Secretary Kearney of HUD replied: "I would like to point out that the economic and market analysis section of Housing Production and Mortgage Credit is geared to analysis of housing needs and market demands in various communities and the determination of appropriate income levels. It is not a broad based staff support function for the Department." Boland then asked: "But the Department would be interested in what effect the curtailment would have upon jobs in the Nation; would it not?" Kearney replied: "Certainly."[17]

An examination of the activities of HUD's Office of Policy Development and Research reveals no programs to explore Congressman Boland's areas of concern.[18] Perhaps this is not the sole responsibility of HUD but rather of an interagency or interfunctional consortium. The answers to the Congressman's questions could be invaluable to state and local governments and private and nonprofit organizations concerned with housing policy.

The gap with regard to basic research in housing should be filled. The period of enchantment with glamorous consulting firms has been followed by one of disillusionment, because of the often questionable performance accompanied by high fees.[19] Agency in-house capabilities, supplemented by the occasional use of outside professionals, have all too frequently, in recent years, been allowed to falter but should be revived and continued.[20]

Ideally, housing should not be considered as a contracyclical measure:

> The use of housing investments as a tool for counter-cyclical short-term economic policy is not to be recommended, both because reductions in housing production may jeopardize social objectives of housing policy and because the effectiveness of such measures occurs after too great a time-lag. Moreover, a "stop-go-policy" disrupts effective planning and continuity of construction operations, thus contributing to higher building costs.[21]

The primary concern of the government should be the provision of the proper number of housing units in terms of needs:

> Housing is needed primarily, however, not to provide
> employment to workers, profits to businessmen, or
> fees to professional groups, but rather to supply a ba-
> sic service. The primary purpose of a housing pro-
> gram should be to see to it that an adequate supply of
> housing that meets recognized standards of health
> and decency is available at charges commensurate
> with family incomes. [22]

However, the economic impact of housing is so widespread that
it has to be examined in a broader context than merely the provision
of shelter.

ASSIGNING PRIORITIES

The efforts to give housing priority are illustrated by the introduction of legislation in Congress to give the Federal Reserve Board
the power to allocate credit on the basis of social priorities, for example, in 1971. The proposal would have imposed varying reserve
requirements on different types of asset; for example, to increase investment in housing relative to plant and equipment, the board could
set higher reserve requirements on business loans and lower requirements on mortgages for housing. This would tend to increase the return on mortgages relative to the return on business loans. At present, reserve requirements can be set only against bank deposits or
liabilities. The board has opposed legislation that would give it the
power to influence the allocation of credit, contending it was the role
of Congress to make such determinations.

The disinclination of the Federal Reserve Board to assign priorities has continued. In September 1974, the Federal Reserve Advisory
Council to the Board of Governors of the Federal Reserve System issued a statement on commercial bank lending policies. The council
commented:

> A regrettable aspect of restrictive monetary policy
> is that it tends to produce an uneven impact, bear-
> ing more heavily on some sectors of the economy
> than others. Therefore banks should make an effort
> to utilize their limited funds equitably, giving con-
> sideration, for instance, to the special vulnerability
> of the home building industry. [23]

In turn, the board recognized that "an active home-building industry is vital to the well-being of local communities as well as of

the nation as a whole, and it is to the interest of banks and other financial institutions to give reasonable support to the financial needs of
that industry."[24] Federal Reserve officials have always contended
that the central bank in the United States has no responsibility for the
individual sectors of the economy.

> However, in the actual application of this policy, the
> credit of the nation has been allocated unevenly with
> the larger and more affluent elements of the society
> willing and able to outbid the more needy sectors in
> the fight for the available funds. As a result, essen-
> tial areas of the economy—such as housing, urban
> development, state and local governments—have been
> consistently starved for credit, leaving the country
> with enormous backlogs of unmet social and economic
> goals.[25]

The passive role of the Federal Reserve, which Congress has
not overruled, contrasts with the actions of other central banks, who
actively promote national economic and social goals. Central banks
in most countries select particular sectors of the economy for prefer-
ential treatment. Housing and agriculture generally obtain more favorable consideration, since the effects of general credit restrictions
are much more severe in those sectors than in the general economy.[26]
The effect on the national economy of residential construction
is far-reaching and is not confined to the expenditures directly made
for housing.* "The income that is received by individuals as a result
of such expenditures appears again and again in the economy in the
form of income to others as each set of recipients pays it out in consumption expenditures or taxes."[27] The multiplier effect for such
expenditures has been calculated at two. The multiplier represents
the approximate contribution to GNP directly and indirectly within a
year from the residential construction expenditures. The National
Association of Home Builders' chief economist, Michael Sumichrast,
calculated the multiplier effects in 1967 of 1.5 million housing units,

---

*An example of the far-reaching effects of housing expenditures
is the ripple effect of a housing slowdown in reducing the income of
the city railroad in Pineville, Oregon. The reduction reflects the
cutback in the forest-products industry and a substantial drop in the
annual payment by the railroad to the city for its operational budget.
In turn, the city property taxes would have to be increased. (Editorial, Central Oregonian, October 3, 1974, in Congressional Record,
120, no. 158 [October 17, 1974]: S19407.)

TABLE 2.3

Multiplier Effect of Housing Expenditures on 1.5 Million Housing
Units, United States
(in billions of dollars)

Expenditures	Cost
Single–family housing	
Construction	16.0
Site improvement	2.2
Multifamily housing	
Construction	5.0
Site improvement	1.0
Related expenditures	
Community development (schools, churches, highways, utilities)	4.0
Additional direct expenditures (brokers, title companies, fees, and the like)	1.5
Durable goods and furnishings	3.0
Total	32.7
Multiplier effect—2 × 32.7	65.4
Related services (taxes, interest, heat, insurance, maintenance and operating)	2.0
Total dollar effect	67.4

Source: U.S. Congress, Senate, Committee on Government
Operations, Subcommittee on Executive Reorganization, Hearings on
Federal Role in Urban Affairs, 90th Cong., 1st sess. (Washington,
D.C.: U.S. Government Printing Office, April 20-21, 1967), pt. 17,
pp. 3547-48.

with direct costs of $33 billion as $67 billion (see Table 2.3). Each
home built provides about two man-years of employment, half on site,
half off site. A study in the state of California indicated that every
job created on a building site produced an additional 1.57 jobs.[28]
    In 1973, the Nixon administration declared a moratorium on any
new commitments for subsidized housing, and it was contended that
this affected new commitments for the construction of 450,500 units.
The economic impact of utilizing the aforementioned multiplier of two

was estimated to be $19,298 million, and, with a factor of 115 workers employed for one year for each $1 million spent on all building and related services and facilities, resulted in a loss of 2.2 million man-years of employment (see Table 2.4).

TABLE 2.4

Multiplier Effect of Housing Expenditures on 450,500 Housing Units,
United States
(in millions of dollars)

Factor	Cost
Construction costs	7,497.7
Supporting facilities	1,403.7
Total	8,901.4
Multiplier effect—2 × 8,901.4	17,802.8
Related services	1,495.2
Total dollar impact	19,298.0
Man-years lost: ($19,298 × 115) = (2.2 million)	

Source: U.S. Congress, House, Subcommittee of the Committee on Appropriations, Hearings on HUD-Space-Science-Veterans Appropriations for 1974, pt. 3, Department of Housing and Urban Development, 93rd Cong., 1st sess. (Washington, D.C.: U.S. Government Printing Office: 1973), pp. 69-70.

HUD differed with the contention that the suspension of the subsidy programs in 1973 would have an adverse impact on housing-related investment, on incomes, and induced consumption expenditures, as measured by the multiplier of two. According to HUD, in 1973 there are two fundamental deficiencies to this assertion.[29]

There is considerable controversy among economists as to the appropriate value that should be used for the multiplier. The value of two is not unreasonable but economists of the monetary school would take a value closer to one.

Second and more important, can fiscal and monetary authorities permit the multiplier process to work itself out at a stage of the business cycle when the rapid growth of the economy at that time was quickly closing the gap between actual and full employment output? Any further stimulus would run the risk of the economy overshooting the target and intensifying the already too powerful inflationary pressures. Continued subsidies would result in a tightening of monetary policy or a tax increase.

The end result would then be aggregate demand and employment levels no higher than those being experienced.

The HUD comments about the inflationary impact in a full-employment economy could be turned around when a slackening of demand called for a policy of expanded housing production to absorb underutilized resources.

In human terms, the critical resource is labor. Though a full-time position in construction involves over 1, 800 hours of work per year, construction workers average only 1, 000 hours of construction work per year.[30] The lack of employment opportunities in the construction field creates problems in terms of retaining a stable and permanent labor force. Because of the insecurity, craftsmen may tend to avoid this field. Prospective apprentices question the value of the long training, for which there may subsequently be no jobs. With more stable employment, there would be less pressure to restrict admission to labor unions. By reducing the fluctuation, there would be a decrease in overtime payments. Without a permanent labor force, transient and temporary workers with questionable qualifications are hired. There is the pressure for wages to compensate for periods of inactivity.

Andrew Brimmer, former member of the Board of Governors of the Federal Reserve Board, in an address to the National Urban League in 1966 stated that, traditionally, construction and related industries have been important sources of employment for Negro men: "Historically the construction and related industries have been prime sources of employment opportunities for Negro men. . . . Thus, with the persistent decline in construction activity, a considerable share of the adverse employment impact has been borne by non-whites."[31]

Analagous to the stabilization of employment is the need for better utilization of heavy equipment. When the fluctuations in construction can be mitigated, the costs for purchasing or borrowing equipment for short periods of concentrated activity are reduced.

INFLATION

The adverse impact of counterinflationary measures on housing is well-enough known, and this analysis of mandatory allocation of funds for housing has to face the question of whether the inflow of funds into the housing sector would accelerate inflationary pressures, with dire effects on the economy.

The viewpoint has been expressed that larger, not smaller, investments, not fewer, but additional, people at work, more goods and services, not less, should be channeled into the proper noninflationary sectors. The confusion stemming from antiinflationary efforts is that there is no distinction between "nonsense" production to serve human prestige and vanity instead of the fundamental needs of shelter and food.[32]

Should inflation be fought by increasing production and investment in selected sectors through curtailment of production or through forced savings?[33]

> Imagine the surprise of a man from outer space if he arrived today and was told inflation was our number one problem and that we were fighting it primarily by "cutting back on production and investment." Clearly, he would think we were mad to try to bring down prices by creating supply shortages. Yet that is what present policy depends on.
>
> We cannot continue a completely demand-oriented policy that assumes our problems can be solved primarily by decreasing spending and so cutting back on the production of goods and services. We will end up both with far fewer goods over the next several years and with a greatly reduced level of capital, thus making inevitable both lower production and a more inflationary prone economy in the future.[34]

Housing is a good example of where increased production can offset inflation. With a housing shortage, rents and prices of existing housing rise and serve to force up the wage-price spiral. An adequate supply of housing has a deflationary role. It enables workers' purchasing power to be maintained and relieves some of the pressure for wage increases. As compared to expenditures on services or goods with relatively short impact or lives, an influx of resources into housing could lead to an adequate supply with a long life span, thus neutralizing inflation.

With the exception of 1949-50, all major expansions in housing starts have taken place during periods when nonresidential construction was stagnant, if not declining. The noninflationary implications are that there would be no overexcessive demand for labor, materials, and financing simultaneously.[35]

HEALTH, EDUCATION, AND THE ENVIRONMENT

An analysis of housing-related influences has to be multifaceted, particularly if the intertwined problems of poverty and slums are to be mitigated or eliminated. The concentration on the low-income group in this section does not preclude the existence of many comparable difficulties for middle- and upper-income persons and communities.

The existence of blighted housing and slums entails enormous expenditures of public resources, with additional private costs. It is not only the slum dweller who suffers; there are the spillover effects, when the spread of fires, disease, and crime reach outside the slum. [36]

Health professionals are aware that no appreciable improvement in the health status of certain population groups can ensue solely from good medical care services unless there are related efforts to improve environmental conditions:

> Acceptable health care for the individual cannot be provided in a contaminated environment. In this nuclear day, citizen's understanding of adequate health care must make a quantum jump forward to acceptance of a tenet long advocated by alert public health agencies; that personal and environmental health are inseparable. [37]

A number of ecological studies have indicated that population groups living in a disorganized environment in deteriorating housing are more prone to accidents and physical and mental illness than those residing in satisfactory housing. [38]

> More than a casual relationship has been demonstrated to exist between inadequate housing and a variety of social morbidities, which like unemployment, poverty and poor education, interfere with the attainment of good social health in the community; and in many instances, a direct association can be seen between the health conditions of residents and the physical condition of the housing in which they live. The relationship of peeling paint to lead poisoning in children, and of broken stairs, defective and inadequate lighting and rotted window sills with inadequate or nonexistent window guards to the incidence of certain accidents in the home is clearly demonstrable. In addition, broken and defective plumbing systems, inadequate heating in winter, infestations of insects and rodents, and poor man-

agement and disposal of waste can be directly associated to the incidence of infections and infectious
diseases. [39]

A review of 40 studies, 16 of European and 24 of American
origin, investigated the relationship of housing to physical and social
pathology. [40] In 26 of the studies (English and American), a positive
association between housing and health or housing and social adjustment was indicated. In other words, poor housing tended to go with
poor health and adjustment, better housing with better health and adjustment. The results of 11 studies were ambiguous or showed no relationship between housing and the dependent variable. Only 3 clearly
had negative findings; they dealt with death rates, tuberculosis, and
mental hospital admissions.

A three-year cross-sectional study beginning in 1954 in Baltimore had two samples, a test sample of 300 families who moved to a
new public housing project and 300 families who elected to remain in
the slums. The basic conclusions were as follows:[41]

> The adjustment findings, stressing the more mod-
> erate rather than the pathological manifestations of
> adjustment, were less dramatic than had been expect-
> ed. In this connection, it must be remembered that
> for all the housing improvement, many other circum-
> stances that would be expected to affect a way of life
> remained substantially the same. These were still
> families at the lowest end of the economic scale.
> Practical family situations remained materially unim-
> proved; in one-third of the families there was no hus-
> band present; and one-third were on public welfare.
>
> The morbidity findings were considerably more
> substantial. Even in a three-year period, incidence
> of illness and disability was markedly reduced in bet-
> ter housing circumstances. This was true, as sev-
> eral of the cross-sectional researches reviewed had
> suggested, of younger persons and particularly of
> children.
>
> The data concerning schools suggested an inter-
> weaving of social and physical variables. School
> promotions, while probably affected by intelligence
> and intellectual achievement as in more general
> school samples, is apparently also related in a sig-
> nificant way to attendance at school. Attendance in
> turn is a function of illness and health, in which hous-
> ing circumstances seem to pay an undoubted role.

Housing plays a critical role in the education of low-income children, especially in connection with overcrowding. Opportunities for study are restricted due to the scarcity of space in which children can study. [42]

The subculture of despair, bitterness, and violence that stems from spending the early years in a slum environment is a handicap that is not without its price in later life. By providing improved housing and less overcrowding early in life, the psychological pressures that lead to higher rates of mental illness in low-income adults than in higher-income groups can be alleviated. For those individuals who are severely disturbed, it is questionable that a change of housing in later life can have great significance.

The resolution of the complex social and physical environmental factors affecting the poorly housed calls for an interfunctional approach. Housing is, and must be, a key component of the solution; yet, potential changes in federal housing policies becloud the place of new housing in any environmental upgrading.

The efforts to institute a program of housing allowances in place of the production-oriented housing programs, in effect since the 1930s, would furnish poor families with monetary allowances to find their own housing, without any geographic restrictions. Funds for the construction of new housing already have been curtailed.

What is the fate of the problem family under the new system? Will they be capable of finding better housing at a reasonable rental outside slum areas? What new types of medical and social service will be needed if they are dispersed and no longer concentrated?

If federal funds for new housing in slum areas are no longer available, will the physical environment deteriorate even further? Will those families with sufficient motivation leave the slums, which could then become an area occupied only by the hard core poor, beset by insurmountable and intractable problems? There has been little study of the impact of housing allowances on those major cities where new construction is most urgently called for.

HOUSING AND ENERGY

Though the immediate effect on the overall energy picture may be relatively small, new housing can, over a period of time, be an important means of conserving energy. New housing can be effective in terms of more economical heating, air conditioning, and waste disposal systems. A panel of construction industry experts affirmed that over the short run, a one-third drop in energy consumption in new buildings was probable by means of combinations of design innovation and the use of existing and "new" insulating materials. [43]

An obvious source of energy savings would be the reduction of automobile travel. To bring about such a reduction, is there a possibility of a massive relocation bringing residences closer to workplaces, as well as a decline in urban sprawl? One view is that this type of shift is unlikely because increases in gasoline prices are not going to cut deeply enough into the pocketbook of the average American family to cut automobile usage. Low-income groups are likely to continue using the automobile but to go to cars that burn less gas. In Europe, despite the high retail price of gasoline, high auto taxation, less personal income, and strong controls on urban growth, the spread of suburbanization has continued unabated. [44]

Another viewpoint is that there will be pressure on firms to move job opportunities from the cities to the suburbs so workers in the suburbs can live closer to their place of work. [45] It is highly improbable that the energy crisis will cause firms to move merely to be closer to employee's residences. There are more critical determinants of location. Furthermore, the work force of a particular concern is apt to be fairly well dispersed throughout a metropolitan area, so that no one location would be entirely satisfactory.

The probability is that over a period of time, new housing will reflect the influence of the need for energy conservation, and, as workers make a choice in terms of housing sites, they will give major consideration to accessibility and alternative modes of travel, with an eye to minimizing commutation costs. There will be a gradual diminution of traveling long distances to work. Obviously, the sooner a high rate of housing construction is brought about, the earlier would these energy conservation measures come into being.

CONCLUSIONS

In terms of determining the proper priority to be assigned to housing, it should not be done with the intention of allocating a level of resources so a specific construction volume can be attained, for which no effective demand may exist, nor, necessarily, to assign housing a higher ranking than for other basic wants.

As to demand, the United States is far from being faced with the predicament of a surplus of housing; rather, it is one of allocating an adequate share of national resources to housing in the face of competing claims for these resources, for example, credit. A severe housing shortage still exists in which both the public and private sectors, singly or in combination, have been unable to attain the desired level of construction.

Regarding competing claims for resources, Supreme Court Justice Lewis S. Powell in the case of San Antonio Independent School

District v. Rodriguez ably stated that basic wants cannot readily be
ranked hierarchically:

> How, for instance, is education to be distinguished
> from the significant personal interests in the basics
> of decent food and shelter? Empirical examination
> might well buttress an assumption that the ill-fed,
> ill-clothed, and ill-housed are among the most in-
> effective participants in the political process, and
> that they derive the least enjoyment from the bene-
> fits of the First Amendment.[46]

Housing does have a special role in the solution of social and
economic problems. Education, health, and social well being are adversely impacted in an environment marked by deterioration and
blight. Though housing cannot be the primary vehicle for solving social problems, the physical and social environment can be signifi-
cantly enhanced by an improved housing stock. Housing can be built
much more quickly than can severe intergenerational economic and
social family problems be cured. There is also a greater degree of
predictability as to what can be accomplished in terms of expenditures
and results, as witnessed by the many ambitious and costly govern-
ment-financed programs, whose legacy has been one to failure.

The ability of the public sector to alleviate social ills is limited
by more than just money. Even the highly publicized "wars" on such
pressing social problems as poverty, crime, and hunger have not
yielded benefits commensurate with their costs; these skirmishes
have, in fact, told us more about which approaches will not work than
which ones will. If this country pursues the strategy of considering
every possible interpretation and every possible solution to complex
social problems, it will run out of time and resources before it can
exhaust all the possible, albeit imaginative, alternatives that can be
produced by its legions of governmental administrators, consultants,
and academicians.[47]

NOTES

1. Joint Center for Urban Studies, Massachusetts Institute of
Technology and Harvard University, America's Housing Needs: 1970
to 1980 (Cambridge: Joint Center for Urban Studies of MIT and Harvard, 1973), and United Nations, Committee on Housing, Building
and Planning, Eighth Session, World Housing Survey: Report of the
Secretary General (E/C.6/CRP/no. 1), January 31, 1974.

2. United States, the President's Committee on Urban Housing, A Decent Home (Washington, D.C.: Government Printing Office, 1968).

3. Joint Center for Urban Studies, Massachusetts Institute of Technology and Harvard University, op. cit., ch. 2.

4. Ibid., pp. 4-6 to 4-8.

5. Marshall A. Kaplan, Review of "America's Housing Needs: 1970 to 1980" Joint Center for Urban Studies of the Massachusetts Institute of Technology and Harvard University, Office of Economic Research, Federal Home Loan Bank Board (Washington, D.C.: Federal Home Loan Bank Board, May 14, 1974), p. 3.

6. United Nations, World Housing Survey, op. cit., p. 13.

7. Ibid., pp. 92-93.

8. U.S. Bureau of the Census, "Vacancy Rates and Characteristics of Housing in the U.S.: Annual Statistics 1973," Current Housing Reports, Series H-111-73-5 (Washington, D.C.: Government Printing Office, 1973).

9. UN Economic Commission for Europe, Committee on Housing, Building and Planning, Financing of Housing (HBP/SEM.2/2), November 15, 1973, p. 68.

10. National Planning Association, Changes in National Priorities During the 1960's: Their Implications for 1980, prepared by Leonard A. Lecht, Report. no. 132 (Washington, D.C.: National Planning Association, September 1972), p. 34.

11. Yves Dube, Housing and Social Capital, Royal Commission on Canada's Economic Prospects (Ottawa: J. E. Howes and D. L. McQueen, January 1957), p. 1.

12. Wallace F. Smith, "Should a House Last 300 Years?" Socio-Economic Planning Sciences 7 (1973): 723, Reprint no. 84, Center for Real Estate and Urban Economics, Institute of Urban and Regional Development, University of California, Berkeley.

13. Ida R. Hoos, Systems Analysis in Public Policy—A Critique (Berkeley: University of California Press, 1972), p. 39.

14. S. George Walters, "Interfunctional Management: A New Dimension of Management Education," Proceedings New York University, Graduate School of Business Administration—Annual Meeting, October 11 and 12, 1973, Middle Atlantic Association of Colleges of Business Administration (New York: New York University), p. 76.

15. Wassily Leontief, Input-Output Economics (New York: Oxford University Press, 1966), pp. 7-8.

16. Anne P. Carter and Wassily W. Leontief, "Goals for the Input-Output Data System in the Seventies," Survey of Current Business 51, pt. 2 (July 1971): 29.

17. U.S. Congress, House, Subcommittee of the Committee on Appropriations, Hearings on HUD-Space-Science Veterans Appropria-

tions for 1975, pt. 6, Department of Housing and Urban Development,
93rd Cong., 1st sess. (Washington, D.C.: Government Printing Office, 1974), p. 349.

18. Ibid., pp. 1196-267.

19. Hoos, op. cit., pp. 243-44; and Douglass B. Lee, Jr.,
"Requiem for Large-Scale Models," Journal of the American Institute
of Planners 39 (May 1973): 163.

20. Maurice L. Spreiregen, "The Bureau of Planning and Program Research: Functions of a Research Bureau in a Redevelopment
Agency" (Master's thesis, New York University, 1966).

21. "Housing Shortage for Low-Income Groups in Southern Europe," Human Settlements 4 (July 1974): 41.

22. Ramsay Wood, "Housing Needs and the Housing Market,"
Housing, Social Security and Public Works, Postwar Economic Studies, no. 6 (Washington, D.C.: Board of Governors of the Federal Reserve System, June 1946), p. 1.

23. Federal Reserve Press Release, September 16, 1974.

24. Ibid.

25. U.S. Congress, House, Committee on Banking and Currency,
Staff Report, Activities by Various Central Banks to Promote Economic
and Social Welfare Programs, 91st Cong., 2d sess. (Washington,
D.C.: Government Printing Office, December 1970), p. v.

26. Ibid., p. 2.

27. M. L. Colean and R. J. Saulnier, Economic Impact of the
Construction of 100,000 Houses (Chicago: The United States Savings
and Loan League, December 1961), p. 3.

28. Wallace J. Campbell (President, International Cooperative
Housing Development Association and Foundation for Cooperative
Housing), paper prepared for International Cooperative Housing Conference of the International Cooperative Alliance, Warsaw, Poland,
September 1972, "Cooperative Housing and Development with Particular Concern for the Less Developed Countries," in Towards New Priorities for Housing (Washington, D.C.: Foundation for Cooperative
Housing, n.d.), pp. 8-9.

29. U.S. Congress, House, Subcommittee of the Committee on
Appropriations, Hearings on HUD-Space-Science-Veterans Appropriations for 1974, pt. 3, Department of Housing and Urban Development,
93rd Cong., 1st sess. (Washington, D.C.: Government Printing Office, 1973), pp. 73-75.

30. Craig Swan, "Labor and Material Requirements for Housing," Brookings Papers on Economic Activity 2 (Washington, D.C.:
The Brookings Institution, 1971): 355.

31. U.S. Congress, Senate, Committee on Banking and Currency, Subcommittee on Housing and Urban Affairs, A Study of Mortgage Credit, 90th Cong., 1st sess. (Washington, D.C.: Government
Printing Office, May 22, 1967), p. 152.

32. UN Economic and Social Council, Committee on Housing, Building and Planning Report of the 8th Session, October 15-26, 1973, Official Records, Suppl. 2 (E/5447.E/C.6/140), 1974, p. 10.

33. Horace J. de Podwin and W. Giles Mellon, "In Lieu of a Surtax: Forced Savings," Letter to Editor, New York Times, November 2, 1974, p. 28.

34. Sherman J. Maisel, Statement, the President's Conference on Inflation, Atlanta, Georgia, September 12, 1974, p. 4.

35. Swan, op. cit., p. 348.

36. Jerome Rothenberg, Economic Evaluation of Urban Renewal (Washington, D.C.: The Brookings Institution, 1967), pp. 160-75.

37. National Committee on Community Health Services, Health Is a Community Affair (Cambridge, Mass.: Harvard University Press 1967), p. 40, quoted in Courtney B. Wood et al., "An Experiment to Reverse Health Related Problems in Slum Housing Maintenance," American Journal of Public Health 64 (May 1974): 474.

38. Wood et al., op. cit., p. 476, fns. 2-5.

39. Ibid., p. 474.

40. Daniel M. Wilner and Rosabelle P. Walkley, "The Effects of Housing on Health, Social Adjustment and School Performance," paper presented at the 39th Annual Meeting of the American Ortho-psychiatric Association, Los Angeles, March 23, 1962.

41. Ibid., p. 12.

42. Oliver C. Moles, Jr., "Educational Training in Low-Income Families," in Low-Income Life Styles, ed. Lola M. Irelan (Washington, D.C.: Department of Health, Education and Welfare, Social and Rehabilitation Service, Office of Research and Demonstration, 1967), pp. 42-43.

43. Marketing Research Committee, Producers' Council, Inc., "Delphi Study, Forecast of Events Influencing the Construction Industry" (Washington, D.C.: Producers' Council, Inc., 1974).

44. B. Bruce Gibbs, "Gasoline Prices and the Suburban Way of Life," The Public Interest, no. 37 (Fall 1974), pp. 135-36.

45. George H. Brown, "Suburban Sprawl and the Energy Situation," The Conference Board Record 11 (November 1974): 35.

46. 93 S. Ct. 1299 (1973).

47. U.S. Department of Health, Education and Welfare, Office of Human Development, Administration on Aging, Indicators of the Status of the Elderly in the United States, prepared by the Institute of Interdisciplinary Studies, DHEW Publication, no. (OHD) 74-20080 (Washington, D.C.: Government Printing Office, 1974), p. 1.

3

FRANCE:
AN INNOVATOR
IN HOUSING

As contrasted to the assertions of a lack of leadership in the field of management, most notably by J. J. Servan-Schreiber,[1] France, historically, has been a pioneer in the area of fiscal policy and taxation. "The tax systems of the Western world have been transformed over the 40-year period starting with the outbreak of World War I. In that transformation France has played, and is still playing, a leading role as innovator . . . no country has surpassed France in number of major innovations in taxation over the past half-century."[2] France can also be described as the originator of such taxing practices as the sales tax, value-added tax, income tax, business tax, land tax, and international tax arrangements.

In few countries are tax incentives as numerous or as varied as in France. Tax incentives to scientific research and development, to export, to the modernization of plant and equipment, to adaptation to competition within the Common Market, to the merger, reorganization, and consolidation of the industrial structure, to regional development and the decentralization of Paris, and to housing construction—all these, and more, may be found in the French tax system. . . . The weight and burden of French taxes . . . make these incentives all the more effective. The greater the weight of taxation, the greater the leverage the government can exert by means of "detaxation."[3]

Among the fiscal innovations for which France is a pioneer is the mandatory contribution by employers, based on wage and salary payments to be utilized for the construction of housing. France, for

some years, has been ahead of such countries as the United States,
Great Britain, and West Germany, as well as all of Eastern Europe,
in respect to construction of new housing units in relation to population. Between 1945 and 1958, an average of 128,000 new housing units
were completed annually. By 1960, the figure reached 295,000, and,
in 1972, there was an estimated completion of 540,000 housing units. [4]

BACKGROUND OF THE LEGISLATION

In France, at the time of the initiation of the mandatory contribution in 1953, there was a severe shortage of housing and an overaged
housing stock in poorer condition than that of other Western European
countries. At the start of the twentieth century, the quality of French
housing was equal to that of surrounding countries. At that time, the
government had not yet entered the housing field but had undertaken,
in response to the requests of philanthropic organizations, to provide
low-interest loans for low-cost housing developments (see p. 46).

During World War I, France did not suffer widespread housing
destruction, but there was a loss in respect to the housing that would
otherwise have been built and the deterioration from the lack of
maintenance. Other problems arose from the war, such as a moratorium on rents due from servicemen and their families and the rent
freeze, which was extended until 1926, after which gradual increases
were permitted.

As part of the 1926 rent control legislative changes, maximum
rents were instituted for all housing, including new construction.
"In fact during the next decade, rents for new housing were too low
in relation to building costs, so that real estate, long a favored investment for the French bourgeoisie and _rentier_ class, rapidly ceased to
attract sufficient capital." [5]

In the following decade, rampant inflation and the world economic problems deterred any substantial housing construction. Of
even greater consequence for housing, the family budget became permanently imbalanced, with too high a share going to food and other
consumer goods, leaving too little for rent; as a consequence, rent
control was retained by legislation until 1939.

Further compounding the severe housing shortage was the re-
jection by French governments of programs to replace traditional
financing methods with direct public investment, as in Austria, Britain, Germany, and Holland. The lack of private funds for housing
could have been offset by the availability of public funds. However,
in 1922 and 1928, legislation was enacted allowing the government to
grant loans. The loan arrangements were deemed trifling and inadequate. [6]

Prior to World War II, French industry assisted in providing
housing for employees, either through individual companies building
housing themselves or, in certain regions, by the cooperative efforts
of local industry. Thus, France entered World War II with a severe
housing problem.

> Her buildings were old and maldistributed, both
> geographically and in terms of family needs, mod-
> ern conveniences did not exist for the mass of the
> people, new buildings lagged behind demolition, so
> that the situation was constantly deteriorating. The
> combination of low fixed rents and mounting infla-
> tion meant that real estate was no longer a profit-
> able field of investment, and the public were becom-
> ing accustomed to assume that rent should be a neg-
> ligible factor in the family budget.[7]

World War II worsened the housing problem. Destruction was
even greater than in World War I: 1.3 million dwellings were dam-
aged and 450,000 totally destroyed.[8] The country entered the postwar
period with a shortage of manpower and materials. In 1914, there
were 950,000 building trades workers, skilled and unskilled, and in
1945, 602,000.[9]
During the building decline of the 1920s and 1930s, many construction workers left the industry. Adding to the difficulties was the
inefficient or low productivity. The larger and more efficient construction firms concentrated on public works, while the smaller and
more inefficient firms engaged in housing.

> However, although the problem of labor of material
> and the inefficiency of the industry (shared it should
> be noted by France's neighbors) are considerable,
> the real difficulty and the constant factor always to
> be emphasized in discussing French housing is the
> disincentive provided by the whole body of French
> housing legislation . . . the control laws and the
> trifling loan arrangements obtaining during the inter-
> war years when construction lagged so badly.[10]

After liberation, the impact of inadequate rents, the slowdown
in construction between the two great wars, and the devastation from
World War II were compounded by a sharp rise in the birthrate, growing urbanization, and demands for improved housing quality. The result was a severe housing crisis.
Opposition to raising rents in the late 1940s was based on the
contention that the price of food should be stabilized first, but price

controls on food were not effective. Nor did rent rises have much effect in stimulating housing construction. With family budgets unable to absorb sizable rent increases, consideration turned to the use of ample housing allowances to allow rents to reach an economic level adequate to attract private capital for new housing.

> Given a public authority which is unwilling to enter
> directly into the building of low rental housing and
> which gives relatively little aid to cooperative and
> other semi-public housing associations, such a con-
> cealed subsidy appears as a possible solution to the
> impasse. It has the further advantage of channel-
> ing any aid available to those groups and persons
> most favored by the Government—families with
> young dependent children.[11]

HOUSING ALLOWANCES

In view of the preference expressed for housing allowances as the replacement for federal housing programs, an examination of the French allowance program is merited. The allowances should not be confused with the mandatory contribution by employers. It is surprising that, despite the extent of the consideration given to housing allowances as a solution to housing problems in the United States, the preferred approach has been a stress on theoretical studies and limited controlled experiments as the basis for legislative decisions, rather than an in-depth examination of the French and other European programs.

The first housing allowance system began in January 1944 with the family allowance fund of the Roubaix-Tourcoing employers association.* It was actually a carryover of a special cost of living bonus paid in 1941 to all textile workers in the area and was calculated as a percentage of the rent paid by the family in accordance with the gov-

---

*"In 1943, Northern France textile manufacturers requested Albert Prouvost to find a solution to the housing shortage. He convinced the employers to set up a rent allowance program in proportion to the monthly rent and the size of the family. The allowance varied from 20 percent for a young married couple to 50 percent for a family with four children. Rent increases were made possible and led to private and public funds being invested in the construction of new housing." (Letter, Albert Prouvost, March 11, 1974.)

ernment policy of a rise in proportion to the number of dependent children. It was followed by a building levy, which subsequently became official policy.

The allowance plan was gradually adopted by other employer associations. In 1944, the cost borne by industry was 4 percent of wages; in March 1945, with inflation and rising wages, the percentage dropped to 2.9 percent, and, in June 1945, to 1.48 percent. When the allowance in 1948 was supplanted by an official housing grant, the cost was only 0.9 percent of wages paid that year. The allowances were based on the amount of rent paid: 25 percent for a family of two persons; 40 percent for three persons, 50 percent for four persons, 80 percent for seven persons, and 90 percent for eight persons.

The legislation finally enacted in 1948 had been enthusiastically sought for several decades by family associations and other concerned groups, but the results were disappointing. There was agreement that the system in terms of calculation was unduly complex; furthermore, because of the acute housing shortage, families eligible for the allowance were unable to upgrade the quality of their housing accommodations by moving. Thus, those occupying the worst housing generally could not move, even when able to pay higher rents. "Finally, the allowances suffered by being associated with the rise in rents. Most people regarded it simply as a device for enabling the state to bear part of the burden."[12]

The housing allowance system has evolved into several different types of aid: dwelling allowances, rent allowances, and removal premiums. The dwelling allowance is an addition to the family allowance. It was instituted in 1968 and is available to tenants, subtenants, and purchasers of housing. The family or household must devote a minimum percentage of its income toward rent payments or repayment of a loan for the purchase of housing. Rent allowances are payable to the low-income aged, to the handicapped, and to those neither aged nor infirm but below a stated income level. Removal premiums are given to persons who move to improved housing as part of urban decentralization measures and to persons who leave a locality with over 10,000 inhabitants to move to a community with fewer than 10,000 inhabitants.[13]

While the housing allowance system received much attention as an imaginative device for subsidizing family housing, the more traditional method of low-interest loans to various building and housing organizations was not entirely ignored by postwar governments.

SEARCH FOR SOLUTIONS

In the postwar search for a vigorous housing program, there appeared to be two prerequisites. The first was to affect a reversal of the public thinking about housing; the second was to locate the institution or program capable of assuming the role formerly held by the private sector with private capital and determinedly spurned by local authorities and the state.

The public's attitude toward housing was indicated by a 1946 survey on the percentage of income considered reasonable for rent, excluding heating costs and local taxes but including other service charges. Some 60 percent said a fair rent was 10 percent or less of family income, while 17 percent said 7 percent or less of family income.[14]

In the first half of the nineteenth century, a number of housing innovations were originated by employers in Roubaix and Tourcoing, in northern France, located near the coal fields. Numerous model housing projects in the area were started and successfully administered. They were sponsored by municipalities or, perhaps more frequently, by charitable or unusually intelligent manufacturers.[15] The growth of the cities was based on textiles, the major industry.

Throughout the nineteenth century, the introduction of new machinery and new materials stimulated the region's growth, which has slowed since 1900. At that time, the twin cities were classic examples of early industrialism, with a mediocre record in terms of health, slums, poverty, and other social problems. Long before it became official policy, a textile employers' association was among the first organizations to adopt a system of family allowances; they were followed by a building program to provide housing for employees, funded by an annual levy on members of the association.

As an aftermath of the payroll tax, the association's activities were expanded, and, in 1943, Le Comite Interprofessional du Logement de Roubaix Tourcoing was formed. It covered all employers in the area, which had a population of about 300,000. The goal was to replace the 15,000 slum dwellings with modern, inexpensive housing. Employees were to be encouraged to buy homes through an affiliated organization, Union Mutuelle Immobiliere de Credit, with financing from a 1 percent levy and, later, a 2 percent levy on each member's payroll. Immediately after the liberation (World War II), labor unions were invited to participate in the fund's activities. By 1953, administration was in the hands of a board of 16 employers' delegates and 16 union representatives. For the textile industry, collective bargaining agreements had special provisions to guarantee employers' contributions.[16] As a result, Roubaix has housing conditions that are among "les meilleures existant dans les grades villes francaises" ("the best existing in large French cities").[17]

The credit for such innovations as the rent allowances and mandatory contributions started at Roubaix-Tourcoing (and subsequently adopted by the national government) should be ascribed to Al-

bert A. Prouvost, head of a major textile manufacturing firm. He
rejected any indication of paternalism, whereby the worker would be
dependent on the employer for housing. His program was intended to
function on a broader scope than just the individual firm, preferably
on a regional basis. In order to build housing, the efforts of employers with the collaboration of employees were to be encouraged by the
government.[18] Prouvost's enterprise still survives, and "there is
a certain wooliness woven into its complex corporate structure."[19]
"Prouvost" is the international identity mark for a number of separate
firms but related through "rather crisscrossed ownership lines and
together informally known in the trade as the Prouvost Group."[20]
(The Group, a recognized world leader for combed wool and all syn-
thetic fibers, both in diversity and volume, has plants in the United
States.)
        The question of what public agency should replace the private
sector and its capital to provide housing for the majority of the populace was equally troublesome, since

> The possibility of national and local authorities di-
> rectly accepting responsibility is slight. Nor is
> there popular demand for this. There is, on the
> contrary, widespread suspicion of government in-
> terference. Direct labor construction such as that
> undertaken by many local councils in Britain seems
> at present out of the question. The substitute fre-
> quently mentioned in recent writings on the subject
> is the employers' associations. And these appear
> to be willing to undertake the task if only as a coun-
> terpoise to the dirigisme implicit in the direct
> housing efforts of the great nationalized industries.[21]

        The housing record of the nationalized industries was particu-
larly good. The proportion of employees in these enterprises occupying new housing or buying new homes was much higher than was generally found throughout the country.

> Of course if the employers subsidized and built low
> cost housing for their workers, the cost would be
> passed on to the consumer. Such a plan would cer-
> tainly be opposed by organized labor, since it would
> tend to "tie" the house to the job. In addition it
> would seriously restrict the mobility of labor, a con-
> sideration in a country with so widespread a man-
> power shortage, it might create solid groups of ten-
> ants of approximately the same income level and

type of employment rather than diversified communities; and it would burden small and medium incomes
disproportionately, since the cost would be reflected
in all types of consumer goods.[22]

The favorable experience with the industry contribution for
housing originating at Roubaix-Tourcoing led to the enactment of legislation on July 11, 1953, to give the government the authority to make
contributions mandatory. On August 9, 1953, Decree 53-701 was issued, setting forth the conditions under which industry must participate. With the passage of the legislation, union participation was considered no longer necessary.

The legislation was enacted during a period when the government, by means of the Second Modernization and Reequipment Plan,
was attempting to stimulate economic activity, by raising the level
of housing construction, as well as to alleviate the critical housing
shortage of the postwar era.[23] A number of other measures to stimulate housing were also instituted. The firm that built housing for its
personnel could, during the first year, depreciate half the expenses
incurred. The government increased its loans for Habitations a Loyer
Modere (HLM) (Dwellings of Moderate Rents). On August 19, 1953,
another decree granted civil servants building loans. Another decree,
on September 30, 1953, enabled local authorities to aid housing by
means of loans or guarantees.

Thus, since World War II, a number of substantive measures
have been introduced to promote housing construction, ranging from
subsidies to reduce interest rates, government investment, loans to
enterprises and households, loan guarantees, tax benefits, and the
mandatory contribution by employers.

As to the banking system, at all times, special construction
loans have been rediscountable at the Bank of France and not included in rediscount quotas for individual banks. Fiscal restraint,
which usually accompanies monetary restraint, tends to affect housing activity more strongly if housing appropriations are cut. During
two major periods of fiscal restraint in the 1960s, the number of residential permits declined when the budgetary appropriations for housing were reduced.[24]

The extent of subsidies granted is such that, in 1968, almost 80
percent of newly built housing was subsidized.[25] At the end of 1969,
only 30 percent of outstanding housing credit was granted by private
banking and financial institutions; however, during the 1960-70 decade,
the private or unassisted sector gradually increased in importance.[26]
About 1 million households, or 6 percent of all households, received
housing allowances.[27]

MANDATORY CONTRIBUTIONS

Decree no. 53-701 of August 9, 1953 established the requirement that employers allocate a percentage of wages and salaries for
housing. The mandatory contribution cannot be considered merely a
tax; it should be considered as an investment in housing for a firm's
employees or as a means of providing housing for other sectors of
the populace. Originally, the contribution was 1 percent, but, on
July 16, 1971, was reduced to 0.9 percent. The proceeds are sufficient only to provide supplementary assistance for the primary financing, which must be secured from other sources.

Participants

All employers with 10 or more employees have to allocate 0.9
percent of the preceding year's wages and salaries for housing. The
determination of the 10 employees is based on the average monthly
number of employees during the preceding year. Originally, the obligation to invest extended only to employers in industry and commerce
but subsequently came to include the so-called liberal professions
(architects, lawyers, and accountants) and various types of professional
and nonprofit organization. The government, local authorities and
their administrative bodies, and employers deemed agricultural in
respect to the social security laws are exempt from the decree.

Investments

The required investment must be made within one year after
the close of the period in which the employee compensation was paid.
The contribution must be paid even if there is a loss for the subject
year. If the actual amount invested exceeds the requirements, the
surplus may be applied against any subsequent liability without any
time limitation.

Previously, the period was 10 years, but, after November 11,
1966, any investment had to remain committed for 20 years. If loan
repayments were made prior to the 20-year expiration date, reinvestment had to be made for the balance of the period. Funds repaid after 20 years revert to the employer.

Penalties

Those employers failing to make the required contribution for
wages during the subject period are liable to a 2 percent tax on the

wages. The yield from the penalty is not put into the general budget but, rather, into a special fund for construction and development, Fonds de Development Economique et Rural, established in 1955. In 1960, the delinquency tax was paid by 9,012 firms and yielded 14,912,290 francs. The penalty was 3.8 percent of the 1959 compulsory investment, 393.53 million francs, and indicates a high degree of compliance.[28]

Forms of Investment

The 1953 decree gave the employer discretion about how the investment is to be made—either direct or indirect:

Direct:
 1. the firm itself builds housing
 2. the firm has housing built on a divided coownership basis according to the Grenoble formula, whereby the employer finances the housing in proportion to his ownership share
 3. by acquiring existing property
 4. by loans and subsidies to employees to build housing

Indirect:
 1. payments to nonprofit collection organizations, authorized by the government to receive the funds
 2. professional associations concerned only with housing construction, formed by employers or trade associations, in some cases with the participation of employees
 3. Comite Interprofessional du Logement (CIL) (Interprofessional Housing Committee) (most important)
 4. chambers of commerce
 5. building societies
 6. family allowance funds
 7. HLM, dwellings of moderate-rent organizations

Housing Characteristics

The investment is largely confined to the construction of new housing and cannot be used for the purchase of existing housing; however, financing of home improvements is permissible. By comparison, rehabilitation has enjoyed a much more prominent place with respect to housing policy and the formulation of housing goals in the United States; yet, the success of rehabilitation in the various public programs has hardly been proportionate to the amount of rhetoric devoted to rehabilitation, and there are serious questions about the economies to be gained from publicly aided rehabilitated housing as compared to publicly aided new housing construction. [29]

Dwellings must be on French national territory and the principal residence of the occupants. An exception is the loan given to a 55-year-old employee who, upon retirement, would make the secondary residence his principal abode.* Housing must conform to minimal construction standards and not exceed surface area and cost limits. There must be an entrance independent of the firm and cannot be used for caretaker's quarters.

Administration

The Ministry of Finance has jurisdiction over matters concerning the financial liability and the amount of money to be invested. The Ministry of Housing and Equipment is responsible for the character and nature of the investment.

Tax Deductions

Investments by means of payments or subsidies to approved housing groups may qualify as a deductible expense for the corporate income tax; however, direct investment by the employer, for example, loans, are not deductible from taxes. The 2 percent penalty tax is deductible as an expense for the corporate income tax. Under specified conditions, contributions to assist employees to obtain housing are exempt from individual income taxes. Company officers and their families are not eligible for any tax free contribution. Grants received by employees are not taxable as income to the extent of F4,000 (about $720), plus F1,000 (about $180) for the wife and each dependent child. This exemption is available only once. [30]

Selection of Employee Beneficiaries

In addition to deciding on the allocation of the funds, the firm can determine which employees will receive benefits. There may not

---

*See page 154 for another example of how consideration is given in Japan to the housing needs of the older worker after retirement. There is a need for such concern and developing appropriate programs in the United States.

be sufficient money to meet all requests for assistance. The basis for priorities varies. In some cases, the crucial factor may be the physical condition of the housing currently occupied; it may be seniority in the enterprise. Most firms contacted require an employee to have a minimum of a year's service.

The employer can stipulate contractually that, under certain conditions, a loan to an employee becomes due immediately, for example, should the employee leave the firm or if the law is violated in respect to the use of the loan. It is not the practice to offset loans or other benefits by lower wages. Since French law specifically prohibits the tying of a work contract to a lease for housing,[31] an employer could not use the loss of housing as a punitive measure.

Direct Investment

A December 30, 1972 decree curtailed the scope of direct investment. For construction, approval must be obtained from the local government entity. The cost of construction cannot exceed stated maxima. The firm's options in respect to giving subsidies was also limited.

The preferred means of direct investment has been loans. The top interest rate is 3 percent, with a minimum repayment period of five years. Loans with an interest rate over 3 percent are not deemed as having met the statutory requirement. However, employers rarely apply interest charges to these loans.

Indirect Investments

The work and responsibility involved in the disposition of the housing funds could be an onerous task, and there is a means for firms to relieve themselves of this burden. They may discharge their obligation by making payments to government accredited and supervised nonprofit collection agencies. The most important of these is the CIL (Comite Interprofessional du Logement).

CIL

The CIL, first organized in Roubaix-Tourcoing, is primarily concerned with housing development; it frees the employers from any direct involvement with the use of the housing funds, while still allowing an option in their disposition. CIL receives the funds and allocates them within the specified guidelines. In the utilization of the funds, CIL brings to bear an intensive knowledge of the housing industry, legislation, and institutions. It does studies on urban and environmental planning, housing needs, land use, and site and housing development.

In 1970, CIL collected more than 1.5 billion new French francs, which enabled the organization to become the promoters of 90,000 homes and apartments. In 1970, 50,000 individual loans were granted. CIL does not actually build housing but does manage. [32]

The income to support CIL's operations comes from the receipt of a percentage of the funds it handles:

3.0 percent on funds equal to or less than 1 million francs
2.5 percent on funds between 1 million and 5 million francs
2.0 percent on funds between 5 million and 10 million francs
1.5 percent on sums exceeding 10 million francs

For the first two years following the creation of an agency, the deduction is 5 percent. [33]

If a firm has not resolved the precise allocation of the funds at the close of the fiscal period, it can lend them to CIL on a short- or medium-term basis. For example, a 6- to 12-month loan without interest can be made, and, at the end of the period, CIL repays the loan; the firm must then find alternative outlets for the balance of the 20-year period. The short-term loans can be extended or converted into other forms of investment through CIL. If a firm lacks sufficient capital to fulfill all the requests for housing assistance for its employees, CIL, if in a position to do so, will advance funds from the short- and medium-term loans to the firm, with the proviso that they be covered by the firm's subsequent contributions.

The loans from CIL may be restricted by the firm providing the funds, who can specify how and to whom the loan is to be made. Arrangements can be made for CIL to give an employee a 5- or 10-year loan with the firm's funds; when CIL is reimbursed, the firm regains the freedom to use these funds for the balance of the 20-year period.

The Union Nationale Interprofessionnelle du Logement (UNIL) (National Interprofessional Association of Housing) is an association of all the organizations that participate in the collection or use of the funds and those that are particularly interested in housing for employees, including CIL. UNIL represents about one-third of French housing construction.

The objections in the United States to centralized decision making from Washington on housing could possibly be resolved through the use of the CIL system on a local or regional basis. Chapter 10 outlines the structure and functions of an organization to manage a contributory system that might be established in the United States.

HLM

As in the United States, there is limited direct construction of housing with government appropriations. Also comparable to the United States is the complexity and multitude of housing programs. France has a number of programs encompassing loans and guarantees to assist construction and both mortgage subsidies and personal subsidies to assist occupants. Furthermore, builders may receive aid in the form of tax relief.

The major component or category of subsidized housing is the responsibility of the HLM; the societies carry out building programs to which the mandatory housing contribution can be applied.[34] An understanding of HLM places the mandatory housing contribution in a better perspective.

In return for its financial assistance to HLM companies, the state has permanent and direct supervisory powers over the groups exercised through the Ministry of Community Facilities and Housing and the Ministry of Economic Affairs and Finance in respect to technical, accounting, financial, and administrative matters; the prefectures are responsible for the fulfillment of the ministry's requirements.

The HLM organizations are a hybrid in that they have the legal character of a private company but retain certain features of a public body. The 1,300 HLM societies differ in terms of their sponsorship and operations.[35] There are mortgage companies, public groups, and cooperative societies.

The approximately 200 mortgage companies, whose origins go back to 1908, furnish mortgage loans to moderate-income borrowers for the construction of a home by a building company associated with an HLM mortgage company.

Some 300 public groups are formed and operated by municipalities or local departments, the French equivalent of states or provinces, as a means of effectuating governmental policies. They are responsible for the planning and construction of rental dwellings for low- and moderate-income families; they can also plan and execute urban renewal programs.

Another 300 fall into the category of quasi-public limited companies. They are the product of private initiative and operated by community organizations or employers concerned with housing for their personnel. They build predominantly rental housing.

The roughly 250 cooperative societies build housing for cooperatives. The cooperative members can rent the housing, with the option of purchasing within a 25-year period. Another program guarantees a tenant the permanent right to live in a rental dwelling with no fear of being evicted because of family or income changes. The tenant makes a deposit of at least 10 percent of the original costs of the housing and subscribes to the society for a sum equal to the loan contract. A complementary family loan determined by both the category of the dwelling and the borrower's family status may be added to the contractual loan.

HLM originated over a century ago. In an effort to "remedy the truly dramatic situation of overcrowded dwellings without air and light, the unhealthy disorder of slums and the heartbreaking conditions of tumbledown suburbs,"[36] trade unionists and middle-class philanthropists, with the promulgation of the 1867 Societies Act, were able to form the first cooperatives to build housing. Gradually, the force of public opinion was responsible for parliament passing the Seigfried Law in 1894 to form Habitation a Bon Marche (HBM), then known as "cheap dwellings."[37] From HBM, the public character of HLM evolved, to become the basis for much of the French publicly assisted housing construction. The Strauss Law of 1906 established the principle that HBM dwellings should be available only to low-income occupants and encouraged local public bodies to give various forms of aid to building organizations. To help workers acquire their own homes, the Ribot Law of 1908 established building societies and included rules for their operation.

A 1912 law, the Bonnevay Law, instituted another innovation, the establishment of HBM public offices to be initiated and managed by local authorities. A 1919 act marked the first instance of state financial intervention in HBM building activities. The state was permitted to grant loans at subsidized interest rates to HBM organizations. The state made up the difference between its costs of borrowing and the loans to HBM at a reduced interest rate. The first detailed building program for the construction of 200,000 low-rent and 60,000 medium-rent dwellings over a five-year period was set forth by the Loucheur Law of 1928. From 1919 to 1939, the government gave subsidies to make up the difference between the going interest rates on loans and an interest level capable of reducing rents to a level suitable for low-income families.

After World War II, reduced-rate state loans with easier repayment terms were granted. The 1949 Minjoz Law enabled savings banks to devote part of their funds to loans to HBM bodies. These loans enabled savings banks to devote part of their funds to loans to HBM bodies. These loans contained a state interest subsidy to reduce the rate paid to banks to the level of reduced rate state loans. In 1950, HBM for low-rent dwellings was replaced by HLM for moderate-rent dwellings. The scarcity of housing was aggravated by the growing demand emanating from urban renewal, deterioration of the housing stock, foreign immigration, war damage, the exodus to the cities, and the increased birthrate.

Financing of HLM

Prior to 1966, the major source of financing was through the reduced interest rate loans coming from the state through an intermediary banking institution covering some 60 percent to 70 percent of development costs. In 1966, La Caisse des Prets aux Organismes de HLM (Bank for Loans to HLM Bodies) was created, with about 90 percent of its funds coming from La Caisse des Depots et Consignation (the Deposit and Consignment Bank). (The banking structure is supplemented by a group of semipublic intermediate financial institutions, one of the most powerful being the La Caisse des Depots et Consignation, formed in 1816. It is the repository of funds from postal savings, savings banks, private insurance agencies, social security, and certain pensions for nationalized institutions and local authorities and has access to central bank credit.[38])

> There is no legal compulsion on the Caisse to obey any political directives emanating from the Government; its "independence" in the management of its funds is guaranteed and it is as important to its clients as the Government's guarantee of their deposits. But as the Government's own banker with its top manager and his deputy appointed by the state, it has a strong incentive to collaborate closely with those responsible for official economic policy.[39]

The balance of its funds comes from state subsidies, interest bonuses, and amortization of loans to HLM. The allocation of loans, terms, and rates are made by the Ministry of Equipment and Housing.

The Loan Bank borrows for 30 years at a rate of 5.25 percent; the amortization rate is 6.69 percent. Loans are then made at a lower rate, of about 4.5 percent, and usually repayable over a longer period. The average mortgage rate is an estimated 4.24 percent. Loans are not made directly to occupants but to HLM societies, which, in turn, make the loans. The difference in the costs of the bank's borrowing and the repayment are compensated for by state subsidies.*

---

*In the United States, the same factor has been a consideration in the passage of federal housing legislation. The federal public housing program to minimize the immediate budgetary impact has used a system of annual subsidies to local housing authorities. One factor in the curtailment of the Federal Housing Administration (FHA) direct loan program was the immediate effect on the budget, whereas the interest subsidies, which replaced the direct loans to avoid this in the long run, proved even more costly.

Up to 1966, loans for the financing of HLM's were included in the budget of the Ministry of Equipment and Housing; then changes were made to include only the annual subsidies in the budget.

The interest rate and term of the HLM loan are dependent upon the social nature of the dwellings, the greater the social nature, the lower the rate of interest and the longer the term. HLM rents are 30 percent to 35 percent less than the rents of comparable unsubsidized dwellings. [40]

In addition to the various types of HLM organization, there are different categories of housing sponsored or built by HLM.

Rental dwellings:

1. Programme Social de Relogement (PSR): relocation housing financed with a 1 percent interest rate loan, 45 years, 95 percent of the cost

2. Programme de Loyer Reduit (PLR): low-income housing, for which HLM local offices receive low-interest rate loans from the government at 1 percent for 45 years, 95 percent of cost

3. Habitations a Loyer Modere-Ordinaire (HLM/O): the bulk of the HLM output equivalent to new private buildings, financed at a 2.95 percent interest rate for 40 years, covering 95 percent of the costs

4. Immeuble a Loyer Normal (ILN), and Immeuble a Loyer Moyer (ILM): for people with incomes slightly above the HLM eligibility requirements but who are still unable to afford private housing; there is limited funding for such housing and thus not too many such units

5. Lodgings-foyers-efficiency apartments: for older persons, single persons, and young migrant workers, operated by private non-profit societies;

6. University residences: constructed for students, together with the Ministry of Education

Ownership:

1. Accession a la Propriete (AP) (HLM Ownership Programs): in 1970, they represented about one out of every four units in the HLM inventory, can be a single-family home or apartment; building organizations grant loans between 80 percent and 90 percent of total cost, with a 2.5 percent subsidy for the first five years, making for a sizable reduction in the 5 percent interest rate for the initial 10 years of the loan

HLM financing, which may reach as high as 95 percent of cost, still requires residual or supplemental assistance; loans or grants may come from family allowance funds, local communities, savings banks, insurance companies, or the employers' mandatory contribution, which "performs an important public service."[41] Supplementary borrowing may be obtained for a shorter period than the subsidized HLM financing.

DISTRIBUTION OF THE FUNDS

The major proportion of the mandatory funds collected prior to 1966, about 60 percent, were channeled through the collection agencies, as contrasted to some 40 percent for direct employer investment. From 1966 to 1970, the proportion for collection agencies increased to almost 80 percent (see Table 3.1). For the next step, the use of the funds (see Table 3.2), between 1958 and 1970, the largest share, approximately 50 percent to 55 percent, went to subsidies. The sharpest changes in this period were the increase from 13 percent to 28 percent in loans and the drop from 27 percent to 5 percent in the purchase of shares in building companies.

In respect to the relationship of the employer participation funds to total financing of new and rebuilt housing between 1958 and 1970, the percentages were some 8 percent to 10 percent (see Table 3.3).

There are some differences in the figures and the definitions for the categories in Tables 3.3 and 3.4. Table 3.4 indicates that in the 1965-68 period, there was an increase in the actual amount of employer participation funds invested in new housing, 1,212 million to 1,800 million francs; however, the percentage of total investment did not vary greatly from 4.5 percent.

The employer funds have had an effect on the increase in residential construction. "The role of French industry in this field (housing) has been of prime importance in the flight housing construction has taken since 1953. According to statistics of the Ministry of Housing, one in four of the total number of houses built since the end of the war has benefited in one way or another from the funds contributed by employer participation."[42]

LABOR COSTS

The housing contribution cannot be considered entirely as a cost, since the employer has the option of investing the funds and could consider them a company asset. But a discussion of costs is in order, since the loans are generally made without interest, and the use of these funds by the firm is lost, either in terms of return foregone or in having to pay for the use of capital borrowed externally; approximately half the proceeds went to subsidies (see Table 3.2).

TABLE 3.1

Source of Funds, by Type of Agency, France, 1953-70
(millions of francs)

Year	Total	Collection Agencies	Direct Employer Investment	Total	Collection Agencies	Direct Employer Investment
	(amount)			(percent)		
1970	2,030	1,616	415	100.0	79.5	20.5
1969	1,819	1,399	420	100.0	77.0	23.0
1968	1,761	1,296	465	100.0	73.6	26.4
1967	1,775	1,308	467	100.0	73.7	26.3
1966	1,566	1,096	470	100.0	70.0	30.0
1965	1,292	821	471	100.0	63.5	36.5
1964	1,097	695	402	100.0	63.4	36.6
1963	948	564	384	100.0	59.5	40.5
1962	844	488	356	100.0	57.8	42.2
1961	765	434	331	100.0	56.7	43.3
1960	696	412	284	100.0	59.2	40.8
1959	678	393	285	100.0	58.0	42.0
1958	630	363	267	100.0	57.6	42.4
1953-January 31, 1958	1,555	987	568	100.0	63.5	36.5

Source: Secretariat General du Gouvernment Direction de la Documentation, "Le Financement du Logement en France," Notes et Etudes Documentaires, July 3, 1970, no. 3704-05, p. 29; and 3'Congres de l'UNIL, 30 Ans de Realisations—Perspectives d'Action: Statistiques, Paris, October 25-27, 1973, p. 5.

TABLE 3.2

Distribution of Funds, by Type of Payment, France, 1958–70
(percentages)

Year	Total	Subsidies	Loans	Payments Made to Acquire Buildings	Shares Bought in Building Companies
1970	100.0	55.7	27.8	11.3	5.2
1969	100.0	54.1	26.8	12.4	6.7
1968	100.0	50.9	27.8	13.6	7.7
1967	100.0	49.4	27.6	13.8	9.2
1966	100.0	51.2	25.0	10.8	13.0
1965	100.0	51.6	22.1	13.3	13.0
1964	100.0	52.5	21.5	12.5	13.5
1963	100.0	51.5	21.5	11.2	15.8
1962	100.0	52.0	20.1	12.4	15.5
1961	100.0	50.9	19.0	13.7	16.4
1960	100.0	49.0	16.2	11.6	23.2
1959	100.0	48.2	15.3	12.0	24.5
1958	100.0	48.2	13.0	11.8	27.0

Sources: Secretariat General du Gouvernement de la Documentation, "Le Financement du Logement en France," Notes et Etudes Documentaires, July 3, 1970, no. 3704–3705, p. 28; and Ministere d'L'Amenagement du Territoire, De Equipement, Du Logement, et Du Tourisme, Statistiques de la Construction, Table 2, April 1973, p. 71.

TABLE 3.3

Major Sources of Financing for New and Rebuilt Housing, France, 1958–67

(millions of francs)

Source of Financing	1958	1959	1960	1961	1962	1963	1964	1965	1966	1967
					Amount					
One percent funds										
Direct investment by employers	267	286	284	331	356	384	402	471	—	—
Utilized by collecting organizations	393	370	400	454	460	527	586	741	—	—
Total 1 percent funds	660	656	684	785	816	911	988	1,212	1,350	1,650
Total financing	6,817	7,605	8,109	8,572	9,186	11,338	13,490	15,373	17,360	20,780
					Percent					
One percent funds										
Direct investment by employers	3.9	3.8	3.5	3.9	3.9	3.4	3.0	3.1	—	—
Utilized by collecting organizations	5.8	4.9	4.9	5.3	5.0	4.6	4.3	4.8	—	—
Total 1 percent funds	9.7	8.7	8.4	9.2	8.9	8.0	7.3	7.9	7.8	7.9
Total financing	100.0	100.0	100.0	100.0	100.0	100.0	100.0	100.0	100.0	100.0

Source: Secretariat General du Gouvernement de la Documentation, "Le Financement du Logement en France," Notes et Etudes Documentaires, July 3, 1970, no. 3704–3704, p. 51.

TABLE 3.4

Employer Participation Funds Invested in New Housing, France,
1965-69
(millions of francs)

Investments	1965	1966	1967	1968	1969
One percent funds in-vested in new housing	1,212	1,350[a]	1,560[a]	1,650[a]	1,800[a]
Total investment in new housing	1,200	29,200	31,100	35,400	39,700
One percent funds invested in new housing (percent)	4.5	4.6	5.0	4.7	4.5
Total investment in new housing	100.0	100.0	100.0	100.0	100.0

[a]Estimated.

Source: Letter and report, "La Contribution Patronale de 1%
a la Construction," French American Banking Corporation, New York,
April 12, 1971.

French wage payments do not accurately reflect the real total
income the employee receives, "Either directly or indirectly (housing, meals, sports, vacations, etc.) or through his high taxes, many
of which end up in the state 'social budget.'"[43] France heads the
nine leading industrial countries in the world on the amount spent for
social aid.[44] An analysis of the annual reports of 37 of France's
largest enterprises shows that, on average, 59.7 percent of their
gross income is paid in wages, salaries, and social security charges
and 35.3 percent to the state in various taxes—leaving 4.9 percent
for investments and dividends.[45]
    An Organization for Economic Development and Cooperation
breakdown of national taxes reveals that the social security imposts,
France's ratio of total taxation to GNP at market prices (1968-70
average) was 36.3 percent, as compared to only 27.9 percent for the
United States. The ratios ranged from 43.0 percent for Sweden to
19.2 percent for Spain.[46]
    Thus, the fact that French wages are the lowest (except for
Italy's) in the six-nation Common Market,[47] must be viewed in the

context of the high level of social benefits. There has been concern
that these high costs adversely affect the international competitive
position of France.* The beneficiaries of the social benefits bear a
goodly share of the increased costs in the prices paid for goods and
services. Assuming the full contribution is a cost, "As employers in
the Common Market pay between 15 and more than 50 percent for social insurance, etc. on top of the hourly wage, the 1 percent can have
only a negligible impact on costs and profits, or on prices."[48]

Consideration must also be given to the benefits the employer
can derive from housing. Adequate housing is a strong inducement in
the recruiting of new employees. Reasonable proximity to the place
of work means less absenteeism and tardiness. High rents and sales
prices for housing could not only deter prospective employees but
could be reflected in wage demands.

LABOR PARTICIPATION

To compensate for their weakness in collective bargaining,
French trade unions have relied upon political action. The political
influence of trade unions although nebulous is significant. Their bargaining power is used primarily against the government and general
public rather than against employers at the industry or plant level.[49]
As with the housing fund originating in Roubaix-Tourcoing, "France
recognizes intergroup arrangements as quasi-public in character, so
that employers and unions develop rules within legal boundaries, which
may become a charter for an entire industry, or in some cases for
the entire economy, binding upon employers and workers not parties
to the agreement."[50]

Thus, the environment in which the housing fund became established, and later developed into French legislation, differs from the
United States, where the provisions of collective bargaining agreements have not been as likely to be institutionalized in the form of
legislation.

> Collective bargaining still plays a secondary role
> in regulating industrial relations in France. The
> State, on the one hand, and the more or less uni-
> lateral decision of the employer, or the other, play
> a more significant part than bargaining between em-

---

*The housing contribution is only a negligible portion of the total
social charges, and it is unlikely that it is a deleterious factor in
respect to France's competitive ability in world markets.

ployers and unions. This is not altogether undesirable
from the point of view of the workers or of French tradition. Government intervention has probably been
more favorable to the workers than bargaining would
have been and it is in the mores of the country to regard law and administrative decisions as more permanent settlements than collective agreements. The tendency to transform habitual or contractual arrangements into law has been unmistakable. Even collective agreements, being mostly based on multiemployer
and multiunion agreements have some of the attributes
of legal regulation. Only recently has there been some
emphasis on plant agreements.[51]

French unions are looking to the government to make changes in
the contribution system, allowing for a greater union role than now
exists. Though the contribution is mandatory, the employer makes
the determination as to how and where the funds will be utilized.
Though favoring continuation of the plan, unions are demanding a
voice in the control and management.

The Confederation Francaise Democratique du Travail (CFDT)
has asked for the establishment of a collective agreement, including
equal participation in management. CFDT asserts that, presently,
sums invested are the property of employers, since the sums return
to the firm at the end of the 20-year period. For employees to manage these sums, the legal nature must be changed in order that the
funds become a deferred salary in the same fashion that social allowances are handled.[52]

The Confederation Generale du Travail (CGT) has requested
for its use the 0.9 percent funds under strict control of the Employees'
Committee with payment to the Public Offices of HLM. Force Ouvriere
(FO) insists on equal management in the control, collection, and use
of the 0.9 percent, without any interference by banking associations
or private promoters.[53]

In April 1972, a resolution was adopted by the Comite Confederal
National (CCN) of CGT-FO:

> The CCN upbraids the Government—which claims
> "participation" to be one of the basic tenets of its
> social policy—for not having seen fit to make provi-
> sion for joint administration of the "housing 1 per-
> cent" at the time it amended the texts governing
> this contribution, the social character of which is
> not open to question.

Considering that the substantial funds constituted
by the "housing 1 percent" no longer can or must be
administered virtually by the employers alone, the
CCN calls for provisions to be adopted speedily so
that the workers—represented by their trade union
organizations—may have their say in supervising the
receipt and utilization of the "housing 1 percent" by
means of joint administration. [54]

EVALUATION

According to an evaluation of the program by an executive in the
residential construction business in France, the existence of the employers' fund has affected housing sales. Almost all French salaried
employees apply to their employers for a loan when buying a home.
The amount of the individual loans may be low, depending upon the
number of applications received and amount in the firm's account.
Employees are restricted to the amount that has been accumulated.
The extremely low or nonexistent interest rates make the loans extremely attractive. The executive comments that approximately 60
percent of purchasers of his firm's homes utilize these loans.

Possibly the major benefit of the housing fund is that institutional lending agencies do not consider these sums as "borrowing"
but rather as coming from the borrower's "personal funds." Normally, a prospective home buyer has to provide 20 percent of the total
purchase price before receiving mortgage financing; the proceeds from
the employer can be included as part of the 20 percent requirement.

The construction executive could not state that the existence of
the mandatory contribution had a direct influence on the demand for,
or the price of, housing, but he did state that "on the other hand, it
is indubitable that the availability of low-cost housing, even though
limited, acts as a positive factor in the sale of houses."

In respect to lessons for the United States, he has a twofold answer: (1) the employers' participation is a direct payroll tax and,
consequently, can be viewed as a measure tending to increase overall
costs, and (2) the pros and cons of a centralized economic policy in
housing have to be measured before any recommendation for or
against can be made.

Another respondent felt that the mandatory contribution could
facilitate decentralization from urban areas. Concern was expressed
that, although the proceeds are not extremely large, there is the danger that the government would be tempted to assume direct control
in respect to their utilization, according to designated political or
economic goals. The flexibility and adaptability of the plan would then
be nullified.

OVERVIEW

With regard to housing policies, France has been a successful innovator, with the incorporation of the mandatory contribution into her fiscal system. The program started on a relatively small scale on a voluntary basis, and only after indications that it could be effective regionally was it adopted nationally by legislation. In contrast to the intergroup arrangements at Roubaix-Tourcoing, which preceded the national legislation, the United States has all too often enacted broad housing legislation without sufficient preliminary study to warrant enactment.

Since the French program has been fully operational for over 20 years, there is an unequalled opportunity to evaluate its pluses and minuses and to determine the desirability of replicating the program in other countries.

The housing fund has been a contributing factor to France's leadership in respect to housing construction. In one way or another, one out of four houses built since the end of World War II has been a beneficiary of the employer-financed program.

There is a minimum of government involvement in the administration of the program. Expenditure of the funds can be sufficiently flexible to take local and regional needs into account. Government supervision is limited to setting broad guidelines and observing that they are adhered to.

From the standpoint of the firm, the contribution cannot be deemed in its entirety a tax, since the firm does have the option of investing in housing or making repayable loans. However, capital may be tied up for as much as 20 years, while the firm simultaneously has to borrow externally at high interest rates and to make loans to employees at below market rates. For most firms, the sums involved apparently are not substantial enough to be a major concern, even though a marginally solvent firm could find the payments burdensome.

Any country considering this type of program must face up to the question of how to distribute the funds efficiently with a minimum of government responsibility for details and administration. Firms are also concerned about the degree of involvement and the costs. Perhaps, the successful operation of the program is due in large part to the existence of a mechanism extending to the local or regional level that handles more than 60 percent of the funds collected, while relieving the government and industry of the administrative burden.

An issue that might be raised by labor is whether the net gain to workers is illusory, since the housing payments by the employer might be made at the expense of wage increases or be passed on to consumers in the form of higher product and service prices. One possibility is that, in view of high income tax rates, the better-paid

employee might gain if he received housing benefits from the employer
rather than in the form of taxable wages. Another question for labor
is the availability of low-cost credit or direct governmental assistance.
Then, how high is housing on the list of labor's priorities? For example, Italian labor has struck to demonstrate concern over the national
housing shortage. Into this complex equation there is a related factor
affecting jobs, that is, the continued ability of firms to compete in international markets if the costs of the housing payments adversely affect prices.

There is an element of inequity in the manner in which potential
beneficiaries are selected. Since the availability of assistance depends
on the balance of the firm's account, the employee in a new firm or
one with a low balance cannot receive the same benefits as if the request were made of a firm with a larger balance. Thus, the extent
of the worker's need for housing does not necessarily correlate with
the ability to secure a loan or other benefits from the employer.
Paradoxically, employees of a new firm are likely to be most in need
of housing, especially when located in an isolated or distant area and
the staff has relocated. This type of firm is unlikely to have any substantial accumulation of funds. Another inequity is the limit to firms
with 10 or more employees; the worker in the small firm is bypassed.

Along with the matter of direct money costs, the cost-benefit
equation for the program has to consider the importance of an adequate supply of housing to an enterprise. Recruitment, wage demands,
absenteeism, and tardiness are affected by the proximity of housing.
Though the control and administration of the program have been
largely in the hands of employers, unions have been seeking an expanded role.

What is most pertinent about the French mandatory contribution
plan is that it has channeled money into the housing sector and has
facilitated housing construction that would have been more difficult
to attain without this assistance.

NOTES

1. J. J. Servan Schreiber, The American Challenge (New
York: Avon Books, 1969).
2. Carl S. Shoup, "Taxation in France," National Tax Journal
8 (December 1955): 328, 338.
3. Harvard Law School International Tax Program, World Tax
Series: Taxation in France, 2/1.1e (Chicago: Commerce Clearing
House, Inc., 1966).
4. "West or East France is First in New Housing," France
Actuelle 21 (December 1972): 7.

5. Cicely Watson, "Housing Policy and Population Problems in France," Population Studies, 7 (July 1953): 18-19.

6. Ibid., p. 6.

7. Ibid., p. 7.

8. International Housing Bulletin, April 1957, p. 59.

9. Watson, op. cit., p. 22.

10. Ibid., p. 24.

11. Ibid., pp. 32-33.

12. Ibid., p. 36.

13. Secretariat General du Gouvernement Direction de la Documenation, "The Financing of Housing in France," Notes et Etudes Documentaires, July 3, 1970, no. 3704-3705, trans. by the Agence Tunisienne de Public Relations, Tunis, 1970, pp. 89-98.

14. Watson, op. cit., p. 44.

15. Arthur Louis Durham, Industrial Revolution in France 1815-1848 (New York: Exposition Press, 1955), p. 200.

16. H. Umrath, European Labour Movements and Housing (Brussels: European Regional Organization of the International Confederation of Free Trade Unions, 1963), pp. 80-81.

17. Pierre George, La Ville (Paris: Presses Universitaire de France, 1952), pp. 97 and 110, quoted in paper by Celia Von de Muhll, "The Urban Structure in France," n.d., p. 33.

18. For an exposition of Prouvost's views, see "Logement Familial," International Congress for Family and Population 5 (1946): 23-29; and Jesse R. Pitts, "Continuity and Change in Bourgeois France," in Stanley Hoffman et al., In Search of France (Cambridge, Mass.: Harvard University Press, 1963, Harper Torch Books, 1965), p. 284.

19. "La Lainiere de Roubaix Is Alive and Worldly Well," France Actuelle 22 (July 1973): 4.

20. Ibid.

21. Watson, op. cit., p. 44.

22. Ibid., p. 45.

23. For background on French planning, see Morris L. Sweet, "Decision Making and French Planning," Business and Government Review 8 (January/February 1967): 21.

24. Jan W. Karcz, "Monetary Restraint and Housing Activity in France," Monetary Restraint and Housing in Selected Foreign Industrial Countries, Board of Governors, Federal Reserve System, Division of International Finance Review of Foreign Developments, pt. 3, L 52 RFD 669 (Washington, D.C., May 24, 1971), p. 2.

25. International Confederation of Free Trade Unions/International Federation of Building and Woodworkers, ICFTU/IFBWW International Housing Committee, The Housing Situation of Low Income Groups (Brussels: International Confederation of Free Trade Unions, 1970), p. 24.

26. Karcz, op. cit., pp. 1, 2, 4.

27. U.S. Department of Housing and Urban Development, Office of International Affairs, European Housing Subsidy Systems—An American Perspective, prepared by Irving H. Welfeld (Washington, D.C.: Government Printing Office, September 1972), p. 15.

28. Harvard Law School, op. cit., p. 223.

29. Morris L. Sweet and William Pincus, A Large-Scale Residential Rehabilitation Program for New York City, New York City Housing and Development Administration, Housing and Redevelopment Board, Bureau of Planning and Program, Research Report, no. 14 (February 1967), p. 4; and Rhoda Radisch, Profile of New York City's Municipal Loan Program, New York City Housing and Development Administration, Office of Programs and Policy Report, no. 15 (December 1967), p. 2.

30. Price, Waterhouse and Co., Information Guide for Doing Business in France, December 1969, p. 50; and Arthur Andersen and Co., Tax and Trade Guide—France, 2d ed. (August 1971), pp. 80-81.

31. Charles S. Ascher, The Administration of Publicly Aided Housing (Brussels: International Institute of Administrative Sciences; and The Hague: Martinus Nijhoff, 1971), p. 20.

32. Union Nationale Interprofessionnelle du Logement Circular, January 1971.

33. Edite par la Federation Nationale du Batiment ("Fiscal Service"), La Participation des Employeurs a l'Effort de Construction (Paris, n.d.), pp. 25, 26.

34. Maurice Langlet, "Public Housing in France," in Public Housing in Europe and America, ed. J. S. Fuerst (New York: John Wiley and Sons, a Halstead Press Book, 1974).

35. Ibid., p. 39.

36. International Confederation of Free Trade Unions/ International Federation of Building and Woodworkers, ICFTU/IFBWW International Housing Committee, Trade Union Activities in the Field of Housing and Building (Brussels: International Confederation of Free Trade Unions, 1966), p. 7.

37. PEP, "Housing in Britain, France and Western Germany," Political and Economic Planning 31 (August 1965): 235.

38. U.S. Congress, House, Committee on Banking and Currency, Activities of Various Central Banks to Promote Economic and Social Welfare Problems, Staff Report, 91st Cong., 2d sess., December 1970, p. 4; and Andrew Shonfield, Modern Capitalism: The Changing Balance of Public and Private Power (New York and London: Oxford University Press, 1965), pp. 167-68.

39. Schonfield, op. cit., p. 168.

40. Langlet, op. cit., p. 48.

41. Ibid., p. 47.

42. Letter, France Actuelle, September 1, 1970, and attached memorandum, Conseil National du Patronat Francais, August 24, 1970.

43. "France's New Secure Society—Part III," France Actuelle 19 (July 15, 1970): 7.

44. "France Highest for Social Aid," Cross Channel Trade, no. 278 (June 1970), p. 12.

45. "France's New Secure Society—Part I," France Actuelle 19 (June 15, 1970): 2.

46. "French Firms' Labor Costs Are High, Too!" France Actuelle 22 (July 1973): 8.

47. Alfred Kamin, ed., Western European Labor and the American Corporation (Washington, D.C.: Bureau of National Affairs, 1970), p. 119.

48. Letter, H. Umrath, Secretary, International Housing Committee, International Confederation of Free Trade Unions/International Federation of Building and Woodworkers, April 20, 1971.

49. Lloyd Ulman and Robert J. Flanagan, Wage Restraint—A Study of Incomes Policies in Western Europe (Berkeley: University of California Press, 1971), pp. 472-73.

50. Frederic Myers, "Labor Relations in France," California Management Review 3 (Summer 1961): 46.

51. Adolph Sturmthal, "Collective Bargaining in France," in Adolph Sturmthal, ed., Contemporary Collective Bargaining in Seven Countries (Ithaca, N.Y.: Cornell University Institute of International Industrial and Labor Relations, 1957), p. 165.

52. Letter, J. P. Bardin, Le Delegue General, Union Interprofessionnelle du Logement, Paris, December 7, 1971.

53. Ibid.

54. ICFTU Economic and Social Bulletin 20 (May/June 1972): 17.

4

ITALY:
THE END
OF A PROGRAM

HISTORICAL BACKGROUND

Italy has a long tradition of legislative action to stimulate the construction of housing. In 1903, the first Italian Council Housing Law, the Luzzatti Law, established enti autonomi (autonomous bodies), now the Istituti Autonomi Case Popolari (IACP) (Independent Institutes for Public Housing), in order to build council housing with public credit institutes.[1]

In 1907 and 1908, legislation was enacted to authorize cooperative societies to borrow from certain public and private institutions on advantageous terms. The state gave subsidies by covering one-third of the interest costs and by exempting new projects from all real property taxes for a period of 10 years. Municipalities were encouraged to assist cooperative housing societies by providing land for building and by granting further subsidies, which could also be given to the special housing agencies, IACP. The Italian cooperative movement was beginning to assume a major role in the Italian economy when the Fascist regime suppressed all democratic institutions.[2]

The end of World War II found thousands of refugees and other homeless persons quartered in schools and other temporary shelters. This was the result of the damage during the war to over 1 million dwellings; in addition, between 1937 and 1952, while population increased about 11 percent, housing production during this period was negligible. In terms of density, size, and sanitation, Italian housing compared unfavorably with that of most European countries.

INA-CASA

Premier Amintore Fanfani set up an organization in 1949 whose primary objective was to relieve unemployment without increasing inflation and, only secondarily, to provide low-cost housing for low-paid workers. The original conception was a "plan to increment the employment of manual workers by building working-class housing."[3]

INA-Casa was established in 1949 for a seven-year period under the Ministry of Labor and Social Welfare (Act of February 28, 1949, no. 43). The formation of an independent and self-administered authority for INA-Casa was due to the reluctance of the Italian civil service to renounce its own independent powers to the political parties, so they were circumvented and operational responsibilities given to the new authority.[4] For organizational purposes, the new authority was placed within the Istituto Nazionale Assicurazioni (INA), a government-owned insurance agency.

The intial funding came partially from U.S.-owned lire from the European Recovery Program (ERP) (Marshall Plan). ERP "funds made it possible to start programs (INA-Casa . . .), which could hardly have been started and operated without American aid."[5] INA-Casa placed major reliance for its income from taxes levied on wages. All persons employed in industry, commerce, banking, insurance, and public administration, except for agricultural workers, were required to contribute 0.6 percent of their wages. Private employers contributed an amount equal to 1.2 percent of the employees' gross wages. The state added 4.3 percent of the total yield of employer-employee contributions, plus a subsidy of 3.2 percent per annum for 25 years of the cost of each dwelling built in the 7-year period, up to a ceiling of 400,000 lire ($640) per room.* A considerable portion of the state's contribution was paid in 7 yearly advances, to facilitate construction. The income from the completed dwellings, rents, or sale prices went into a revolving fund to be used immediately for further construction.[6]

INA-Casa housing was constructed by a public company, IACP, and cooperatives and was to be fully paid off in 25 years, although the total sum of the interest and amortization was considerably less than the general loan.[7] The occupant came into possession of the dwelling after a 25-year period, during which time he repaid little more than three-fourths of the cost of the building (the remainder subsidized by the state) without any interest charges.

---

*Since World War II, there has been such extreme fluctuation in the relationship of the Italian lira to the dollar (between 575 and 650 lire) that no conversion of the currencies has been attempted in this chapter.

The key to the regional distribution of housing was the number
of unemployed workers, the number of workers making payroll contributions, density of existing housing, and the amount of war damage.[8]
At least one-third of new construction had to be in southern Italy and
the islands.

Because of the temporary nature of INA-Casa, it could only
build in special cases. As a rule, funds had to be allocated to experienced public authorities or to undertakings or to cooperatives that
built housing for their own employees or members. Private undertakings that advanced the cost of construction projects recovered their
expenditures in due course by exemption from payments to INA-Casa.
Decentralization was prescribed as far as possible through the use of
existing agencies to implement the plan. Thus, employer and employee
contributions were collected by the National Insurance Institution, application for allocation of housing was handled by provincial labor offices, and management of rented buildings was entrusted to provincial
popular housing institutions and the National Housing Institution for
Civil Servants.[9]

Business undertakings financed their projects by withholding
their own and their employees' contributions, which would otherwise
be paid into INA-Casa. "Cooperation by undertakings . . . has proved
most valuable. They have proceeded with remarkable speed in the
construction of housing for their own personnel, and their projects,
taking their place in the annual construction programmes have resulted
in greater conformity with the needs of the workers and of productive
industry."[10]

In its 14 years of existence, INA-Casa invested some 975 billion lire ($1.56 billion) and produced 349,100 housing units. Some
135 million working days were attributed to INA-Casa. During the
1950s, public housing, largely under INA-Casa auspices, accounted
for 16.3 percent of total new housing, whereas in the 1960s, it was
about 6 percent.[11] The INA-Casa housing was deemed architecturally
satisfying by the American architect, G. E. Kidder Smith.[12]

According to G. Parenti, it would have been preferable to make
the primary objective housing construction rather than raising the
level of employment. In the current discussions on new housing programs in Italy, almost nothing is said about the employment objective.
This change in attitude parallels the U.S. experience, whereby today,
the original employment objective of the federal housing programs of
the 1930s is of minor importance. Yet the cyclical impact of housing
expenditures in a national economy cannot be ignored and will be discussed in this study.

In his review of Italian housing policy, Paul Wendt questioned
the equity of this method of financing:

The INA-Casa program can be subjected to specific
criticisms. The method of financing the program
through payroll taxes paid by employees and employers is unfair and regressive. Clearly, the share of
the tax paid by employers actually falls upon the
workers' payroll. But only a small portion of workers actually receive any benefits from the program
for which they are taxed. An important criterion
for any government housing program is the degree
of flexibility with which it meets changing social or
economic conditions. Because financing of the INA-
Casa program is linked to wage payments, expenditures for the program depend upon wage and employment trends rather than more suitable criteria. [13]

An early evaluation of the program by Parenti suggested the removal of restrictions:

The most interesting aspect of the Fanfani method,
and one that renders the experiment significant for
other countries, is that it permits an extensive and
integrally conceived programme to be launched without any substantial change in existing institutions.
This in turn makes it possible to test the adequacy
of the institutions and to increase their efficiency or
to devise without undue haste reforms in their organization or working. Finally, it may be appropriate
to suggest that schemes of a similar kind should not
be limited like the present Plan to the construction
of homes for the workers; they should extend without restriction to the planning of all the work involved
in substantial building projects of any kind. This
would make it possible to avoid the laborious search
for expedients that has been the cause of so much
trouble to the authorities of the Fanfani Plan. [14]

GESCAL

The end of the postwar reconstruction period, along with political changes, resulted in the phasing out of INA-Casa; it was replaced
by Gestione Case ai Lavoratori (Gescal) (Workers' Housing Agency)
in the Ministry of Labor and Social Welfare, under the Act of February 2, 1963, no. 60, with a life of 10 years. Employee and employer
contributions were reduced to slightly less than one-half the INA-Casa

rate. Worker contributions were set at 0.35 percent of wages, employer contributions at 0.7 percent of gross wages, and government subsidies at 4.3 percent of total workers' contributions, plus a maximum subsidy of 600,000 lire (approximately $1,000) per room, raised on May 1970 to 1 million lire (approximately $1,600) for new construction. To compensate for the low civil service salaries, there was a separate organization to handle payroll contributions for these workers.

Gescal did not do any actual construction; primarily, it drew upon the services of IACP, as well as building cooperatives. IACP is under the jurisdiction of the Ministry of Public Works; whereas Gescal is in the Ministry of Housing and Social Welfare. IACP-managed housing is for the needy and low income, while Gescal housing was intended for industrial workers. After completion of construction, Gescal managed the housing.

Under Gescal financing, a mortgage could cover up to 85 percent of the maximum cost per room for construction or purchase and 25 percent of the value of improvements. A revolving fund used contributions of 15 million lire (approximately $24,000) per year. The interest rate was 2.65 percent for a 20-year term. The annual repayment cost was 6.5 percent. On the other hand, conventional mortgages covered about 45 percent, with a term of 15 years to 25 years and a 7 percent interest rate. Gescal and IACP housing were to be exempt from taxes for 15 or 25 years, depending upon how the land was acquired.

From 1963 to 1970, Gescal expended 462.4 billion lire ($740 million), which built 29,827 housing units, almost all in apartment buildings, accounting for 37.5 percent of public investment in housing but only 2.1 percent of total housing investment. At the end of 1970, Gescal had accumulated in its till 650 billion lire, or slightly over $1 billion dollars in contributions.[15]

In 1971, Gescal contracted for projects amounting to 163 billion lire, but the ability to translate this into completions was questioned. The Economist reported:

> Gescal has no problem about the intake of funds; its
> kitty is everlastingly replenished from one of the
> numerous deductions on the payslip of every employee
> in Italy before he receives his net wages, with match-
> ing contributions from his employer. But Gescal's
> difficulty is in regurgitating its funds.[16]

And in an Italian business magazine the comment was made: "The amount of financial resources utilized is even greater if consideration is given to funds commited but not spent on projects planned, contracted and authorized."[17]

A proposed seven-year plan for Gescal, 1970 to 1976, provided for annual expenditures of some 180 billion lire. The ability of Gescal to utilize these funds was viewed skeptically by Giovanni Alessandri, in an article:

> The report's projection of Gescal's spending capacity denotes a fair dose of optimism, in view of what has happened in the past. Things being as they are, these allocations seem to be miles above what the authority will actually be able to spend in the light of past experience, even though these figures fall far short of public housing requirements. Assuming that all the money is spent within the time envisaged, this would still only account for public expenditures on homes amounting to 5 percent of the total spent by the entire building industry in normal years, and at the most 7 to 8 percent of that spent during the years when the industry was in a recession.[18]

Among the Gescal projects is the total financing of a new town some 10 miles from the city of Rome, in Spinacento and within the Rome jurisdiction. The new town was planned for 26,000 families, and construction began in 1966. In the early 1970s, it was not yet close to completion but did have 10,000 people as residents. Construction is by private contractors through IACP. There is both conventional and industrialized housing.

Gescal has been slow to build housing; one factor was the inability to contract quickly with builders. Then, after construction was completed, there was the problem of determining who was to be admitted. Originally, tenant selection was by lottery, but this system did not last very long, and the lottery never really got off the ground. Admission standards are not uniform throughout the country. The housing shortage has led to conflicts over admission; for example, there has been resentment over migrants from the south receiving preference over senior workers.

The Gescal housing has not been self-supporting, and Gescal funds have been used to cover deficits. Tenants have frequently refused to pay rents. Another problem has been the lack of adequate maintenance by tenants.

Gescal's management problems have been duplicated in the United States with publicly aided housing. For example, in New York City, the occupants of subsidized limited-profit housing have resisted the imposition of increased rentals or carrying charges needed to make the housing companies self-supporting or to reveal their incomes by allowing the city access to their city income tax returns.

The rents for Gescal housing have been moderate: about 35,000 lire for a three-bedroom apartment under the redemption scheme and 25,000 lire for a rental. The redemption scheme provides for the tenant becoming the owner after 30 years. Most of the housing built under INA-Casa, the predecessor to Gescal, will soon become privately owned. About half the Gescal housing is under the redemption scheme. The unions have opposed the redemption plan, preferring rentals; the redemption plan hinders mobility, and unions prefer large housing estates or public housing in the center of cities and towns.

LABOR'S ATTITUDE

In contrast to the limited power of French trade unions, the Italian trade unions have increased their strength since 1969. They negotiate directly with the government and are influential in housing policy and legislation. Labor unions in the United States have not shown as intense an interest in housing, other than passing resolutions about the need for housing. The construction unions have demonstrated greater concern for housing, but a good share of the interest is based on ensuring that government funds are sufficient to provide an adequate level of employment.

The concern of Italian labor for housing transcends considerations of employment; labor actively seeks remedies for the housing shortage in Italy. The seriousness of the housing crisis caused a nationwide general strike on November 19, 1969, with a demand "for an organic, global housing policy."[19] During the night of November 17, virtually on the eve of the strike, the Cabinet approved plans to allocate over 1,700 billion lire for workers' housing "in order to meet the urgent requirements for homes, which have recently become acute, particularly in urban centers."[20]

Opposition has been expressed by labor to continuing the employee contribution to Gescal, preferring that the money be raised from the capital market system. However, the IACP borrowing experience did not prove successful; it sought money in the open market. The state's role has been largely confined to subsidizing interest payments. As with other borrowers in Italy and elsewhere, IACP had to meet the unequal competition of Eurodollars and other high-yielding securities.[21]

The general secretary of the Italian General Confederation of Labor called for funds to be obtained from the public sector:

As regards funding the financial resources to implement a new housing policy in Italy I should point out

that the workers' movement and the trade unions have
unanimously decided that by 1973 an end must be put
to the existing system of contribution to the public
housing building sector now, while money must also
be raised from the capital market and credit system.
This will obviously call for a massive transfusion
of funds into the public sector, which we feel is of
primary importance to defend and enhance the standard of living of the workers and to affirm the concept of "the home as a social service."[22]

A shift to financing for housing from the capital market and
credit system has a weakness in that the flow of funds into housing,
as exemplified by the United States, fluctuates too sharply. In contrast to dependence on these sources, there is the alternative of utilizing the employment-related tax to counterbalance the feast or famine
of housing credit.

THE HOUSING PICTURE

There are multiple causes for the poor housing record and the
large amount of unspent public funds in meeting the needs of those
segments of the populace most in need of housing. Procedures for
disbursing and controlling expenditures of public funds are excessively
drawn out on the part of Gescal and national and local governments.
Public authorities concerned with housing are highly fragmented and
overlap in jurisdiction, for example, Gescal and IACP. A 1958 report by the Ministry of Public Works on the Housing Problem in Italy
discussed the need for centralized governmental housing activity directed by a single organization.[23] In the 1970s, responsibility for
working class housing remained divided among some 100 large and
small public bodies, "an intricate bureaucracy feeding on the thousand
rivulets through which the scant available resources are dispersed."[24]
This duplication constituted an enormous waste of energy and
resources. A need to merge these agencies and ensure that the funds
allocated for public housing were actually spent was expressed. Although Gescal solved the problem of financing by ensuring continuity
of contributions, "the intricacy of the bureaucratic procedures regu-
lating urban planning, the house projects and construction and the extremely fragmentary nature of the interventions, contrary to the initial hypotheses, prevented an approach based on large scale programmes."[25]
Not only in Italy is there a necessity to simplify the governmental housing structure and operations. So numerous and involved is

the housing legislation enacted in the United States that one feature of
proposed housing legislation in recent years has been to reduce and
simplify the multiplicity of programs. So complex are the different
housing programs that they have fostered career specialists capable
of making them operational. Moves by the Nixon administration, initiated by the then Secretary of HUD Romney to decentralize the department have only led to further chaos.

Another problem in Italy is the shortage of building sites caused
by the lack of municipal funds for expropriation and the required public works or infrastructure. Law no. 167 stipulates that public housing can only be built on urbanized land compulsorily purchased by
municipalities. There are limits on allowable construction costs that
deter contractors.

Speculation has raised land prices to a point where housing construction is impeded. The Minister of Public Works has noted that
"the biggest obstacle in implementing all the schemes that have been
financed in the past and being certain of the costs involved have been
the difficulties in purchasing all the land needed for public works."[26]

> Property speculation in Italy has reached heights in
> terms of real power and overall effect on the economy
> not found in any other part of the world. It is diffi-
> cult to evaluate the resources which have been swal-
> lowed up by real estate speculation in the country
> over thirty years. The figures involved run into thou-
> sands of billion of lire and some calculations based
> on statistics in the last three years will serve to high-
> light the seriousness of this problem, which has now
> reached an intolerable level. It is estimated that
> total investments on housing in the public and pri-
> vate sectors combined has been 11,000 billion lire
> of which as much as 4,000 billion have been used to
> purchase development land, i.e. devoured by the
> maw of speculation.[27]

The demand for housing stems not only from the shortage and
the poor condition of the inventory but also from the mobility of the
Italian populace. As many as 20 million persons have flocked into
cities with over 50,000 population since 1951.[28] Over the past 12
years or so, 15 million Italians have changed residences.[29]

A substantive cause of the acute housing crisis is the transformation from an agricultural to an industrial country with urban centers, where employment can be found. Planning forecasts did not
foresee the extent of the migration.

> The enormous demand for accommodations in the
> large metropolitan areas is the price that is now be-
> ing paid for a policy involving massive concentration
> of investments in relatively few areas of the country,
> where the creation of an increasing number of jobs
> has acted like a magnet to workers who have flowed
> in from other areas. [30]

In Milan, large workers' housing projects have been built in locations that are almost diametrically the opposite of those selected
for comparable housing in the United States. The city is growing in
the wrong direction in an unplanned way, with schemes being set up
haphazardly too far on the outskirts and cut off from the center—thus
bringing about a situation whereby the lower-income groups are dis-
dained by the large city. [31] Since it is almost impossible to utilize
land within town boundaries, Gescal and IACP housing projects have
been built on the outskirts or in outlying areas. In the United States,
the judicial rulings and attempts by HUD to disperse publicly aided
housing within cities and to suburbs have met strong resistance.

Private enterprise has been so successful in providing luxury
housing that the market for such housing has become saturated. On
the other hand, the need for housing for less-affluent households has
not been satisfied, despite the funds in the Gescal kitty.

> Nor should it be forgotten that the very considerable
> supply of housing over the last twenty years, which
> has provided around 20,000,000 rooms as compared
> with an increase in the population of 6,800,000, i.e.
> about three rooms for each inhabitant, has largely
> been brought about by the activities of private enter-
> prise, since the public sector's contribution to meet-
> ing the total demand for housing has averaged about
> 13 percent over the period, and in recent years has
> declined to the almost negligible proportion of just
> over 6 percent. The disastrous results of such un-
> balanced growth have been two fold. On the one hand
> the private market has become saturated, and on the
> other a huge and unsatisfied demand for homes from
> the less privileged members of society has been
> created. The only way to remedy this state of af-
> fairs to the benefit of the community as a whole is
> to raise the level of public investment in housing to
> a very substantial degree and set aside a special
> permanent fund for this purpose in the State budget.
> Public housing, reorganized in this way would be pro-

vided with proper infrastructures and social ameni-
ties, and would then be offered to tenants exclusively
on a rental basis, with priority being given to the
availability of rented accommodation over the right
to own a home. At the same time all the incentives
that the Government can muster to attract private
enterprise to build workers' housing would be mobil-
ized.[32]

The aforementioned preference for rental over ownership varies
from the continuing statements in the United States about the desirability of homeownership programs for low-income groups. The experience with the FHA Section 235 subsidies for owner-occupied housing
has not been the most favorable. All too often in the United States,
homeownership is proposed for low-income families not always capable of assuming the added responsibilities. Homeownership, by
tying them down geographically, limits the mobility needed for employment opportunities. Also homeownership programs for low-income families may be based on the purchase of undesirable houses
in blighted areas, which entails a high degree of risk on the part of
the purchaser. A skeptical viewpoint on the benefits of homeownership has emerged on the part of HUD.[33]

NEW LEGISLATION

Early in 1971, parliament was presented by the government
with a comprehensive housing reform bill aimed at increasing the
supply of public housing. Enactment of the housing reform law (no.
865, October 29, 1971) was a victory for the government parties,
which considered housing a major factor in the social and economic
reforms deemed necessary for Italy's future development. The bill
could also be attributed to the large-scale political and trade union
mobilization, culminating in the general strike of November 19, 1969.
A goal of the legislation was to raise the public share of new housing
from some 5 percent to 7 percent to 25 percent. The legislation provided that all appropriations for low-cost housing be merged into a
housing fund to be administered by the central government through
the Committee on Residential Construction (CER), which is in the
Ministry of Public Works. General policy direction and guidance
are furnished by the Interministerial Committee for Economic Planning (CIPE). Housing authorities of the regional governments, coor-

dinated within CER, would develop regional housing plans. * Implementation of the plans would be the responsibility of housing cooperatives and IACP. If the cooperatives and IACP's are unable to utilize
the funds available under the new law, the regional governments could
use such semigovernmental agencies as Istituto per la Ricostruzione
Industrialie (IRI) (Italian Institute for Industrial Reconstruction), now
the fourth largest enterprise in Europe.

Most germane to this review of Italian housing policy was the
proposed liquidation of Gescal and some 125 other housing agencies.
The government issued a ministerial decree that confirmed its commitment to Gescal for a year, through December 31, 1973, the organization and operations to remain unchanged. "If the present government manages to survive for another year, it is highly probable that
Gescal will also continue to survive."[34] Former Prime Minister
Guilio Andreotti suggested that the 1971 law could be improved and
did not close the door on further legislative changes. In the summer
of 1972, Gescal set aside 26 billion lire for a study and research
project, with the purpose of reducing costs and modernizing Italian
construction practices.

A total of 54 billion lire was appropriated for 1971-73 for various housing programs; this encompassed 2 billion lire annually for
interest rate subsidies, reducing the rate to 3 percent for mortgages
granted to agencies, corporations, and individuals. The mortgages
could be up to 75 percent of the total cost of land and construction.

The housing bill gave the regions, as previously mentioned, the
responsibility for distributing the appropriated funds that were to be
spent on housing construction over the next three years. The program
would supposedly result in a basic shift in the construction industry
and produce a sizable quantity of low-cost social dwelling units. The
program entailed some 1,283 billion lire. An additional 1,189 billion lire would be furnished by Gescal prior to ending its activities
in 1973. The total of 2,472 billion lire would be sufficient to build
an estimated 240,000 dwellings. Based on past experience, the
trade unions were skeptical about the successful implementation of
the program.[35]

CONTINUATION OF GESCAL

There was no unanimity on the decision to discontinue Gescal.
Former Minister of Labor and Social Welfare Carlo Donat-Cattin

---

*There has been a continuing effort in recent years to shift the
responsibility and administration of federal housing programs away
from Washington to the states, regions, and municipalities.

favored continuance. The Liberal Party sought to have Gescal transformed into a financial institution providing interest subsidies. The
Socialist Party opted for a change from payroll contributions to appropriations to be utilized for rentals.

The General Secretary of the Italian General Confederation of
Labor, Aldo Bonaccini, proposed that, within three years, Gescal
should be dispensed with, as should all the other organizations of a
similar nature, large and small alike. "This is the initial framework
which in our view should form the starting point for housing reform,
the State controlled corporations should be placed at the service of
this reformed policy only as executive and operational organizations.
Yet this task cannot be assigned to them alone. Building cooperatives
can also play a vital role in this field."36

Industry would not object to a change from the payroll tax system.
The percentage ratio of fringe costs to payroll costs in the United
States was 18 percent; in Italy, it was 51 percent.[37]

The outlines of the new approach to construction of low-cost
housing based on Law 865 are becoming more specific.[38] Gescal is
to be succeeded by the formation of a new financing body, tentatively
entitled FINCASA, designed to get low-cost housing programs off the
ground as part of a 3-year funding plan for 1974-76 and the forerunner
of a 10-year program. The 10-year program calls for the construction of 300,000 housing units at a cost of $5.5 billion dollars: $2.8
billion for subsidized housing as a state responsibility and $2.0 bil-
lion for conventional housing to be sold or rented at controlled prices.
Funding was to come from state interest subsidies and a 3-year exten-
sion of Gescal contributions, even though the organization was no
longer legally in existence. Article 4 of Law 865 declares that state-
owned companies, such as IRI, can use unexpended funds of IACP and
building cooperatives.

An organization change is the involvement of ITALSTAT (part
of the aforementioned IRI group) and the Industrialized Building Development Company (SVEI), with a subsidiary financing body for each of
the numerous Italian regions. The ownership of SVEI is divided as
follows:

Sectors	Percent
ITALSTAT	51.0
Montedison (largest chemical company in Italy, privately owned)	
ENI—state-owned petrochemical company	24.5
Through subsidiary ANIC	24.5

The regional financing companies are ITALSTAT entities, formed by IRI to deal with the supply of civil infrastructure in Italy. A prototype for the regional financing companies was initialed on July 1973 by SVEI, the regional government of Tuscany, and the League of Regional Cooperatives. In the 5-year period 1973-77, the agreement provided for the construction of 25,000 low-cost apartments for $410 million. If finally ratified, there would be one financing company for each region, and every IRI bank would be involved. In the event the president of a region needed funds for low-cost housing, rather than applying to banks for a loan, he would apply to a regional financing company.

> From a practical point of view the central financing
> body and the regional financing bodies might well be
> out of step with each other. The former cannot, be-
> cause of extremely lengthy bureaucratic procedures,
> supply cash to the latter—who ought to be able to guar-
> antee cash on the barrelhead to the regions. [39]

"Italstat will be calling the shots in the Italian building industry and public works programs,"[40] "and there has been disagreement on the merits of the new concentration of power in Italstat."[41]

> Eugenio Cefis, chairman of Montedison, may well
> have been right when, in his speech at the Modena
> Military Academy, he stated that major decision cen-
> ters will not be so much in the cabinet or in Parlia-
> ment but in the executive offices of the big companies
> and labor unions—all of which are developing inter-
> national cooperation.
>
>   An efficiently run ITALSTAT with fingers in every
> pie can easily replace the various notoriously ineffi-
> cient public administration of various sorts. One
> would do well to note en passant, that the latter are
> democratically administered to a greater or less ex-
> tent; the former is not. [42]

The conventional builders have been fearful of their ability to survive in the face of IRI's move:

> We feel that IRI's entry into residential building is
> neither opportune nor positive from an economic
> point of view. The country already has a building
> industry which is capable of erecting any type of
> modern building using the latest systems. Why
> should state owned companies replace private build-
> ers?[43]

IRI

The entry of IRI into housing could have implications for housing policy in other countries. The IRI formula has been directly or indirectly adopted in other countries:[44] British Industrial Reorganisation Corporation, French Industrial Development Institute, Australian Industries' Development Corporation, Canada Development Corporation, a new IRI-type state-holding company in Sweden, and a proposed expansion of the existing West German Federal Holding Company. If IRI is successful in its housing ventures, the results could be significant as a forerunner of similar activity elsewhere.

IRI was created by Mussolini in 1933 during the great depression, when the Italian banking system was threatened with collapse. Banks held large quantities of securities—to prevent collapse of the banks, IRI took over the bank assets, thus acquiring industrial holdings in practically every field of endeavor. These holdings represented some 30 percent to 35 percent of Italian industry. Though public ownership was envisaged as a temporary measure, it did not occur. In addition to four major banks, IRI controls the radio and television network, turnpike system, commercial airlines, and firms in cellulose, paper, glass, textile, and mercury. It also manages a number of holding companies, telephone service, shipping lines, shipyards, iron and steel works, automobiles, aircraft, railway and mechanical equipment, and electric utilities—a total of 140 diversified joint stock companies, which are run as private enterprise. At the end of 1970, IRI's assets were 8,210 billion lire.[45]

It may have started as a salvage operation, but only some 10 percent of its financing comes from state grants; the other 90 percent is obtained on the same conditions as private enterprise, from banks or other medium-term financing sources.[46]

IRI is itself a holding company for the group of companies; it is 100 percent state owned, even though companies within the group have sold shares to the public. IRI has been responsible for the attainment of the government's strategic goals, yet left free in the employment of tactics to achieve such strategy. Though state owned, IRI management has been allowed flexibility. The higher in the pyramidic structure, the greater is the awareness of IRI as a state rather than private enterprise organization.

At the level of the operating companies, subject only to constraints-imposed guidelines resulting from government policy, management is pretty much free to operate as if in a private environment —hiring and firing, purchasing in the most favorable markets, and taking the initiative in new products and markets. The profit criteria differs from the private sector in the length of the acceptable time horizon in that there is a longer range time outlook.

Giorgio Ruffolo, Secretary General of the Economic Planning Department of the Budget and Planning Ministry, makes a number of cogent comments on the new Law 865:

> Financial resources are centralized on paper but continue in reality to flow through a number of unsynchronized circuits.
>
> The "choral" participation of all those concerned seriously complicates the procedures involved. In passing through the legislative offices, the Ministerial working parties and the parliamentary committees, the decision-making process weaves like a paper serpent: the flow-chart tracing the application of the law would be of sufficient length to make a commemorative column erected in honor of bureaucracy.
>
> The battle for the unification of the agencies is far from being won. In essence defunct, the original agencies live again as "agencies in liquidation," a form which may easily become immortal, as it has crossed the threshold of official death.[47]

According to Dr. Ruffolo the miracle of Boethius is being witnessed in the case of the agencies as he is said to have taken his head in his hands and walked a distance after he had been beheaded and a lady remarked: La distance n'y fait rien; il n'y a que le premier pas qui coute (distance is nothing, only the first step counts).[48]

Ruffolo's comments about the unlikely dissolution of government agencies are confirmed by the delays in liquidation.[49] By December 31, 1973, Gescal and several other operating housing agencies were to be liquidated and their properties to be transferred to IACP, subsequently, the mandatory contributions were extended through April 1974, and then it was decided that Gescal would continue through 1974 under the control of the Minister of Public Works, with the guidance of a committee on the dissolution. The organizations to be dissolved would limit their work to the completion of programs launched in 1972 and still in progress or already contracted for. Then, the Gescal contributions were extended for a three-year period.[50]

The work to be completed involves costs of approximately 1,318 billion lire and the services of some 1,300 employees who have been requested to remain for another year to oversee the completion of the projects. The unions representing employees of the dissolved agencies insist upon a "global solution" that does not permit the liquidation of teams of bureaucrats and experts; the unions to obtain an "agree-able" solution have threatened to go on strike. Those teams of bureaucrats and experts constitute a rich source of technical capabilities for the state.

The problem of relocating the personnel of the former Gescal and other agencies is "exquisitely" political and seems destined to cut directly into the developments of Law 865. "Two-and-one-half years after the launching of the reform by the House, the debate on post-Gescal is still totally to be heard."[51]

CONCLUSIONS

Both in France and Italy, the genesis of the present government involvement in housing programs began to develop around 1900, some 30 years before the U.S. federal government took any comparable steps. The mandatory payroll programs emerged around 1950 as a means of solving the acute French and Italian housing shortages brought about by World War II. The enactment of the Italian legislation was abetted by Marshall Plan financial assistance and was designed to give priority to the objective of relieving unemployment; the goal of supplying additional housing was deemed secondary. However, the employment goal did not continue to receive the first priority.

After almost one-quarter century since enactment, the French legislation is solidly entrenched; whereas in Italy, it is close to expiration. Whether the difference in status and acceptability is due to the drafting and inherent soundness of the legislation or due to one country having a tradition of stability and a more favorable economic and social environment are factors to consider. Without attempting to assign weights to each factor, the French legislation allows for greater flexibility in choices and functions in a country whose environment is more favorably disposed to make it more effective. For example, there is no mass movement to the French urban centers from regions of poverty, such as the Mezzogiorno in Italy.

Only the French employers provide the funding, but, in Italy, the employee and government also contribute. The Italian system does not give the employer the flexibility that is built into the French counterpart. Flexibility or options could be a key factor in gaining acceptance from industry for the initiation of a new program of mandatory financing. The Italian collections are, for the most part, distributed through government agencies not noted for their efficiency; whereas the French employer has the choice of using a government-approved agency. The French funding covers a smaller share of the costs of housing than does the Italian and thus is tied in with other methods or programs of financing. Therefore, Gescal has had greater importance in allowing construction to start.

Any plan calling for a direct contribution from employees can anticipate labor opposition. Yet, labor has accepted the social security system with its employee tax in the United States, although since all members benefit, social security cannot be equated with housing in terms of taxation. Those not benefiting from the payroll tax in terms of improved housing would question the necessity or equity of such a tax.

The absence of a payment by French employees may actually result in correspondingly decreased real wages; however, French labor does not appear to be concerned with this point but more with gaining a voice in the administration and allocation of the funds. On the other hand, Italian labor has sought to change the method of financing.

The Italians are not alone in having been unable to solve the management problems in Gescal; they plague public and publicly aided housing elsewhere. Gescal faced the commonly shared matters of deciding who should be given preference for admittance, how to keep tenants from falling into rent arrears, and how to indoctrinate them to maintain their apartments properly.

An interesting aspect of the Gescal scheme has been the redemption scheme, whereby tenants can eventually acquire ownership of the housing. In view of the limited success to date in devising a means for public housing tenants to assume ownership, the feasibility of the redemption mechanism being adopted in the United States should be further explored.*

Although there is no totally parallel organization to IRI in the United States, the entry of IRI into the housing field as a replacement for the more traditionally oriented government agencies or builders, if successful, could have far-reaching effects outside Italy. Continuing with the comparison to the United States is the contrast in locational preference for housing in the center of Italian cities and towns. [52] In the United States, the exodus out of the cities for those able to do so is approaching epidemic proportions. Are there factors in the Italian preference that can be discerned and possess a commanality with respect to application in the United States that might stem the trek out of central cities?

The plethora of housing programs and agencies in Italy has been also recognized in the United States. Both the administration and Congress have agreed that housing programs be consolidated and simplified.

---

*In connection with homeownership for public housing occupants, one such program was designed for low-income families as part of federal public housing (Turnkey III) but was suspended in favor of public-housing leasing. Volume was limited.

A major conclusion that emerges from the Italian experience with Gescal is that the employment tax did raise ample funds for housing purposes. The problem has been the disposition of the proceeds, getting them into the construction pipeline, and translating the funds into housing completions. The causes of the difficulty are to a considerable extent indigenous to Italy. But consideration for adopting this type of plan within the United States or other countries necessitates that any mechanism be designed to ensure that the proceeds are efficiently and productively distributed.

NOTES

1. "Organization and Disorganization of Housing in Italy," Italian Planning Reports (Milan), no. 1 (January 1969), p. 3.

2. H. Umrath, European Labor Movement and Housing (Brussels: European Regional Secretariat, International Confederation of Free Trade Unions, September 1953), p. 95.

3. Giorgio Ruffolo, "Building Waste: Urban Rent and Administrative Quasi-Rents," Review of the Economic Conditions in Italy 28 (March 1974): 144, fn. 1.

4. Marcello Vittorini (lecturer in urban planning, University of Naples), quoted in Leo Sisti, "Muscling in on Housing," Successo, no. 12 (December 1973), p. 96.

5. Italian government, General Secretariat, International Reconstruction Committee, The Development of Italy's Economic System Within the Framework of European Recovery and Cooperation (Rome, 1952), p. 269.

6. G. Parenti, "Workers' Housing and the Unemployment Problem in Italy: First Results of the Fanfani Plan," International Labour Review 69 (January 1954): 31.

7. International Housing Bulletin, March 1956, p. 52.

8. Ibid., August 1955, p. 120.

9. Parenti, op. cit., p. 33.

10. Ibid., pp. 34-35.

11. Letter, U.S. Embassy, Rome, July 1, 1971.

12. G. E. Kidder Smith, The New Architecture of Europe (Cleveland, Ohio, and New York: World Publishing Company, Meridian Books, 1961), p. 161.

13. Paul F. Wendt, "Post World War II Housing Policies in Italy," Land Economics 38 (May 1962): 129.

14. Parenti, op. cit., p. 46.

15. U.S. Embassy, Rome, op. cit.

16. "Colombo's Castles," Economist 237 (December 12, 1970): 86.

17. Francesco Forte, "How to Curb Speculation in Housing," Successo, no. 2 (February 1971), p. 114.

18. Giovanni Alessandri, "La Gescal," Aggiornementi Sociali, quoted in ibid.

19. Agostino Rosso, "The Houses the Government Didn't Build," Successo, no. 5 (May 1970), p. 192.

20. Ibid.

21. Economist, op. cit.

22. Aldo Bonaccini, "Expropriated Land Should Be Made Available on a Fixed Time Basis," Successo, no. 2 (February 1971), p. 117.

23. Ministry of Public Works, Housing Problem in Italy, 1958, cited by Wendt, op. cit., pp. 116-17.

24. Ruffolo, op. cit., pp. 144-45.

25. Ibid., p. 144.

26. Salvatore Lauricella, "Eliminate Speculation and Control Industrial Siting," Successo, no. 2 (February 1971), p. 117.

27. Marcello Vittorini, "In Three Years, Speculation Has Swallowed up 4,000 Billion Lire," Successo, no. 2 (February 1971), p. 126.

28. Francesco Perri (President, National Association of Building Constructors), "Take Away Unearned Income but Don't Expropriate," Successo, no. 2 (February 1971), p. 120.

29. Vittorini, op. cit., p. 126.

30. Perri, op. cit., p. 120.

31. Rosso, op. cit., p. 196.

32. Lauricella, op. cit., p. 117.

33. U.S. Department of Housing and Urban Development, Housing in the Seventies (Washington, D.C.: Government Printing Office, 1973), pp. 4-108 to 4-109.

34. Letter, Centro di Documentazione, Milan, February 23, 1973.

35. "Construction Boost," International Housing Bulletin, no. 2 (1972), p. 6.

36. Bonacini, op. cit., p. 118.

37. Michigan International Labor Studies, Program in International Business, Labor Relations and the Law in Italy and the United States (Ann Arbor: University of Michigan Graduate School of Business Administration, 1970), 4:141.

38. Sisti, op. cit., pp. 92-93.

39. Ibid., p. 92.

40. Ibid.

41. Ibid., p. 95.

42. Ibid., p. 96.

43. Ibid.

44. Stuart Holland, ed., The State as Entrepreneur (London: Weidenfeld and Nicolson, 1972), p. 243.

45. Ibid., p. 311.

46. Christopher Layton, "State Entrepreneurship in a Market Environment," in ibid., p. 53.

47. Ruffolo, op. cit., p. 148.

48. Italian Planning Reports, op. cit.; and Edward Gibbon, The Decline and Fall of the Roman Empire, abridged by D. M. Low (New York: Harcourt, Brace and Company, 1960), p. 543.

49. "Dopo la Gescal C'e il Vuoto" (After Gescal, Nothing), Mondo Economico 6 (February 16, 1974): 18-19.

50. Sisti, op. cit., p. 92.

51. "Dopo la Gescal C'e il Vuoto," p. 19.

52. For a review of locational preference in the United States, see S. George Walters, Morris L. Sweet, and Max D. Snider, "When Industry Moves to Interurbia," Sales Management 82 (February 20, 1959): 89; and Jonathan Lindley, "The Economic Environment and Urban Development," lecture, National Planning Association, April 28, 1967, p. 94; both included in S. George Walters, Morris L. Sweet, and Max D. Snider, Marketing Management Viewpoints: Commentary and Readings, 2d ed. (Cincinnati: South-Western Publishing Company, 1970). On post-World War II policy for rebuilding European city centers, see Karl H. Stein, "Some Observations on the Evolving Retail Pattern in Europe," Economics and Business Bulletin (Temple University) 10 (March 1958), in S. George Walters, Max D. Snider, and Morris L. Sweet, Readings in Marketing (Cincinnati: South-Western Publishing Company, 1962), p. 825.

5

EMPLOYEE HOUSING
IN SPAIN

In the transition from a developing nation to one capable of absorbing sizable industrial growth, Spain's housing problems have assumed greater magnitude, not only because of the increased shortage but because the character of needs has changed due to the more affluent citizenry and the movement from rural to urban centers. As one means of reducing the housing deficit, Spain, even prior to France and Italy, enacted legislation prescribing that firms provide housing for their employees. Housing is considered sufficiently important that, in contrast to practice in the United States and other countries, a good share of Spanish collective bargaining contracts have dealt with employee housing and the right to occupy such housing has been negotiated in some labor agreements.[1]

EFFORTS AT AMELIORATION

The housing plight of the wage earner has long been a matter of concern to the Spanish government; even though attempts at improvements were made, the problems still remained. One such attempt occurred in the mid-nineteenth century reign of Isabella II, when a royal decree was promulgated in the Queen's name, proposing the betterment of living conditions for the Spanish people "whose slender means and miserable wages" did not allow them to pay for suitable dwellings.[2] The Queen promised to aid every legal effort to improve sanitation in the poorer districts of industrial cities, whose working-class quarters were deemed to be a menace to health. It was agreed to facilitate any plans for construction on the outskirts of such cities for one or more dwellings "in which comfort and adequate space shall be combined with low rents and accommodations suited to habits of this portion of the population."[3] There is no evidence of the goals ever being realized.

In 1904, the Seville Chamber of Commerce, Industry, and Navigation built six cottages in honor of the King's visit to the Alcazar. They were awarded to the most faithful wage earners, who were recommended by the city's employers: one dock laborer, one female and one male operative, one employee of the tobacco factory, and so forth. The fortunate recipients were life tenants, and their heirs took full possession of the property.

The town council of Seville appropriated $1,000 a year for construction of workmen's cottages, to be rented at 4 percent of cost to those wage earners able to prove the longest period of service with any one employer. After 20 years of occupancy, no further rent was required, and, if the head of the family died prior to the end of the 20-year period, the widow and minor children remained rent free.

The Cheaper Houses Act of June 1911 gave the state the power to create agencies and programs for low-cost housing construction for workers by means of housing cooperatives, interest free loans, and subsidies. The law provided for the organization of local juntas dedicated to the improvement of workmen's dwellings. The nine members in each junta had to consist of an architect or contractor, a physician, and a member of the town council. All were nominated by the alcalde and appointed by the civil governor of the province in which the town was located. Two of the members were elected by the 50 principal subscribers to the building fund and two by the workmen's societies represented on the junta of social reform. Two had to be concerned with social betterment.*

Building societies approved by the local juntas and legally registered could receive legacies, donations, and subventions accorded by the state, province, or municipality. All property designated for the construction of workmen's dwellings were exempt from direct taxation, that is, taxes on net profits, property, inheritance, transfer, and stamp duties.

Municipal lands could be expropriated by the societies. Private building sites suitable for "cheap" houses and not utilized could be expropriated within three years after promulgation of the law in the interests of general welfare.

When tenements were condemned as unsanitary and the owner refused to make the necessary improvements, a city could expropriate (only for the value of the land). With the proceeds realized from the

---

*This early interfunctional attempt to gain a cross section of interests may be compared with current recommendations for development corporations, p. 202.

sale of the wreckage or surplus land, new housing could be placed on the site. To guard against abuses of power, protests could be made to higher authorities.

Under the same law, city governments or cooperative building societies could issue bonds for the construction of workmen's dwellings and mortgage the property. The state guaranteed the payment of interest by the building societies. Interest subsidies were granted to building societies, except those paying dividends in excess of 4 percent. Housing built under this law was given tax exemption for 20 years or as long as it conformed to the original use. It could be sold to tenants.

In the 1920s and 1930s, new legislation facilitated public aid for construction of housing, but due to the paucity of resources, the aid was more significant in theory than in results. In 1935, under the Unemployment Act, one of the means devised to combat unemployment was residential construction through financial assistance and tax exemption.

THE OBLIGATORY INVESTMENT

The law of December 20,1943 obligated industrial enterprises to invest in housing for employees to the extent of 20 percent of their obligatory social reserves. On March 3, 1944, this reserve had to be transformed into an Obligatory investment in protected housing." On July 17, 1946, all newly established firms, even if not compelled to accumulate a social reserve, were required to build homes for workers. On October 31, 1947, the obligatory social reserve was changed to the obligatory purchase of bonds. The bonds carried a low interest rate of 3 percent and could be redeemed only with the construction of housing.

The December 1943 act was further amended by a July 1946 act, whereby establishments with more than 50 workers had to provide housing facilities if access to the place of work was difficult. Workers could either rent or purchase these dwellings by installment payments.

Private enterprise could build directly or contract with a local government entity or syndicate to provide the housing. The firm was

---

*Protected dwellings were intended to resolve housing problems of the moderate-income groups. The benefits consisted of tax exemption, long-term interest-free loans, building grants, and the right of compulsory purchase (Ministerio de la Vivienda, Secretaria General Tecnica (Ministry of Housing, General Staff Office), Architecture, Housing and Urbanization in Spain (Madrid, 1963), p. 70.

offered the benefits of eminent domain, tax exemption, preference in obtaining building materials, and loans at reduced interest rates. If rented to workers, rents had to be moderate. If the work contract was terminated, the occupants had the right to remain for at least a month.

A May 27, 1955, decree stated that, if a firm expands or moves elsewhere, it must submit a detailed report covering its labor and housing needs in the new location. If there was a housing shortage, the industry had to agree to build directly or have it done through state organizations. An investment of at least 10 percent of the capital required for the installation and its operation had to be made. Initially, a deposit of at least 5 percent of the capital was necessary as a guarantee.

Effective July 1, 1955, all industrial, commercial, and banking institutions with over 50 employees were obligated to build housing within a five-year period equivalent to 50 percent of the families or 20 percent of their regularly employed personnel, respectively.

To facilitate such construction, the National Housing Institute agreed to lend 50 percent of the cost of land and construction, repayable within 50 years, without interest. As a further incentive, enterprises were to be given tax benefits for the amounts invested in such construction, and, perhaps, of greater importance, they were entitled to cash in for the actual value, the social reserve paper they had been required to invest in previously.

The July 24, 1968 act provided that undertakings employing more than 50 workers in any one locality could be compelled to build dwellings for their staff or, as an alternative, grant loans for the acquisition of "officially protected dwellings." Only new construction is allowed, no rehabilitation or purchase of existing housing. Most firms prefer to extend loans rather than become involved in construction. The loans are at 3 percent, with a minimum repayment period of 10 years, and cover 80 percent of total costs.* The loans come from a revolving fund and must be reinvested. The employee can secure the remaining 20 percent from a savings bank at 6.5 percent to 8.0 percent interest with a term of about 16 years.

EFFECTS

The worker usually buys a cooperative from a private promoter. If the employee leaves the firm and occupies a rental apartment, he

---

*The Spanish legislation differs from the French legislation in that the employer provides the major share of the financing, 80 percent, whereas in France only supplemental financing comes from the employer.

is given six months in which to vacate; however, if in a cooperative, he remains, but the firm takes a rigid stance in respect to repayment. The possibility of having to vacate in the face of a housing shortage leads to a preference for loans for purchase of housing over residing in employer-owned housing. Until recently, there was little job mobility, accentuating the tendency to buy rather than rent. But growing mobility has led to greater consideration to renting, and the government may be opting for more rentals.

If left to themselves, firms would not become involved in housing for employees. The ministry has jurisdiction and sets housing quotas for firms. Those firms relocating or setting up new facilities in new areas are more cooperative, for example, Michelin in 1960 established a plant with 300 employees in Burgos, where there was insufficient housing. Banks have been cooperative in working out housing for their employees.

Employees prefer less paternalism and better salaries. The benefits to the employee from employer assistance are the savings in interest costs and, for those who are poor credit risks and would otherwise be unable to borrow, the ability to secure financing.

CONCLUSIONS

In reviewing the Spanish legislation obligating industry to assume the financial burden of supplying employees with housing, questions arise: one is whether there is merit in industry rather than government having this responsibility; and second, should industry become closely involved with the life of employees outside the workplace? In comparison with France, industry in Spain under the obligatory legislation is the major source of the funds rather than merely supplying a supplement to borrowers.

Spain has recognized the importance of housing in economic growth and has not been willing to delay for untold years the resolution of the housing problem. In a rapidly industrializing country, with a government lacking adequate resources and the administrative capability to mount a full-scale housing program capable of solving the housing crisis—which, incidentally, few developed nations have accomplished—there is a basis for shifting the responsibility to industry. Industry does benefit from a labor force that is suitably housed. As compared to government subsidies, there may not necessarily be any appreciable savings to taxpayers in having industry finance housing for employees; the costs to industry could be reflected in product prices. The government also provides subsidies for this housing. It may also be possible in the case of exporting industries to shift the cost of the subsidies outside Spain. Regardless of the incidence of

the costs, Spanish industry is apparently reluctant to become too
closely involved as a supplier or landlord of housing and has opted for
loans for the purchase of housing. Yet, the increased mobility of labor
counteracts the preference of industry to avoid becoming a direct supplier and points up the need for allowing industry to limit its direct
connection in the use of the funds.

NOTES

1. Fred Witney, Labor Policy and Practice in Spain (New York:
Praeger, 1965), p. 52.
2. Katherine Coman, "How Spain Provides for the Housing of
Her Wage Earners," The Survey 32 (July 25, 1914): 431.
3. Ibid.

6

LATIN AMERICA: HOUSING AND SOCIAL SECURITY

Latin America's serious housing shortages and overcrowding are due to population growth and lack of construction. Unemployment for the growing labor force has been a problem of great magnitude, and housing policy has been formulated not only to resolve the housing shortage but also to provide employment. The construction sector has become a prime source of jobs, particularly for migrant workers coming to urban areas.

Since 1960, there have been major changes in housing finance, with a decline in the use of the traditional mortgage credit systems and, starting with Brazil, the creation of new national entities drawing upon social security funds. The allocation of social security funds to housing has drawn worldwide attention and the adoption of similar plans. For example, the attention of African governments has been directed to the desirability of investing a proportion of the funds collected under social security plans in mortgages for the benefit of lower-income groups; whereas in the United States, there has been limited attention given to the possible use of social security funds for housing with the exception of a recommendation by the Congressional Joint Economic Committee that the Social Security Trust Fund and Civil Service Retirement Trust Fund could increase purchases of government-sponsored housing agencies' securities and thus reduce interest rates paid by these agencies.[1]

Perhaps, as presently constituted, social security could not be linked to housing. But in a period when the existing concept of social security is being reappraised, it would be appropriate to review the Latin American programs, even though doubts have been expressed about their feasibility in the United States:

The social security institutions in these countries are
divorced from the central government and its financing
so as to provide greater assurance of the availability
of benefit payments. They make a large variety of
investments in the private and public sectors of the
economy, including mortgage loans, in a manner akin
to the life insurance companies in the United States.
Their semi-autonomous status and the reasons for
it have no parallel in this country.[2]

The Brazilian and Mexican programs provide prime examples
of the link between social security and housing. To indicate the vari-
ance within Latin America, the evolving Chilean program that is based
on a tax on profits is covered.

BRAZIL

The Housing Crisis

According to the 1960 census, 8 million dwellings, about one-
half the housing stock of Brazil, were considered unfit for habitation.
With the population growing at the rate of 3 percent per annum,
500,000 new housing units were required to keep an already critical
shortage from growing worse. Though housing was deemed a priority
item, the weak economy allowed meager financial support from the
national budget. Loans for construction and homeownership had
reached a point where credit was obtainable only for very short periods and at extremely high interest rates. A down payment of 40 percent to 50 percent was necessary to purchase a single-family house,
and the outstanding balance had to be paid within two or three years.[3]

To resolve the housing crisis, Law no. 4380 was enacted on
August 21, 1964. It provided for the creation of the Banco Nacional
de Habitacao (BNH) (National Housing Bank), which was given the task
of formulating a national housing plan and finance system. BNH was
also given the sole responsibility for implementing the national housing plan, as well as the management of the entire housing finance system. The designation of a bank rather than a ministry or other specialized government department reflected a basically financial approach to solving the critical housing problem. The legislation was
designed to stimulate construction of low-cost housing and to finance
the purchase of privately owned housing, particularly by lower-middle-
income groups. Some 60 percent of the BNH investments had to be
applied to the construction of dwellings for low-income occupants.

In the mid-1960s, the task of meeting the goals of the national
housing plan appeared impossible. To strengthen the national economy,
the government reallocated resouces, so as to leave little in the national budget for housing. A system for mobilizing sufficient investment capital in housing had to be devised to replace the piecemeal federal budget allocations.

Source of Housing Funds

BNH and the Ministry of Planning approached the problem of
capitalizing the bank "by involving the source of capital with the employment system of the beneficiaries of the housing programme, i.e.
the future occupants of low income housing. The incentive for home
ownership and an improved standard of living among the people was
used as a means for mobilizing investment capital."[4] Thus, the piecemeal federal budget allocation was replaced in 1966 by the massive
resources of the national social security fund and savings from the
national savings and loan system. The new law mandated employers
to contribute an additional 8 percent of employees' salaries into a personal account for each employee held under the supervision of the Central Bank. The contribution is allocated to the Funda de Garantia de
Tempo do Servico (FTGS) (Guarantee Fund for Time of Supervision),
which is part of the social security system. It was specifically established for the retirement and unemployment benefits of employees, and
its resources were made available to BNH. BNH borrows from FTGS
at 5 percent, necessitating the bank to obtain at least a 5 percent return from its loans. In 1973, the bank's budget was $1.5 billion.

There is a personal account in each employee's name; and for
those employees who so prefer, the employer can hold their account
in trust under the provisions of a previous labor law. Deposits for
employees receive no interest for the first four years, but from the
seventh year, 7 percent is guaranteed. The employee can draw upon
this account only for specific reasons:

1. if the employee or member of his family is ill
2. if he is discharged from his job and remains unemployed
3. if he retires
4. if he wishes to purchase a home through the bank

Though any Brazilian citizen can use the bank to purchase a
home, its policies and operations are directed in favor of low-income
families. The interest rate for homeowners' mortgages ranges from
1 percent to 10 percent, depending on gross family income. An employer willing to provide housing for his staff can obtain financing

from BNH on an equal-sharing basis; his contribution is usually in the
form of land.

The initial allocation of FTGS funds to BNH went to housing;
they were then made available for the financing of integrated urban and
local government planning, sanitation (water, sewerage, and pollution),
training of technical personnel, activating industries for building materials, and construction, electricity, and highways. With the use of
FTGS resources, BNH was able to establish the Brazilian Savings and
Loan System, which began to finance middle-income housing, employing the technique of seed capital to inaugurate savings associations.
The interfunctional effects of BNH on the Brazilian economy are illustrated in Figure 1.

Monetary Correction[5]

Brazil has pioneered in minimizing the effects of inflation; the
method has received much attention in the United States as a putative
solution to the high degree of inflation. All financial instruments except equities are pegged to inflation, based on the use of monetary correction: "basically it is a device to make nominal monetary claims
match real monetary value, a normal balance that inflationary distortion disrupts."[6] To mitigate the impact of inflation, mortgages are
linked to wages. The usual arrangement with mortgages for low-income borrowers is to have the payment set at approximately 25 percent of salaries, and, as salaries rise, payments rise accordingly.
With the adjustment of the interest rate, the proportion of interest
and principal per payment would vary and the amortization period of
the mortgage would change.[7] "During the period of the creation of
BNH and contrary to the expectations of many traditional economists,
as to the feasibility of the National Housing Plan (especially those who
regard housing only as a consumer product) inflation was gradually
restrained."[8] (See Table 6.1.)

Accomplishments of BNH and the Payroll Tax

The accomplishments of BNH, of which the payroll tax is
an integral part, have been impressive for a developing country. In a
little less than three years after the bank started, construction of
publicly aided housing units reached 500,000; in the previous 28 years,
they totaled slightly less than 164,000.[9] In its first nine years, BNH
financed the building of almost 1 million homes; completion of an additional 2 million dwellings is contemplated by 1980. Some of the worst
slum communities in and around major cities have been eliminated.

FIGURE 1

Induced Savings, Voluntary Savings Campaign (with Incentives from
BNH), SBPE, Brazilian Savings and Loan System

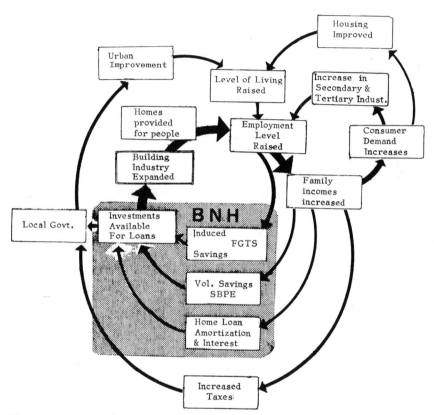

*Diagram shows the effects of BNH as a stimulating, strengthening and integrating
organization that increases employment opportunities, augments family incomes, improves
community and urbanization facilities, raises levels of living and provides more
savings for expanding the cycle of investment*

Source: Morris Juppenlatz, "Brazil: Urban Planning as a
Function of the National Government," Journal of the Royal Town
Planning Institute 58 (February 1972): 63.

TABLE 6.1

Rate of Inflation, Brazil, 1963-69
(percent)

Year	Inflation	Growth of GDP
1963	73.7	1.5
1964	90.8	3.0
1965	57.1	4.5
1966	38.5	5.0
1967	28.6	6.5
1968	24.0	8.4
1969	21.4	9.0

Source: Morris Juppenlatz, "Brazil: Urban Planning as a Function of the National Government," Journal of the Royal Town Planning Institute 58 (February 1972): 64.

Unemployment has been reduced, especially for unskilled workers who have found jobs in the construction industry. BNH estimates that 200,000 jobs are being created annually from the construction boom, and another 800,000 workers annually obtain indirect employment benefits.[10] In terms of housing, the most significant factor has been the additional investment in housing.

> Over the four year period of January 1967 to December 1970, the Bank from this fund and through the multiplier effect of its investment on the employment situation of the country, and in particular the building industry (wherein nearly 500,000 new jobs were created in the year 1969 by BNH investment), through an intensive campaign to reintroduce the habit of savings among the people, and by the sale of real estate bonds (with guaranteed monetary correction against inflation), the BNH mobilized the equivalent of $1,500 million for investment into the housing and urbanization sector of the country. Its annual budget for 1971 was in the order of approximately $1,000 million, and the system has become almost self-generating, to the extent that it is expected to increase by 12 percent each year.[11]

Problems of the System

The accomplishments of the Brazilian financing mechanism are noteworthy, but there remain problems that should be discussed, if a balanced picture is to be given. There are questions about the continued ability of FTGS to continue as the major source of funding for the National Housing Plan. What occurs when the fund has to fulfill its original mandate, that is, social security payments? To prepare for such a contingency, the bank undertook an extensive advertising campaign to increase savings accounts, and began, by the sale of real estate bonds with the monetary correction factor, to offset inflation.[12] The importance of FTGS to the BNH is underscored by the fact that the resources secured from the fund are over twice those received from the Savings and Loan System (see Table 6.2).

The elimination of the slum communities was not done without having to face the social costs of relocation. The difficulties encountered with efforts in Brazil to improve housing conditions of low-income families are applicable to other Latin American countries:

> Another aspect of housing cost which is present but difficult to quantify is the social cost involved when the spontaneous and natural way for low-income urban settlers to upgrade their own situation is deflected. The fact, however, that such families sometimes have to be transported to public developments in hand-cuffs; and that there is a widespread history of delinquency of housing payments on pre-built facilities, even where there are rigorous tenant selection procedures, demonstrate that orthodox developmental processes conflict with the basic requirements of these persons.[13]

One of the first major projects was the construction of new communities on the perimeter of the larger cities planned for the rehousing of the occupants of worst favelas. In spite of the dismal living conditions, many favelados were hesitant to leave their traditional communities for sterile, lifeless homes many miles away.[14] Yet, they were made to move, and strong feelings of resentment still persist. They frequently are uncomfortable and not adjusted to life in the poorly constructed high-rise buildings or row houses.

Most of these communities are too distant from town centers; two or three hours daily is spent on travel in buses. The discontent led the bank to cancel any further forced moves, leaving unsolved the problem of the worst-housed urban dwellers.

Table 6.2

National Housing Bank Resources and Obligations, Brazil, 1965-68
(thousands of U.S. dollars)

| | Period to | | | |
	1965	1966	1967	1968
Available resources				
NHB capital	28,030	43,225	62,567	82,729
FTGS	—	—	193,014	465,000
Brazilian Savings and				
Loan System	—	25,986	84,319	216,820
Obligations undertaken				
Induced savings	3,722	77,356	315,084	776,601
Yielded investments	25,287	142,515	787,725	1,583,450
Units, houses	19,952	57,983	228,396	398,260

Source: Teodoro Rosso, "How Brazil Finances Social Housing,"
Build International 3 (May 1970): 132.

Another weakness is the failure of many low-income borrowers to make their regular monthly payments. The bank discovers that the new borrower cannot make the payments after he has already been granted a loan. Obviously, this points to the need for better screening of credit applicants, unless, as with the FHA in the United States, political pressures lead to a relaxing of credit standards, with a subsequent rash of defaults.

As compared to other mandatory systems, for example, the French, the Brazilian Bank, in accordance with the philosophy and policies of the federal government, is most paternalistic.

Its officials decide who should move, where and, in some cases, when they should move—even the type and size of home they will purchase. As with so many facets of contemporary Brazilian life, people have little or no choice. The government may be well meaning, but it does not feel citizens can decide for themselves what is in their best interests. And the government has almost exclusive authority to decide what should be and what should wait.[15]

The aforementioned difficulties are not necessarily due to defects in the underlying legislation but rather arise out of the indigenous Brazilian political and cultural tradition and from the administration of the legislation. Adoption of the model by other countries should not be entirely precluded; there has been international acclaim in respect to the Brazilian model, influencing the housing finance systems of other countries, such as Argentina, Mexico, and Ghana.

While the United States is unable to find a consistent housing program and constantly seeks new ways to solve its housing difficulties in respect to financing, Brazil has, over a 10-year period, succeeded in channeling funds into the housing sector. "In spite of its problems the dynamic innovative and beneficial performance of the bank cannot be overlooked. It promises to be the principal catalyst for urban development in Brazil for years to come."[16]

MEXICO

INFONAVIT

The Federal Political Constitution of 1917 states that workers are entitled to decent housing, and, on this basis, labor legislation was enacted that obligated employers to provide housing under certain conditions, such as seniority, location, and size of the workplace. Through the initiative of President Echeverria, the legislation was modified in December 1971 to become effective May 1972. It provided for a major program to meet the need for 2.3 million housing units, for, unless steps were taken to alleviate the need for housing, the shortage would increase to 3.2 million units by 1980. The objectives were not only to increase the supply of housing but also to stimulate the growth of the economy and reduce unemployment.

The means of achieving these ambitious goals was through the creation of the Instituto del Fondo Nacional de la Vivienda para los Trabajadores (INFONAVIT) (Institute of the National Housing Fund for Workers). It is basically a banking organization with considerable autonomy, whose control is shared by workers, employers, and the federal government. Its resources come from a 5 percent payroll tax on employers. The government as an employer also contributes 5 percent of the wages for its 700,000 employees. Initial operations are financed by an interest-free loan from the government of 2,000 million pesos ($160 million). Wages of farm workers are exempt from the tax. The proceeds from the payroll tax are not considered as part of the workers' salaries, although they do receive benefits at a later time. The payment by companies is deductible for corporate income tax purposes.

Firms that had ongoing programs for building or financing homes for their employees had to submit details to the fund in order to have their payroll contribution calculated. Workers in these firms had the option of asking that existing plans for furnishing housing be discontinued and that there be compliance with the new 5 percent payroll tax.

Government officials stress that unionized workers will have no priority in the lottery system to be formed to decide who gets the new housing. Loans to workers are granted without any down payment, at an interest rate as low as 4 percent, with a 10- to 20-year term, and life insurance paid by INFONAVIT. Loans can be used to construct housing, repair and enlarge existing housing, or pay off previously incurred housing indebtedness.

> For example, a worker earning the minimum wage may purchase a house worth 30,000 pesos (US $2,400) on an installment payment of 190 pesos per month (US $15.20); the worker with an income of 1,800 pesos per month (US $144), one worth 50,000 pesos (US $4,000) on monthly installment payments of 325 pesos per month (US $26.00). The dramatic mistake of undertaking housing programmes beyond the economic reach of majority groups of workers is thus being corrected.[17]

With conventional financing for a 50,000 peso home, a bank would ordinarily require a 3,000 peso deposit and payments of 500 pesos monthly for 20 years at an interest rate of 6 percent to 10 percent. Under financing by INFONAVIT, in no case need an employee pay more than 20 percent of income for housing. First priority for this housing is given to stable families with two or more children. The preferred type of housing has an average size of 50M, at a cost of some 50,000 pesos ($4,000).[18]

For the first 10 years, although the 5 percent contributions are credited to the worker's account, they are "locked in," but at the end of the 10-year period, the program should be self-supporting, and a worker could withdraw the entire principal without any interest payment "hopefully to invest in the private Mexican economy for his own retirement."[19]

The plans to carry out large-scale construction to the extent of 5,000 million pesos annually ($400 million) for 100,000 low-cost housing units in both urban and rural areas are expected to have a salutary impact on employment. The 100,000 housing units should generate some 126,000 man-years of employment—74,000 direct and 52,000 indirect. The employment effects are similar both for single-

family homes and low-cost multifamily units.[20] Substantial growth is
expected in the construction and building materials sectors. It is estimated that, once the program is in full swing, at least 250,000 new
jobs in the construction industry alone will have been created.[21]

The effectiveness of employment stimulation under this program
depends on the lack of leakage and degree of recovery of the loans and
the rechanneling of the funds back into the construction of housing,
particularly when loans have been granted to pay off previously incurred indebtedness. Another consideration is to what extent the building industry becomes more labor or capital intensive. High prices
for land would reduce the effectiveness of housing funds as employment generators.

The employment of 126,000 persons annually represents some
1.5 percent of the total labor force in 1972. The direct employment
share of 74,000 persons is over 10 percent of the labor force in construction and 27 percent of the net estimated net annual increase in
the urban labor force. The unemployment in the construction sector
of some 70,000 persons could theoretically be absorbed by the genera-
tion of the direct employment of 74,000 workers.[22]

Construction of the 100,000 housing units would have an effect
on the entire economy. In the case of the value of total output, a unit
of final demand for housing requires aggregate output of a little more
than double in the whole economy. The value of output effect breaks
down as follows: 48 percent in the housing sector and 52 percent in
the rest of the economy. A unit of final demand for housing elicits
from the economy aggregate investment needs of about 2.3 units—or
$1 expended on housing has a multiplier effect of $2.30.[23] A 1961
study of the economic impact of the construction of 100,000 new single-
family houses in a one-year period calculates a multiplier effect in
the United States of 2, fairly close to the Mexican figure.[24]

In Mexico, the effect of one unit of expenditure on housing is
about 0.29 units of import requirements of all types (intermediate
consumption and investment). A 1 million peso ($80,000) expenditure
on housing generates total import needs of 290,000 pesos ($23,000).[25]
This proportion may be more applicable to Mexico than other countries, particularly those developing nations for whom one of the benefits from housing is that import expenditures are low.

Accomplishments

It is perhaps premature to expect much in the way of accomplishments from INFONAVIT, but, after three years, "the programs
sets aside a total of 2,250 million pesos ($190 million) in housing
credits. Over 4 million workers are enrolled in this program and

44,000 are receiving benefits directly."[26] INFONAVIT has financed the construction of 51,196 housing units, of which 13,232 are completed, 13,389 are under construction, and 9,947 have been started; 14,626 standard model houses have been completed; it has acquired 19 million square meters of land in a number of cities for future development.[27]

INFONAVIT plans to carry out a large-scale program of housing construction, expending 5,000 million pesos ($400 million) annually for 100,000 low-cost housing units. The housing will be built with supporting community services in clusters of from several hundred units in the center of Mexico City to totally new communities of 14,000 units. Two new communities are under construction: El Rosario, with 14,000 housing units, scheduled for March 1975 completion, and Ixtacalco, with 5,700 units on some 184 acres, costing an average of from $4,000 to $4,500.

The program should have a strong economic impact on the Mexican economy and, in the initial stages, is considered potentially inflationary in terms of the reallocation of scarce resources needed to meet the program's objectives (but not necessarily in terms of the employment of unskilled labor). If the 5 percent payroll tax is the equivalent of a deferred wage increase, there is less immediate purchasing power for workers, that is, assuming workers do not demand pay increases, regardless of the funds set aside for them.

For business firms, there are the added costs over the tax deduction features. But there is relief from any direct obligation to furnish housing to employees, which could entail considerable expense in terms of prolonged labor negotiations and the administrative, financing, and construction responsibilities embodied in previous legislation. Employers in the United States have not found demands for housing a significant factor in their collective bargaining.

CHILE*

A number of Chilean manufacturing firms, even prior to the passage of legislation mandating that funds be set aside for housing, did a great deal to supply their employees with housing. However, the passage of Law no. 7,600, on October 29, 1943, gave considerable impetus to employers' housing building efforts "since most business-

---

*Senor Enrique Labarca Ricci, Subdirector Juridico, Ministeri de la Vivienda y Urbanismo (Deputy Director, Legal Department, Ministry of Housing and Urban Development), was most helpful in providing information for this section.

men prefer to carry out housing programs themselves rather than to throw money down what they conceived to be the government's bottomless well."[28]

The Housing Tax

Law no. 7,600 was instituted to increase the financial resources devoted to housing and to stimulate private firms to construct housing for employees; it called for a tax of 5 percent on the annual profits or earnings of private industrial and mining enterprises and 4 percent on niter enterprises, with the proceeds to be used for the construction of low-cost and sanitary housing, then in short supply. Those firms subject to the tax could build housing for employees with their funds and offset the tax by the imputed value of the housing based on a government appraisal. The housing could not be sold without government authorization, which was given only when sold to the firm's employees. When sufficient housing had been provided for employees, the tax was reduced to 2 percent. The costs of repairing and upgrading could be considered an offset to the 2 percent tax. Property taxes did not have to be paid.

A broad housing policy was embodied in Decree no. 2 of 1959.* The coverage of the 5 percent tax was expanded to include commercial firms, banks, and agricultural enterprises. Additional offsets were allowed against the tax: the amount of the loans given to employees or cooperatives for the acquisition or the construction of economic dwellings. Economic dwellings were defined as not exceeding 140 square meters and without any luxury features in the construction.

CORVI (Corporacion de la Vivienda), the autonomous government housing construction agency, administers or manages the disposition and usage of the housing proceeds, which are limited to the construction or acquisition of economic dwellings. The limitations apply to funds invested in savings accounts, in savings and loan associations (Asociaciones de Ahorro y Prestamo), and funds contributed to Economic Dwelling Construction Societies (Socieda des de Viviendas Economicas). The societies are private entities especially authorized by CORVI to receive the proceeds of the housing tax and are usually called

---

*Decree no. 2 of 1959 is stronger than a presidential decree. A simple presidential decree can be modified or voided by a subsequent presidential decree; whereas Decree no. 2 has the force of a law in that it encompasses the express authorization of the National Congress and, in turn, could only be changed or overturned by another law.

5 percent societies. They can only construct dwellings and are not
allowed to acquire economic dwellings.

Reinvestment

A policy obligating reinvestment was instituted. The proceeds
from the sale of new economic dwellings or the repayment of loans
was to be reinvested in the acquisition or construction of other economic dwellings. The obligation to reinvest continued for 30 years
after the application of the funds or the demise or dissolution of the
contributor or legal entity.

In 1966, the 5 percent CORVI tax was imposed on a number of
U.S.-owned mining enterprises, which were later nationalized.
Previously, as foreign enterprises, they had been exempted. The
Anaconda enterprises have contributed a total of over $50 million for
the CORVI tax, resulting in the construction and sale of over 6,000
dwellings to employees. Tax payments from the Braden Corporation
provided their employees with over 3,000 units.

In 1968, a new law stopped the 5 percent societies from receiving new contributions from the 5 percent tax. They could only operate on the basis of a revolving fund from existing revenues. The same
legislation granted the President of Chile the power to add a 40 percent surcharge to the 5 percent tax under certain conditions. This
discretionary power could raise the effective tax rate to 7 percent.
The various pieces of legislation and other CORVI tax regulations
were combined into a comprehensive law, no. 16,959, of January 10,
1969.

Law no. 17,332, of 1970, modified the housing tax by no longer
allowing the tax to drop to 2 percent as under Law 7,600. When there
is an adequate supply of housing for employees, up to 40 percent of
the 5 percent tax can be used for repairs, additions, improvements
of housing areas, and construction of buildings for communal use or
benefit. The remaining 60 percent can be paid to the treasury or applied to savings accounts.

Prior to the 1970 legislation, the firm was the owner of the
housing and could voluntarily sell them to employees under terms
and prices set by CORVI. However, dwellings acquired or constructed
with CORVI funds are deemed a public utility and can be expropriated
in favor of the employee occupants. When the firm does not want to
sell, the employees can request CORVI to expropriate and have the
units sold with terms of payment for 20 years. As a last resort, the
value of the housing is set by the courts.

The tax payments can be deposited in savings and loan associations but cannot be withdrawn for 30 years, or upon the death of the

contributor, or upon the termination of the activities of the enterprise. During the 30-year period, the funds can be used in their entirety or partially for the acquisition or construction of economic dwellings. There are annual adjustments to compensate for inflation. The same limitations also apply to savings accounts for housing.

The housing tax can only be deducted from income taxes if it is paid to the treasury; it does not constitute a deduction when otherwise allocated. When the proceeds of the taxes are loaned, they constitute an investment that can be recovered and become part of the firm's assets. Juridically it is a long-term housing investment selected by the contributor but made within the framework of government guidelines.

Changing Emphasis

There has been an increase in emphasis on making employees become owners of housing by promoting loans to employees or to cooperatives formed by employees, these loans constitute the largest proportion of housing from the tax proceeds. The loans to the employees are channeled through the savings and loan associations or savings accounts for housing.

The change in the emphasis of the legislation has been from the direct investment by the employers or managers toward the 5 percent societies and, later, toward the financial institutions. The change has not been deliberate but, rather, has occurred as a result of the provisions in Decree no. 2 (1959). When the tax was established in 1943, the only outlet for the proceeds was for the firm to construct dwellings with its own funds for employees' housing.

In 1959, with the other choices available (5 percent societies, loans to employees, savings and loan associations, and so forth), it became easier for the contributor to avoid having to buy land, hire architects and construction firms, and manage property. Also, the firm apparently was tying up more of its funds than it would by other means of allocation. When Law no. 17,332 (1970) allowed the expropriation of the housing constructed directly by the firm, there was little incentive left for direct construction.

NOTES

1. UN Economic and Social Council, Economic Commission for Africa, Report of the UNECA Task Force on Financing of Housing, Building and Regional Planning (E/CN. 14/585, E/CN.14-HOU/99), December 14, 1972; and U.S. Congress, Joint Economic Committee, Interim Report on an Action Program to Reduce Inflation and Restore

Economic Growth, 93rd Cong., 2d sess. (Washington, D.C.: Government Printing Office, 1974), p. 19.

2. Leo Grebler, "Broadening the Sources of Funds for Residential Mortgages," Ways to Moderate Fluctuations in Housing Construction, Federal Reserve System, Board of Governors Staff Study (Washington, D.C.: Board of Governors of the Federal Reserve System, December 1972), p. 204.

3. Benedicto Ferri de Barros, "The National Housing System of Brazil," California Savings and Loan Journal 41 (December 1968): 12.

4. Morris Juppenlatz, "Management of the Planning Process: A Case Study in Brazil," paper presented at Town and Country Planning Summer School, Southhampton, England, 1971, p. 3.

5. Francis E. Hassey, "Indexing: An Inflation Lesson from Brazil," New York Times, sec. F, April 7, 1974, p. 14; George Lefcoe, "Monetary Correction and Mortgage Lending in Brazil: Observations for the United States," Stanford Law Review 21 (November 1968): 106; and "When Rising Prices Get Brazilians Down, They Just Index Up," Wall Street Journal, October 14, 1974, p. 1.

6. De Barros, op. cit., pp. 12, 13.

7. William A. Ellis (Director, U.S. Agency for International Development and Minister for Economic Affairs, American Embassy, Brazil), Testimony, U.S. Congress, Senate, Committee on Foreign Relations, Subcommittee on Western Hemisphere Affairs, Hearings on United States Policies and Programs in Brazil, 92nd Cong., 1st sess. (Washington, D.C.: Government Printing Office, May 1971), p. 180.

8. Morris Juppenlatz, "Brazil: Urban Planning as a Function of National Government," Journal of the Royal Town Planning Institute 58 (February 1972): 64.

9. Teodoro Rosso, "How Brazil Finances Social Housing," Build International 3 (May 1970): 136.

10. Roger S. Leeds, "What Brazil Is Doing about Urban Blight," Johns Hopkins Magazine 25 (May 1974): 6.

11. Juppenlatz, "Management of the Planning Process," p. 3.

12. Rosso, op. cit., pp. 135-36; and Juppenlatz, "Management of the Planning Process," p. 3.

13. Charles C. Boyce, Confronting the Problem of Low-Income Settlement in Latin America, Working Paper Series, no. 4 (Iowa City: University of Iowa, Institute of Urban and Regional Research, n.d.), pp. 18-19.

14. Leeds, op. cit., p. 7.

15. Ibid.

16. Ibid.

17. J. Silva Herzog (Director General, INFONAVIT), Address, Asamblea Constitutiva, Mexico, 1972, pp. 30-31, quoted in G. Araud

et al., Studies on Employment in the Mexican Housing Industry, Organization for Economic Cooperation and Development, Development Center Studies, Employment Series, no. 10 (Paris, 1973), p. 40.

18. Ibid.

19. Don G. Campbell, "Portable Pension Problem—Has Mexico Solved It?" New York Daily News, February 12, 1973, p. 38; and Robert B. Teska, "Mr. Nixon Could Learn from Mr. Echeverria," Planning, 39 (October 1973): 28.

20. Victor L. Urquidi and Adalberto Garcia Rocha, "Housing Construction and Employment in Mexico: Introduction and Overview," Studies on Employment in the Mexican Housing Industry, Organization for Economic Cooperation and Development, Development Center Studies, Employment Series, no. 10 (Paris, 1973), p. 41.

21. "Federal Labor Laws Re: Worker Housing," Semi-Monthly Digest, the Mexican Chamber of Commerce of the United States, no. 743 (New York, April 1, 1972), p. 4.

22. Urquidi and Rocha, op. cit., p. 41.

23. Ibid., p. 34.

24. M. L. Colean and R. J. Saulnier, Economic Impact of the Construction of 100,000 Houses (Chicago: The United States Savings and Loan League, 1961), p. 3.

25. Urquidi and Rocha, op. cit., p. 35.

26. Teska, op. cit., p. 28.

27. U.S. Department of Housing and Urban Development, Office of International Affairs, "Mexico—Workers' Housing Fund Institute," HUD International Information Series no. 25 (November 5, 1973), p. 4.

28. Robert J. Alexander, Labor Relations in Argentina, Brazil and Chile (New York: McGraw Hill, 1962), pp. 335-36.

YUGOSLAVIA:
A CHANGING
HOUSING POLICY

Prior to examining the Yugoslavian employment-based mandatory housing contribution system, a discussion of the background factors in a socialist economy is in order. In addition to the contrasts
with Western economies, the nature of socialism in Yugoslavia differs
sharply from the economies of other Eastern European countries.

HOUSING POLICY

In the period following World War II, housing was treated as a
"social good"; welfare rather than economic factors were deemed to
be of primary importance. Implicit in this policy was the responsibility of the state to supply apartments of suitable size and quality.
Rents were not intended to be set at a level that would cover amortization, maintenance, and operating costs. Subsequently, rents have
been permitted to rise to an economic level, whereby, in 1948, they
were 1 percent of income; in 1950, about 2.5 percent of the average
urban household income; in 1966, 4.6 percent; and, in 1970, an estimated 5.5 percent.[1]
Another factor entering into the formulation of housing policy
is the reaction, since 1948, to a centralized government with strong
controls over economic planning and the ensuing movement of power
away from the central government. The movement matches the makeup
of the diverse Yugoslav populace, representing a variety of nationali-
ties in six republics and two autonomous districts, which result in
strong feelings of self-determination.

WORK ENTERPRISES

The shift of power away from the central government has also been reflected in the growth of autonomy by work enterprises with power by workers to allocate earnings. A basic unit of decision making in the Yugoslavian economy is the work enterprise, a legal entity able to control production and investment and free to establish product prices. It, however, is subject to a complex set of legal and fiscal regulations.

Workers in an enterprise are the managers, profit sharers, and employees. They elect a workers' council, some 10 percent of the employees, which, in turn, elects a management board, who next select a director. The council is the major management body; it distributes earnings, including profits, to workers and to the various enterprise funds. The board more closely directs the firm; it prepares proposals for consideration by the council and executes its directives. The director operates the firm in accordance with the decisions and directives of the council and board.

WORKERS' WAGES

The underlying principle of income allocation in the work enterprises is that the workers control the enterprise through their councils and do not receive wages and salaries in the Western sense. They are not considered to be hired employees with a right to be paid; rather, they are in the category of operators or managers of socialist funds and, thereby, have to bear the risks of management, with earnings supposedly not representing an enterprise cost. Since 1961, workers have been given earnings in the form of personal earnings. Workers' income is dependent on the profits and losses of the enterprise.

The workers' share is calculated by a complex point system, which decides a worker's income at three levels: his personal efforts, the collective efforts of the work unit, and the efforts of the enterprise as a whole.[2] Despite the principle that workers must bear the risks of management, as well as their own responsibilities, there is recognition that the existence of the worker and his family depends on income from employment, whatever the actual performance of the firm. There are two safeguards to assure a minimal income. "Actually the guaranteed incomes are quite low and workers experience a considerable loss."[3]

> (1) A guaranteed personal income level is set by the Government on the basis of the last yearly average personal income per person employed by the cor-

responding branch of industry. If an enterprise is
unable to pay the guaranteed minimum, there is the
communal reserve fund, to which all enterprises
contribute, and from which the difference is given
to the firm. After the enterprise has improved its
financial position, this sum must be returned to the
communal fund. If no improvement is forthcoming,
the workers' management can be suspended, judged
bankrupt and liquidated. The guaranteed income is
distributed according to the firm's own point system.

(2) A minimum personal income is fixed by law
and is the same for all industries and all enterprises.
It is paid out of commune funds. [4]

COMMUNES

Communes that are not coterminous with city or town boundaries
have important economic functions. They frequently furnish investment funds for the start of new enterprises or the expansion of existing ones. In addition to providing funds, the commune may be a guar-
antor for bank loans to the enterprise or may subsidize enterprises
deemed worthy of further growth; it is the principal debtor in the event
of bankruptcy of a firm within its jurisdiction. Although the enterprise
is under no legal compulsion to follow the commune's recommendations, the political, economic, and moral influence is considerable.
If firms could finance investment from retained earnings, the commune
would have less influence; but few firms can do this.

HOUSING ENTERPRISES

Initially, housing enterprises, another unique feature of the
Yugoslavian economy, were largely involved in the management and
maintenance of existing housing. Subsequently, they were given ownership and management of both industrial and public housing, became
active in the construction of housing, and served to pool capital for
housing. All funds accumulated by housing enterprises through de-
preciation reserves and any balances remaining from rents after
amortization and payment of maintenance and operating costs were
channeled into new construction.

The control of housing enterprises is not easily categorized.
The workers' council or staff of a housing enterprise has a role in
the control, but there are limitations to their power in terms of mean-
ingful policy decisions. There is an additional, and perhaps more

powerful, control system based on the functions performed by the enterprise and exercised by those served, that is, the residents through their representatives on the assembly. For example, the assembly of Dom, one of the two main housing enterprises in Ljubljana, with 21,000 dwellings, consists of 191 members elected by those living in the housing owned or managed by Dom.[5]

In a small organization—less than 30 members—a merger of the workers' council and assembly is allowed. To illustrate, in a small housing enterprise, the assembly consisted of the eight staff members, six representatives of the block housing committees, and five from the enterprises furnishing the bulk of the financing from local firms and the commune.[6]

In a large organization, the next step is for the assembly to elect from among its members an executive or management board with various interests represented—the organizations furnishing money, mainly industry and commerce, also communes, individual owners of dwellings bought from the housing enterprise, and the staff of workers' council.

The housing enterprise has no voice in tenant selection. The right is retained by those who have invested in the enterprise. Of the 21,000 dwellings managed by the aforementioned Dom, 11,000 are at the disposal of communes, 5,000 of firms, and 4,500 of private owners. In a small commune outside of Ljubljana, of the 906 dwellings in the housing enterprise, 27 percent, or 244, of the allocation rights belonged to the commune and the remainder to firms.[7] The division of allocation rights varies considerably throughout the country.

Each organization (work enterprise, commune, and so forth) that finances housing can establish its own point system for determining admission priorities to a corresponding number of housing units that it controls. Prior to July 1959, housing was allocated by state administrative action before workers' organizations took over. The work enterprise supplying housing for its employees sets its own rules on the allocation of housing, following full discussion among the workers. The assembly of workers may delegate the right of selection to a committee, but complaints against its decisions are directed to the assembly. There is no administrative or judicial appeal against these decisions. The working man is assumed to be protected because as a member of a workers' organization he participates directly or indirectly in the adoption of these statutes. The committee to select occupants is composed exclusively of workers from the enterprise.

In the event of termination or separation from employment, action may be brought for eviction. Legal provision is made for the eviction of tenants who are transferred and receive quarters at the new work place.[8] If the worker wants to continue to live in work en-

terprise housing, he must arrange for the financing to purchase it
from the enterprise.[9]

HOUSING FUNDS[10]

The next and key step in this examination of the Yugoslavian
housing system is to discuss the development of the mandatory housing
fund. In 1951, steps were gradually taken to separate housing finance
from the governmental budget and tie it to the available funds of enterprises for whose workers new housing was being built.

Prior to the enactment of the Federal Social Plan for 1955,*
preference was given to development and industrialization, and the investment in housing was low; a special contribution for housing was
introduced and has, in various forms, become a major source of
housing funds. It became incumbent upon constituent republics, districts, towns, and communes to allocate at least 3 percent of their
revenues to housing credit funds. In 1956, a special law set contributions for housing at 10 percent of net personal income of workers,
other employees as well as of all socially insured persons such as
employees of private organizations and self-employed.** By a decision of the Federal Executive Council,† and subsequent regulations,
the minimum down payment for loan applicants was 15 percent of the
value of the housing. The minimum repayment period was set at 50
years, and the minimum interest charges at 1 percent. The use of
the funds was gradually expanded to include a set proportion for public utilities and schools.

The first housing reform in 1959 made major changes in housing policy, with a stronger emphasis on housing economics. Credit
terms were made more stringent, with larger down payments, shorter
repayment periods, and higher interest charges. The increased
stringency was considered necessary to ensure maximum mobilization
of public and private resources for housing. As a result, enterprises
and other organizations raised the allocation from their welfare funds
to supply housing for their workers.

In 1960, the mandatory housing contribution was cut from 10
percent of net personal income to 4 percent of gross personal income.
The tax proceeds went to a system of credit institutions, with enterprise social service and housing funds the principal source of housing
finance. In addition to these sources, there was almost the same

---

*Official Gazette FPRY, no. 56/54.
**Official Gazette FPRY, no. 57/55.
†Official Gazette FPRY, no. 31/57 and 47/58.

amount from communal funds. The pressure exerted by workers for
the resolution of their housing problems then was concentrated on the
firm.

The Economic Reform Act of 1965 compelled many business enterprises to concentrate on solving their business problems. They
were unable to assign further resources for housing, and, in the cases
of liquidity problems, were permitted to use funds previously designated for housing as working capital. It was estimated that, in 1967
and 1968, some 700 million to 800 million dinars earmarked for
housing were allocated to other uses.

Economic measures were taken in 1968 to foster the expansion
of housing construction, with the viewpoint that "housing construction
can have a broader economic impact when it has reached a level where
it begins to have an accelerated effect on economic activity, the rise
in employment and stabilization of economic trends."[11]

Almost all federal functions in the housing sector were transferred in 1971-72 to the republics and provinces; republics then enacted
legislation for the allocation of resources to housing. Notwithstanding
great differences among the republics and provinces in the degree of
economic development and the need for housing, the rate for mandatory
contributions imposed on personal incomes ranged from 4.5 percent to
6.0 percent, as compared to the previous federal legislation setting
the rate at 4.0 percent. A new mechanism for the allocation of resources to housing was initiated in this same period. Resources were
directed by work enterprises and communes to the financing of housing for workers of enterprises with a low level of accumulated funds
and, also, to the subsidy of rents.

Other sources of funding for housing were a mandatory allocation by banks of savings for housing purposes, assuming the bank was
in a strong enough position to do so, and the amortization payments
on loans by the commune housing funds, which were taken over by the
banks in 1965. In addition to the mandatory contribution from personal
incomes collected by work enterprises, the enterprises could supply
additional moneys for housing.

According to a survey, the most commonly intended use of remittances by Yugoslavian emigrant workers in other European countries was for housing construction and improvement. The enormous
increase in the construction of private housing has been to a significant extent financed by their remittances.[12]

THE OUTLOOK

About 50 percent of all funds for new construction come from
banks, 30 percent from firms, 15 percent from private savings, and

the remainder from the communes.[13] As to the future, it is considered likely that work enterprises will no longer contribute, and the total cost of residential construction in the public sector will be borne by the rents, less management fees and bank credit. Construction costs are intentionally being allowed to rise and lift housing prices, which are to be paid for by the occupant.[14]

As contrasted to Western countries, where housing subsidies are becoming more pervasive and available to higher-income groups because of the rising cost of housing, Yugoslavia is moving in the opposite direction, that is, of letting rents cover costs and reducing the extent of government assistance. There have been substantial moves made toward the decentralization of housing policy and management and away from the central government; whereas, in the United States, decentralization has been an elusive goal in the formulation of federal housing legislation.

The housing enterprise serves as a means of bringing together funding from diverse sources and yet allowing the investors to have a voice in the allocation of housing; it also is a mechanism for giving a number of separate groups control of the enterprise.

The use of a percentage of personal income as a means of allocating resources for housing works well in an expanding economy with the housing sector benefiting; yet, the opposite situation must be considered where the economy is declining. Those persons in marginal firms, as well as the low-income and the self-employed, do not benefit to the same extent in a system that is tied to contributions for housing from work enterprises. There appears to have been recognition that not all firms can meet the required housing contribution and still remain solvent.

NOTES

1. Gordon Rose, "Recent Housing Policy in Yugoslavia," Social and Economic Administration 4 (January 1970): 33-34.
2. Rudolph Bicanic, Economic Policy in Socialist Yugoslavia (London: Cambridge University Press, 1973), p. 109.
3. Deborah D. Milenkovitch, Plan and Market in Yugoslav Economic Thought (New Haven, Conn.: Yale University Press, 1971), p. 215.
4. Bicanic, op. cit., p. 110.
5. Rose, op. cit., p. 25.
6. Ibid., p. 26.
7. Ibid., p. 27.
8. Charles S. Ascher, The Administration of Publicly Aided Housing (Brussels: International Institute of Administrative Sciences; and The Hague: Martinus Nijhoff, 1971), pp. 32, 37, 58, 183.

9. Katherine C. Lyall, "Joint Capitalist Socialist Enterprise: A Yugoslav Experiment," in "Yugoslavia," Pratt Planning Papers (March 1972), p. 44.

10. Unless otherwise indicated, sources are Stojka Milojevic, "Housing," Yugoslav Survey 8 (February 1967): 93; Bozidar Popovic, "Housing Policy," Yugoslav Survey 8 (November 1967): 63; and Stojka Milojevic and Ivan Jeremic, "Housing," Yugoslav Survey 14 (May 1973): 89.

11. Milojevic and Jeremic, op. cit., p. 95.

12. Organization for Economic Cooperation and Development, Yugoslavia (Paris, 1973), p. 39.

13. Rose, op. cit., p. 28.

14. Rose, op. cit., p. 30.

8

ROMANIAN HOUSING
ACHIEVEMENTS
AND PROSPECTS

Romania has a socialist system in which the Communist Party is the leading political force. In this country, about the size of Oregon, with a population of approximately 21 million, the apparatus of the party oversees all activities and the state owns all of the major means of production, including land and housing. The state is also the sole participant in foreign trade and controls internal trade through the regulation of retail prices.

Romania has experimented with decentralization and federalization in pricing, foreign trade, in enterprise management through the creation of centrales (holding companies that manage a cluster of enterprises), and in the development and administration of housing programs. Results were regarded as uneven; in some cases, decentralization went too far. Thus, in 1974 and 1975, the trend toward decentralization and federalization have been largely reversed, through a return to centralized control.

By establishing a political dialogue with China and the West, especially the United States, Romania has become a political maverick among the Communist countries. It is reported that she plays a relatively independent role in Comecon and in the political-military arrangements of the Warsaw Pact.[1] However, in the housing sector, she is less of a maverick.

RECENT ECONOMIC TRENDS AND POLICIES

Romania is bent on "catch up economics." The goal is to transform the country from an agricultural to an industrial producer. Economic plans for the 1976-80 period were adopted by the party in November 1974. This five-year plan calls for investment to rise 10.5

percent to 11.4 percent a year.[2] Romania's allocation of resources
to investment is, as of 1975, the highest in Eastern Europe and one
of the highest in the world. Industrial production and national income
are planned to increase by 9 percent to 10 percent annually.

Great emphasis is placed on increasing coal output, metallurgy,
engineering, electronics, machine building, and chemicals.[3] The output of agricultural products remains a fundamental problem. These
new directives call for agricultural output to increase over the average of the past Five-Year Plan by 25 percent to 30 percent. In spite of
major social programs and a relatively low average population growth
of 0.9 percent, sizable housing needs remain unfilled. The housing
problem remains sufficiently bothersome so that the 1976-80 Draft
Plan includes the following statement: "A main objective of the policy
of raising the living standard of the population is the acceleration of
housing construction."[4]

The Draft directives of 1976-80 call for mandatory allocations
and subsidies of state funds or state-granted loans to be commissioned
for the construction of 815,000 apartments. And this time "the state
will ensure the materials for the building of dwellings in villages by
the rural population," something not always done in the past, with a
consequent failure to meet housing targets.[5] Planning in the East or
West is a very uncertain thing, but it does appear in Romania's case
that the targets of the last Five-Year Plan (1971-75) will be met in
four years and six months. The report in Table 8.1 on the 1971-75
plan was presented to the Eleventh Party Congress in November 1974.

In Table 8.1, consider the volume of foreign trade as it reveals
the tremendous drive for foreign trade markets. Recognize too that
the volume of goods and retail sales continue to show a very modest
increase. (Housing performance will be covered in the next section.)

A study of the 1976-80 plan reveals that the building materials
industry is projected to grow at an average annual rate of 7 percent to
8 percent (see Table 8.2). It is not likely that all of that increase
will find its way into housing. A portion will go to the industrial-man-
ufacturing area and to ensure that the requirements of other national
investment programs will be met. It is also expected that part of this
additional output will be used in joint ventures with other countries.
So far as housing needs are concerned, the draft plan includes the
statement, "and meet the population's requirements in better conditions."[6] The key economic and social targets of the 1976-80 plan are
stated in Table 8.2.

The essence of Romania's housing policies and happenings present and future can be gleaned by a reading of closing paragraphs of the
text of the 1981-90 economic and social development plan.

TABLE 8.1

Eleventh Party Congress, Report on Five-Year Plan, Romania, 1971-75

Item	Directives of Tenth Congress	Envisaged in Five-Year Plan for Five Years	Forecast Results for Four Years	Forecast Results for Five Years
Social product, average annual growth rate (percent)	—	10.1	10.9	11.5
National income, average annual growth rate (percent)	7.7-8.5	11-12	12.1	12.6
Overall industrial production, average annual growth rate (percent)	8.5-9.5	11-12	13.7	14.1
Overall agricultural production, growth of annual average as to average in 1966-70 (percent)	28-31	36-49	30	37.0
Total investments in national economy (thousands of millions lei)	—	540	413	558
Volume of foreign trade, percent growth as to 1970 (constant prices)	—	61-72	78	98
Labor productivity in socialist industry, growth as against 1970 (percent)	37-40	42	30.2	42
Growth of personnel in national economy (thousands of persons)	400-500	1.000	980	1.300
Volume of goods, retail sales, average annual growth rate (percent)	5.4-6.2	7-8	8.3	8.7
Real remuneration, growth over 1970 (percent)	16-20	20	13	24
Peasantry's real incomes from agricultural output, growth over 1970 (percent)	15-20	22-30	31	35

Source: Draft Directives of the Eleventh Congress of the Romanian Communist Party Concerning the 1976-1980 Five Year Plan and the Guidelines for the Economic and Social Development of Romania in the 1981-1990 Period (Bucharest: Romanian News Agency, 1974), p. 5.

TABLE 8.2

Key Economic and Social Targets, Five-Year Plan, Romania, 1976-80

Target	1980 Versus 1975	Annual Average Rate in 1976-80
Social product	147-154	8-9
National income	154-161	9-10
Gross industrial output	154-161	9-10
Gross agricultural output (annual average for five-year period)	125-131	4.6-6.0
Distribution of national income (average for five-year plan period; percent versus total national income)		
Consumption fund	66-67	—
National fund of economic and social development	33-34	—
Total investments in economy (five-year period)	165-172	10.5-11.4
Foreign trade volume (five-year period)	172-180	11.5-12.5
Number of personnel	116-119	3-3.5
Labor productivity (with present working week)		
In industry	138-142	6.7-7.2
In building-assembly	150-156	8.4-9.4
In railway transport	120-126	3.7-4.8
Cut of expenditures per 1,000 lei marketable output in the national industry	6.5-7.0	—
Total real incomes of population	135-137	6.2-6.5
Remuneration fund	151-155	8.6-9.2
Real remuneration	118-120	3.4-3.7
Real incomes of peasantry per active person, deriving from work in agricultural production cooperatives and individual farmsteads	120-125	3.7-4.6
Volume of goods retail sales	140-145	7.0-7.7

Source: Draft Directives of the Eleventh Congress of the Romanian Communist Party Concerning the 1976-1980 Five Year Plan and the Guidelines for the Economic and Social Development of Romania in the 1981-1990 Period (Bucharest: Romanian News Agency, 1974), p. 15.

Ensured will be the necessary material groundwork for the expansion of the cultural and artistic horizon of all citizens, for the development of physical culture and mass sport. In the 1975-90 period, 2.5-3.0 million flats will be built, with a bigger weight of new 3-4 room flats and increased useful area in each flat; in this way the housing question will be solved by and large.

New housing spaces, building of social and cultural establishments, the laying out of rest and recreational parks, the growing level of technical communal equipping—water supplies, sewerage, modern street networks and public transport—will radically change the face of our towns and villages.

11. The development envisaged will go hand in hand with deep-going qualitative changes in the country's social structure. It is estimated that, following the measures of raising the birth rate, of consolidating the family and of mother and child protection, in 1990 Romania will have some 25 million strong population. The number of persons employed in economic and social activity will stand at over 11 million. The working class will represent the overwhelming majority of the country's population in 1990. Labour force employed in agriculture will be continually reduced, amounting to 12-15 percent of the total gainfully employed population in 1990. The ranks of the intelligentsia, particularly of the technical, will expand.

As a result of the development on modern bases of industry and of agriculture, and of the other branches, of the introduction of mechanization and automation means in production, of the growing general training level of the population, the process of gradually removing the essential differences between village and town, between physical and intellectual work will proceed on a growing scale, accentuating the homogenization of society.[7]

Of all the countries examined in this volume, only Romania is willing to state that by 1990 "the housing question will be solved by and large."

Perhaps it is the qualifier "by and large" that reassures us that the Socialists will not continue to define and regiment housing need so narrowly as to have solved the problem for all time.

Housing Policy

It would take an oyster knife to separate a Romanian housing plan from the country's plans for industrialization. The volume of total investment in the Romanian lei (12 lei for the U.S. tourist dollar; a commercial rate of 4.97 lei for the dollar; and a custom valuation rate of 200 lei for the dollar) and the relative commitment to housing can be seen from Table 8.3.

Romania's annual investment in housing has remained relatively constant, yet numbers of conventional apartments show increases. The data are incomplete. Category definitions may not always be consistent. Could it be that the quality of the apartments has been reduced? Most probably, more effective production of building materials and site-project management may have occurred.

The primary concern of the country is to achieve and maintain an average annual growth rate of 14 percent to 15 percent per year and achieve industrialization.

> This single national objective creates some opportunities and sets certain priorities for the use of the human and economic resources of Romania. It is the general policy of the Party and the Government to aim harmoniously for balanced growth and development of towns and provinces. Some zones of Romania remain less developed. The development of these under developed zones is especially considered in each five year plan. [8]

Within the context of housing there are two categories of unique national plans that must be considered:

1. The Five-Year Plan, the current plan, covers the period 1976–80.
2. Annual plans: These plans cover all economic and social targets and tasks including housing; it is the annual plan that actually brings about housing and development through:
    a. supplying finance and materials
    b. identifying the specific location for housing

Housing is constructed by zone or territory. Thus, geographic areas with the highest economic development have the highest land services and housing development priority. These plans may involve new construction and/or rehabilitation or demolition of older buildings.

TABLE 8.3

Centralized Investments from State Funds, 1971-75*

(millions of lei)

Selected Sector	1971	1972	1973	1974	1975	1971-75
Industry	42,800	54,900	62,300	62,300	58,900	281,200
Building industry	3,700	3,300	3,400	3,900	4,200	18,500
Agriculture (including forestry and water management and other farming activities)	14,100	13,700	15,900	18,100	19,600	81,400
Loans to producing cooperatives	2,100	2,200	2,600	2,900	3,200	13,000
Transportation and telecommunication	8,300	8,600	10,200	12,400	14,100	53,600
Trade, public catering, hotels, silos, storehouses	2,500	2,400	2,300	2,800	3,200	13,200
Education, culture, health protection	1,700	1,800	1,900	2,000	2,200	9,600
Science	800	900	800	1,100	900	4,500
Housing construction	2,400	2,500	2,700	3,000	3,700	14,300
Municipal utilities	1,500	1,200	1,400	1,700	2,300	8,100
Total investment	75,800	87,200	97,800	103,400	105,800	470,000

*Excludes decentralized investment from enterprises, cooperatives, and people's own funds. Centralized investment normally accounts for 85.5 percent of all investment. With the reversal back to centralization, the distinction and practice of decentralized funds has been abolished as of 1974. The Romanian Library, New York, N.Y., reports in July 1975 that actual combined expenditures for housing and municipal utilities were: 1971, 4,600; 1972, 5,400; 1973, 6,100; 1974 planned (centralized and decentralized combined), 5,900; and August 1975 planned, 14,800.

Source: "Five Year Plan 1971-75" (Article 17, Volume of Total Central Investment), Official Bulletin of the State 1972, Bucharest.

TABLE 8.4

Housing Volume, by Funding Source, Romania, 1971-75*

State Funds	Private Housing Supported by State Credit, Construction, Land, and Tax Concessions	Private Housing, Utilizing People's Own Funds (state releases building materials for purchase)
250,000 apartments	250,000 apartments	30,000-40,000 houses

*Primarily urban housing; rural housing is not included.

Housing Funds

There are three financial mechanisms at work in the housing sector and three sources of funds. Their relative importance during the last Five-Year Plan can be seen in Table 8.4. During the period 1971-75, government housing officials informed the author that 60,000 private houses were added in each of the five years of the plan, or an additional 300,000 units.

Through 1985, Romanian housing experts are planning for an additional 800,000 urban apartments funded through mandatory subsidies of the first and second type, as identified in Table 8.4. With respect to the 1975 figure, the 1985 targets represent a 60 percent increase.

Strategy Adopted Relative to Housing

Relating housing development to industrial development targets is the key. Housing strategy is a function, in fact, a residual of plans for accumulating the base for industrial manufacturing plant capacity. New industrial plant locations in rural areas and expansion of existing industrial sites involving a need for land development, infrastructure, and housing receive priority for the mandatory housing allocations.

While there continues to be a fundamental problem of low agricultural output, considerable rationalization and mechanization has already occurred. Agricultural cooperatives and state firms control 91 percent of the land. For example, agriculture's share in the labor force in 1950 was 73.3 percent. By 1973, it had dropped to 44.0 percent. In other words, much mechanization has been introduced to increase food supplies and allow agriculture labor to shift to other employment sectors. These trends compare in the United States to 15.3 percent of the labor force in agriculture in 1950. By 1973, the labor force so employed fell to 4.6 percent.[9]

In the 30 years since the end of World War II, major structural changes have occurred. Development of the secondary manufacturing sector has proceeded rapidly. Rationalization and mechanization have taken place in the primary or agricultural sector, and the labor force has shifted from primary to secondary and tertiary sectors, that is, services.

A recent essay by Romania's Prime Minister, Manea Manescu, who is also actively engaged as a professor and chairman of the economic department of the Academy of Economic Studies, confirms these structural changes by examining shifts in national income for the same sectors (see Table 8.5).

As observed by Romanian housing professionals, the normal housing strategy is for large population and housing concentrations to occur, complete with urban sprawl. Such a phenomenon is not unknown in the Bucharest region. Romanian planners do not want the labor force to move to just a few population centers but, rather, through "planning," to shunt the labor force to smaller, less-developed villages and towns.

Romanian housing experts stressed the great deal of discussion and study that occurred regarding the reemployment and related housing strategy appropriate for labor, freed as a result of economic development programs. Especially stressed was the discussion during 1973 and 1974, as they were refining future five-year housing plans. They were preoccupied with developing programs, to avoid the rapid growth of a relatively small number of already heavily populated industrialized areas.

Special studies were commissioned to outline a plan for "territorial development," which would provide for the rechanneling of freed labor away from large population sectors.

In some respects, the Romanians, their love for city life, especially in Bucharest, the Paris of the East, with its population of 1.6 million, is like the feeling of large city lovers in Latin America. Bucharest has always been the place where "the action is"—political, social, and economic status is to be found in "sunny downtown" Bucharest. Even today, the best opera, ballet, and television reception of that famed U.S. detective Columbo are all there.

Down the scale, Constanza on the Black Sea, Ploiesti, and Timisoara and Iasi, all at around 200,000 to 250,000 population, have

TABLE 8.5

Basic Shifts in National Income Structure, Romania, 1938-73
(percent)

| Year | Sector | |
	Industry	Agriculture
1938	30.8	38.1
1960	44.1	33.0
1965	48.9	29.9
1973	58.1	18.5

Source: Manea Manescu, Social Present and Future of Romania
(Bucharest, 1974), p. 3.

appealed to Romanians as cosmopolitan sectors. In its efforts to
decentralize and initiate a form of territorial development, Romanian
planners have been confronted with this longing for city life.

Another student of Romania has commented on another dimension of territorial housing development. How to keep them "down on
the farm," near the new plant, is now a strategic problem.

> Their establishment [geographic dispersion of cen-
> trales and manufacturing plants] therefore requires
> a fairly massive shift of engineers, accountants,
> and economists from the center to the provinces.
> Most of the persons affected object rather strenuously
> to the transfer. They make use of whatever influ-
> ence they possess to remain in the capital city,
> transferring to positions which pay less but confer
> the right of residence in the capital . . . if there
> are any oranges to be had in Romania they are to
> be found in Bucharest. The top flight surgeons are
> to be found there also and the best in schools and
> universities.[10] [And it might also be added, the
> best housing.]

A special study, entitled Romanian Territorial Social and Economic Development 1976-1990, was reviewed with the writer at the
executive committee office of the Committee for the People's Councils' Problems, a focal point for housing planning, implementation,

and audit. (The office, by the way, is centrally located in Bucharest, within sight of the famous Grand Hotel Athenee Palace.) The purpose of this study is to propose strategic and tactical plans for identifying and creating opportunities for employing freed labor forces, especially from agriculture, and utilizing them in new manufacturing activities close to their present geographic residence. This strategy also involves improving or expanding villages and towns, plus local support services, for example, schools, hospitals, and transport.

Territorial economic development programs have been outlined for 250 newly emerging urban settlements on a county by county basis. The county of Dolj is typical. It lies west of Bucharest and now has four towns and one urban center. Over the period of the plan (through 1990), this county will have four new urban centers and nine new villages, all with related housing developments. The aim is to achieve this same balanced, developed activity in each of Romania's 39 counties.

Some villages are a considerable distance from an urban center. There exists, even before the start of the intensive territorial development program, the problem of adequately housing and serving the population. In these cases, the strategy calls for the creation of additional urban housing centers, with a uniform balance of supporting facilities and services, that is, schools, clinics, industrial training institutes—all supporting newly established industrial plants. This territorial approach calls for schools and specialized worker institutes to be located in such a way that these services will not be more than about 9 milies to 12 miles from where a person lives. Medical consultations are planned in the same way. Each village is being served by a general practitioner.

According to Romanian housing specialists, some 8 million persons now reside in towns and 12 million in villages. In the next 15 years to 20 years, planners project a total population ranging from 25 million to 26 million. Apparently, precise population projections are not always a prerequisite to successful planning. Implementation of the proposed territorial plan would result in an urban population of 14 million and a rural, newly developed, and revitalized village population of 12 million. This kind of geographic decentralization, intensive development, and managed labor mobility is well under way.

Thus, Romania's new housing strategy is to place industrial working centers close to existing places of residence and to create a self-contained economic unit of agriculture, expanded industrial activity, and appropriate support services (thus enabling Colin-Clark's and Rostow's stages of economic development to take place in predetermined geographic confines).

Parts of this program have been enacted into law, but careful consideration of the two main ideas continues and seems to be reviewed on a site by site, industry by industry, basis.

The two main ideas, as confirmed by Romanian housing specialists, are the following:

1. If we spread and geographically disperse, there will be a lowering of efficiency in industry. We may not receive the benefits of long production runs provided by large plants with integrated operations. Further, instead of one large integrated industrial park with nearby housing, hostels, and schools, we will have to duplicate such facilities and thus experience heavy, greater social costs.

2. If we put the working places closer to the residents and solve the problems of services, transport, water, supplies, sewage, and necessary investment, our industrial and social costs will be lower. We will avoid the frequently damaging psychological impact of changes when peasants are uprooted. Further, we must disperse in order to take into account, and successfully reduce, the problems of environment—deterioration, chemical, thermal, electrical, air pollution, and other harmful effects.

Housing planners in Bucharest are concerned with another aspect of territorial development. Should not the greater part of rural agricultural processing be transformed close to the growing area? These agricultural-processing industries should also link with the new clusters of primary, secondary, and tertiary activity.

And so the planners and housing specialists in Romania continue their deliberations.

> Should we concentrate and centralize, or should we decentralize?
>
> Would experience indicate that great concentration is not a happy solution?
>
> Perhaps we should decentralize but not all industries. It should be done on an enterprise by enterprise basis. It may be that we should keep our large industrial platforms (great industrial parks devoted to producing a given product line, for example, garments: fourteen thousand workers on two floors, two shifts, producing mens apparel complete with supporting services, i.e., 300 person studying group, clinic, school, housing, foreign trade company, and so on).[11]

There is little doubt that heavy industry will expand, guided by the "concentrated" principle. Selected industries might easily be geographically dispersed. One example might be the production of component parts, such as gears, electric motor assemblies, and so on.

HOUSING FOR U.S. RESIDENTS

It is difficult for Westerners to fully understand the cultural differences that exist in an Eastern European country, especially the differences in housing quality. Some notion of the cross cultural interface is to be found by conversing with those U.S. managers now assigned to Romania by their companies and living in Romanian housing developments. Generally, apartments made available to foreign managers are at the upper end of the quality scale.

A good case in point is the Control Data joint venture in manufacturing with the Industrial Centrale of Electronics and Automatization (CITC) in Bucharest.* The new joint company manufactures computer peripheral products; the company is 45 percent owned by Control Data Corporation of the United States and 55 percent owned by the Romanians. The company's initial social capital is $4 million, contributed on the basis of the ownership share. Part of the capital consists of such assets as licenses, equipment, technological know-how, plants, components, training, and so forth. Working capital will be raised through bank borrowings guaranteed by the parents. The output of the plant will be sold to both Control Data and to CITC and both of these organizations are free to market these products worldwide. Both Control Data and its partner, CITC, expect to realize a profit from this joint venture.

A reading of the agreement indicates many provisions designed to provide for the welfare of U.S. personnel participating in the venture, that is, salary levels, duty free import and reexport of cars, net income transfers abroad, and so forth.

Control Data also had to prepare the managers and their families because of the Eastern European environment. The procedure was as follows:

First, a number of technically qualified people were selected as candidates for the U.S. representatives of the joint venture. These candidates, their wives, and their teen-aged children were then processed through a system of multiple interviews to determine their suitability for this assignment. A highly skilled psychologist was used in this screening process to assure that (1) the husband-wife team was one of harmony; otherwise, the rigors of the new environment could break down their ability to cope with adversity and to ad-

---

*In this case, we are grateful for inputs from Hugh P. Donaghue, Assistant to Chief Executive Officer, and Ambassador C. Bogdan. Conversations regarding this venture took place in Bucharest, at the World Trade Institute Conference, New York City, November 1974, and the University of Mighican Romanian Conference, December 1974.

just functionally to language differences, culture shocks, and so forth; and (2) the family group could be prepared for an interpersonal relationship with the Romanian people.

This careful screening process was actually only one element of a total systems approach to full functioning and effective management of the joint venture with the Romanians. It resulted in the selection of six candidates (wives and families) to represent Control Data in this enterprise.

The second phase was the training of these families for their new role. Initially, the families were moved to a secluded environment where they were given two weeks of intensive language training. Interspersed with this instruction were elements of interculture communications training. Miniature language laboratories were prepared in advance, utilizing Cannon Repeat-coders. (In this system, language tapes are provided so that the students can listen, speak, and hear themselves in the learning cycle. This training included the teenaged children.)

After an intensive two-week, day-and-night language training, the families returned to their homes to prepare for the physical move. Documented guidance on what to bring with them, what to put into storage, and their actual needs versus the "nice-to-have" articles were provided. During this stage, which lasted six to eight weeks, the language labs were still made available, so that individual language study could continue.

The last stage involved a return to Washington, D.C., where intensive training in Romanian studies was conducted.

Some notion as to the differences in housing quality can be appreciated by examining some of the "social" clauses of the Control Data Romanian venture, as reported by the American participant.[12]

Housing

In Bucharest, the normal apartment size is between 400 square feet and 600 square feet, depending on the size of the family that occupies these apartments. Since this was about one-half the size for a comparable American family, two apartments were sought and acquired for each family. Control Data paid for the leasehold improvements required to combine two apartments into a single unit. The work was performed by local Romanian labor. These apartments were made available to the American families in the latter half of July.

Food

The American employees had the privilege of using the facilities of the foreign trade company, TERRA, for the purchase of food from the West, to supplement their local purchases. Even with this arrangement, more and more of their purchases were made in the local marketplace.

Education

Fifteen school-age children attended the International School in Bucharest. Although only in the school for a short period of time, they seemed to be adjusting quite well. The only problem turned out to be transportation to and from school. That was solved by buying the Romanian equivalent of a Volkswagen bus and hiring a driver to transport them back and forth between the apartment complex and the school. This was an unexpected additional cost to Control Data.

Health

The Americans in Bucharest have access to the Diplomatic Clinic, which, as its name implies, was established for the diplomatic corps in Romania. In addition to this, however, Control Data arranged for a private hospital air service that operates in Vienna to fly out any of its people with serious ailments or injuries.

For the convenience of its people, Control Data purchased one Fiat 132 for each family. Also, membership in the Diplomatic Club was provided. Under this arrangement, each family was to be flown to some major city in Western Europe for a one-week vacation each quarter.

Control Data's experience to date indicates that the first 90 days of adjustment are the toughest. Incidents that were of major concern during the first 90 days are now occurrences that are simply shrugged off and quickly forgotten. In response to the question, "Would you do it again?" Control Data responded affirmatively.

HOUSING AND THE INDIVIDUAL

Every village in Romania has the right to decide and to make recommendations concerning housing. The percent of state funds for housing must be related to population and the level of current and proposed economic activity in the area. The local council is the administrator involved.

It is interesting to note that, when an individual fails to pay rent to the housing enterprise, he is taken to court. It is customary for the court to give the defaulter an opportunity to pay. Failure to do so results in condemnation, and the housing enterprise is empowered by the court to go to the employer and retain the rent from the worker's salary.

In addition to state funds being allocated for housing, each industrial enterprise can use some of its moneys for "necessary" housing. "Necessary" means the housing of those experts who must be on call to ensure the smooth functioning of the plant. Apartments are also built by enterprises to attract and hold young singles and young marrieds as employees of the plant.

Romanian housing experts report that each enterprise contributes from their surplus (beyond the profit target) as much as 95 percent toward the state central fund for housing. Every industrial organization contributes its extra profits from which state housing is financed. The percentage contributed is a matter of administration, rather than a set percentage, as is being used in Yugoslavia, for example.

Money is available that is a credit loan from the state. Some loans are from 15 years to 20 years, with a down payment. The enterprise works closely with its employees on this matter, in fact, arranging priorities for individual workers. The enterprise guarantees that the employee can pay the necessary moneys and recommends that he can rent an apartment or build. Legally, the land is reserved for the life of the building, such as for 99 years. The resident pays 1 lei (1 U.S. tourist dollar equals 12 lei) for each square meter per year, up to 150 square meters, or 12 lei per month for land. Rents are low. Depending on the individual's income, they may be high. Credit is available for low-income groups—20 percent to 30 percent of the value of the flat may be obtained. The loan term ranges from 15 years to 25 years, depending on income. If a citizen does not have money for the down payment, the state will advance these monies at 8 percent to 10 percent. Rental flats relate on a per capita basis of about 10 square meters. With three members in the family, the state allows two rooms, not including an area for the kitchen, balcony, and bath annex. A private house can have as many rooms as desired by the owner, subject to height, land area, zoning restrictions, and loan limits.

Credit is also available for private homes. These may be sold but not for profit. The guidelines for sale price of state-owned properties to individuals can involve 1,400 lei per square meter, one-fifth for the balcony, and then at 300 lei per square meter. To approximate U.S. dollars custom valuation of 20 lei could be used. There is no housing tax for the first 10 years, and then it ranges from 400 lei to 500 lei.

Inside maintenance must be done by the occupant. This leads to a fair amount of moonlighting and special arrangements between resident and craftsman. Resort houses have been hotly debated in Romania. It is now possible to own two homes. Owners of a resort home may rent to others and use proceeds to expand and modernize. New housing needs continue to be great. With increasing incomes and broader material horizons through exposure to the West, the pressure on the state for more housing must be considerable. Perhaps some of this pressure will be lessened as a result of a reduction in the number of years for which the state will extend credit.

Before November 1, 1974, a tying with incomes of 0 lei to 1,500 lei, 1,501 lei to 2,000 lei, and over 2,000 lei had, respectively, 25 years, 20 years, and 15 years to repay.[13] Even though interest rates have been reduced, this benefit has been offset by shortening the repayment period to 10 years, 8 years, and 5 years.[14] The net effect could be to cut effective demand (see Table 8.6). A significant development has been a sharp drop in the proportion of dwellings and apartments built solely from People's Own Funds.

NICOLAE CEAUSESCU—ROMANIA'S NUMBER ONE HOUSING CRITIC

A recent visitor to Romania asked a native, "If President Ceausescu is the number one man, who is number two?" "Well," he said, "Ceausescu is indeed number one. Number two is Ceausescu. And number three is Ceausescu."

So it is in housing (and every other sector). Ceausescu is the chief policy maker, planner, and catalyst. He is the overseer, the chief critic. It is a fantastic role he plays.

Romania has a very ambitious housing plan, but it has been apparently difficult to manage and control. In his closing speech at the Plenary Meeting of the Central Committee of the Romanian Communist Party of June 27-28, 1966, President Ceausescu admonished the members of the Central Committee for the practice of incorporating in productive investments (including enterprise investments) the cost of the social, cultural, and public utility works within the perimeter of some "constructions" or even in the locality where the enterprise plants are being built. The president charged these practices

> are now leading, in certain cases, to an artificial
> documentation of the costs of productive investments,
> of the funds for the amortization of industrial con-
> struction, and this bears negatively on the costs of
> products. In the future, social (including housing)

TABLE 8.6

Classification of Dwellings Turned Over for Occupancy According to the Number of Rooms for Habitation

Dwelling	1965 Amount	Percent	1970 Amount	Percent	1971 Amount	Percent	1972 Amount	Percent	1973 Amount	Percent
Total										
One room	16,460	13.6	26,548	16.3	16,973	11.3	14,054	10.4	10,770	10.8
Two rooms	61,790	51.1	87,528	53.8	81,091	54.4	74,481	53.0	85,699	55.3
Three rooms and over	42,765	35.3	48,669	29.9	51,541	34.3	51,418	36.6	52,427	33.9
Total	121,015	100.0	162,745	100.0	150,207	100.0	140,553	100.0	154,896	100.0
State and Cooperative Organization's Funds										
One room	7,226	14.2	14,819	20.7	6,759	12.2	4,986	9.4	6,556	10.3
Two rooms	29,381	57.6	42,658	59.6	36,212	65.1	35,479	66.8	43,478	68.6
Three rooms and over	14,352	28.2	14,102	19.7	12,629	22.7	12,660	23.8	13,383	21.1
Total	50,959	100.0	71,609	100.0	55,600	100.0	53,125	100.0	63,417	100.0
People's Funds with State Aid										
One room	—	—	1,642	5.8	1,056	2.9	977	2.6	2,562	6.0
Two rooms	—	—	16,459	58.2	20,760	57.7	18,787	50.3	23,247	54.1
Three rooms and over	—	—	10,178	36.0	14,194	39.4	17,562	47.1	17,115	39.9
Total	—	—	28,279	100.0	36,010	100.0	37,326	100.0	42,924	100.0
People's Own Funds										
One room	9,234	13.2	10,057	16.0	9,157	15.6	8,691	17.3	7,652	15.8
Two rooms	32,409	46.3	28,411	45.2	24,722	42.2	20,215	40.4	18,974	39.0
Three rooms and over	28,413	40.5	24,389	38.8	24,718	42.2	21,196	42.3	31,929	45.2
Total	70,056	100.0	62,857	100.0	58,597	100.0	50,102	100.0	48,555	100.0

Source: Socialist Republic of Romania, Anuaral Statistics, Bucharest 1974, p. 274.

and cultural "constructions" will have to be financed
separately, with the respective funds being incorpor-
ated in the budget for social and cultural activities.[15]

As mentioned earlier, housing is an integral part of the Romanian planning system. The keystone of the planning system is the Five-
Year Plan. It is spaced out by years, itemized by economic units,
and drawn up concurrently with the drafting of the general development
lines for a further five-year period. Thus, the planners and the managers are looking at a 10-year span, and for some branches of activity,
especially the national housing plan, the time period may be even
longer. The present central housing plan, emphasizing territorial development by small geographic units, extends to 1990. At present,
Romania is elaborating the Five-Year Plan for 1971-75, and involved
in developing the guidelines of the national economy of 1976-80. During the month of September 1974, the draft version of the 1976-80
plan was made available to Romanians.

All of this activity is carried out under the direct leadership of
the party and the State Central Commission. Some two years are generally involved in developing the Five-Year Plan. The principal emphasis of any plan is the future of the economic units, or the enterprises, the basic nuclei of the national economy.[16] Housing development, though closely tied to the economic objectives, is a residual activity.

The difficulties of identifying costs, establishing prices, and allocating resources are apparent to the Romanians. In his December
6, 1969, address, the president stated:

> One of the main drawbacks of the price system in
> our country lies in the fact that a series of prices
> are established without the social expenditure incor-
> porated in the given products being taken into account,
> and that the criteria of the law of value which still
> governs in one form or another any economy based
> on commodity production, are being ignored. It is
> only within the framework of correctly established
> prices that the enterprises can take action aimed
> at reducing cost prices, at increasing efficiency and
> eliminating losses in the case of some products.[17]

The president thus takes issue with those socialists and economists who have maintained that, in a socialist society, prices no longer
fulfill an important economic function. What is being said in Romania
is that a price system is an absolute necessity. Without it, enterprise
managers cannot adequately analyze, allocate, and manage. The solu-

tion, however, envisioned by the president, was the establishment of
a pricing committee at the central level. It now exists, and in some
cases it establishes price ceilings.

It is generally felt that if the old system of managing the housing
stock with planned losses had been continued, Romania would have had
great difficulty, not just in maintaining the existing housing stock, but
also in expanding it. Foreign visitors to Romania even now can see
that this policy may have favored postponing necessary maintenance
of housing. The results of the earlier policy of neglect in maintenance
have been observed in the poor condition of the building by foreign businessmen visiting the offices of the centrales and trading companies
in Bucharest.

Thus, in 1970, the president envisioned the increase in rents
contributing to the national budget more than 700 million lei. He was
quick to point out that the general increase in wages and salaries for
the same year would mean additional incomes amounting to over
10,500 million lei.

The government viewed the decision to increase housing construction and the change in the system of rents as prerequisites for solving
the housing problem.

Lower cost housing is also a Romanian concern. At the June
19, 1968 Plenum of the Communist Party of Romania, President
Ceausescu cited the need for blueprints for dwellings whose costs
would start from 20,000 lei up to some 50,000 lei a flat and other
types, whose cost would range from 30,000 lei to 40,000 lei. This
range would relate to the needs of people with different incomes.
This approach is also viewed as making possible a greater standardi-
zation, and, thus, rationalization, in the manufacture of building supplies and materials.[18]

At a 1971 Executive Committee meeting, the president of Romania chided the Ministry of Building Industry for a practice that managers in socialist and capitalist countries sometimes use. The device is to indicate to top management that the dollar value of the plan
has been filled, when, in reality, the actual units of capacity have not
been achieved. Unscrupulous managers in any system are not above
placing unfinished objectives in the planned targets for the next year.
The Romanian leadership will have none of this, and now requires that
unfinished objectives be reported and funded separately. "In these
conditions, those guilty of delay of not having observed the drafts of
construction and of commissioning will be penalized."[19]

The penalties for managers in housing (and other sectors) in
Romania for failing to meet their planned targets is somewhat unique.
If an activity falls 10 percent below its planned quota, the top management, and indeed down through and including all workers, may suffer
a 10 percent reduction in their income. Larger failures may entail

removal from their jobs. Labor mobility of the U.S. type is not possible in Romania. Once fired, only the state can rehire. Part of the
penalty may involve putting the manager into limbo for a considerable
period. A certain portion of programmed time on Romanian State
Television is reserved to show pictures of those managers who have
failed. Thus, there are strong incentives for meeting quotas.

The scope of planning and management for housing has also been
uneven in Romania. Housing plans have not, in some instances, provided space for commercial and service units to maintain and operate
the building. The situation was sufficiently serious for the president
to insist that standards for commercial facilities per 100 or 1,000
residents be established, and that these spaces be built at the same
time the housing development was being constructed.[20] Housing developments have been placed under managers who have never previously managed a housing development.

Consider this sequence of events: "In 1966–1968, more than
155,000 flats have been made available, enabling over 500,000 people
to move into new dwellings."[21] The pressure of housing need is critical. Party and state leadership have sought to increase the number of
new apartments by building cheaper apartments in 1969. Instead of
building 62,000 apartments, 90,000 less-expensive apartments were
constructed. These 90,000 lower-rent apartments enabled working
people with smaller wages to improve their housing conditions.[22]

Bucharest has received special attention, and the experience,
in the capitol, according to the president, has proved that good homes
can be built with a reduced expenditure of materials and money.

> The cost of a flat including flats of categories I and
> IV comes to an average of 35,000 lei, about half the
> cost of the previous years. The responsibility for
> further reducing costs and rationalization of the
> labor force has been made a permanent concern of
> the Municipal Party Committee and of the Bucharest
> City Peoples Council. Notice the centralization
> trend in controlling and solving housing problems.[23]

As indicated earlier, houses in Romania may be constructed by
the state; individuals may construct houses utilizing their own private
funds, or private funds may be combined with state funds for housing
construction. By 1970, it became apparent to the party and state leadership that the housing goals in the private sector were not being met
—not because the funds were not available, but because the Five-Year
Plan did not provide for building materials and supplies for use in the
private sector. The president immediately called for a revision in
the forecasting and planned methods underlying the housing plan. A

survey of building materials for tens of thousands of dwellings built
annually in the villages had not been taken into consideration, nor had
the demands of some urban dwellers. The president requested that
the residential construction needs for cement, iron, reinforced con-
crete, bricks, and prefabs should be provided for and sold through
the Socialist Trading Network. It was hoped that these changes would
ensure the supply of the material needed for urban and rural construction for private citizens. A further deficiency was noted at this time
—the forecast for building materials and supplies had been stated in
the plan in terms of their value in lei, instead of actual quantity.[24]
Since prices had changed and the accounting information system was
frequently based on average costing, the inventory of needed material
was just not produced.

To further correct this problem, the county people's councils
were given the authority, by the president, to organize their own enterprises to produce brick and lime and to set the prices for these
products. Further, decentralization was extended to the communal
people's councils and to the agricultural production cooperatives, to
produce their own building materials.

At this same Executive Committee meeting, the president set
forth the goal of the Socialist Republic of Romania and the purpose of
each Five-Year Plan:

> Increased profitableness . . . as I have already said,
> we must not only eliminate completely the abnormal
> economic phenomenon of planned losses, but it is
> also necessary for each unit and even each product
> to bring profits. By achieving this, we shall demon-
> strate, in fact, the advantages of a planned social-
> ist economy.[25]

It may be strange to hear a Socialist president talking of profits, but what this suggests is that Romania is paying close attention
to the technology of profit center management. In addition to learning from doing, it is importing from U.S. schools of business administration and industrial firms the techniques of establishing and managing profit and cost centers. The Rutgers Graduate School of Business Administration Interfunctional Management Program, which is
based on profit center management, has been established at the Academy of Economic Studies in Bucharest with cooperation and funding
from the Office of East European Programs, U.S. State Department.
Management techniques, including return on investment, net present
value, discounted cash flow, and project-site management, among
others, are in great demand. Manufacturing enterprises and housing
developments must be managed and controlled through these vehicles.

According to President Ceausescu, any infringement of the principal of profitableness cannot but boomerang sooner or later in a negative manner on the efficiency of the national economy, and, as a whole, on the general development of society. The Romanians are out to demonstrate that their version of a socialist system, with profit and cost center control, is more profitable than the capitalistic system.[26]

Some theorists in the United States have comforted themselves with the notion that the Communists are coming closer to our system and that we are coming closer to their system. The validity of this "convergence theory" is doubtful. The Romanians, at least, seek out the best of the capitalistic system and incorporate it into their own, in a drive for economic efficiency and profitability.

Romanian housing policy has been faced with some enormous problems. Prior to 1967, the quality of the Romanian housing stock had suffered enormous losses through lack of maintenance. The level of rents charged was well below the revenues necessary even to maintain the property. Beginning in 1967, and parallel with an increase in per capita incomes, the state increased rental charges. Thus, the principal of economic self-management was introduced in the administration of housing, with the expectation that it would lead to the elimination of large losses resulting from the extremely low level of rents. Romania continues to experiment, but the 1990 target is there: "to solve by and large" the housing problem.

Employees of enterprises or other government units are given preference for housing. The government "company" recommends and guarantees their ability to pay.

In the past 20 years, total population has grown from 15.8 million to almost 21 million—in urban areas, from 3.7 million to approximately 8.5 million. Romania's response to the growing urbanization is now aimed at territorial development, urban redevelopment, and improvement of the existing housing stock.

During this same period, 1.6 million dwellings have been built in towns with state and private funds, and, in the villages, 2.3 million new homes have been completed. According to the vice-chairman of the Architects Union, during the 30 years since World War II, some 12 million people, more than half the population, moved into new homes. Over the next 5 years, 815,000 new apartments will be financed from state and citizens funds. Further, hostels to accommodate 200,000 newly married young people will also be constructed. From 1976 to 1990, President Ceausescu envisions the building of 2.5 million to 3 million dwellings.[27]

But is it enough? Can housing, can consumer goods, can the standard of living continue to take a back seat to the fantastic drive for industrialization? The investment rate or accumulation rate in 1975 is expected to be 35 percent, and to continue through 1980 at 33 percent.[28]

According to an analysis by Paul Lendvai, Romania is at a critical juncture.[29] Internally, there is a frenzied drive to complete plan quotas ahead of schedule. Politically, there is criticism of the high investment rate. Romania is now on its fourth planning commission chairman in a little more than two years. Outside, the Russians, and perhaps a jealous neighbor or two, hope that citizen unhappiness will make Romania less freewheeling, especially in the international arena.

Austerity is the name of the game, especially fuel. The use of installment credit may have sparked automobile purchases and temporarily solved capacity problems. Now the car owner has little or no gas. In 1973, Bucharest at night was indeed a second Paris, bright, gay, and full of light. In 1975, it must surely be one of the darkest, but still safest, cities in Europe. The reduction in loan terms for housing could be another aspect of the austerity drive.

But the promise is there. Imagine the boldness of thinking (and promising) 3 million flats by 1980 and an inflation-free per capita income of $3,000 in 1990—approximately the level now of Belgium. When you consider the track record of the 1971-75 plan and housing targets reached and exceeded, the credibility gap may not be all that great.

But the question still remains: How high a price will Romanians pay for establishing their brand of socialism? Recall neighboring Hungary, with accumulation rates of 27 percent, reduced to 25 percent in order to provide for a higher standard of living in 1973.[30]

President Ceausescu has set the pattern. He publicly proclaimed it many times during his five-hour speech to the Eleventh Party Congress: "Let us not forget for one moment that no society, no people can consume more than it produces. The future of the country depends not on what is consumed at a given moment, but first of all on the material means for the continuous growth of the national wealth."[31]

Conditions in the 1970s have improved, but by Western standards there is still deprivation. Over time, this deprivation may pose a serious challenge to continuing the present policies and priorities. But Romania appears alert and sensitive to the dilemma of unfilled housing needs versus the drive for industrialization.

By requiring enterprises to contribute 95 percent of their excess profits over plan to housing, Romania may have developed an interfunctional solution for increasing productivity. If workers help the enterprise to exceed the profit plan, they get back much of the excess profits in the form of new housing. The business and government interface of housing construction, finance and plan requirements for constantly improved productivity could be a key factor in accelerating economic development.

Furthermore, in the 1976-80 plan, housing's planning priority as of July 1975 appears to have been improved. For example, in 1974, planned housing investment from all sources (government budget, enterprises, and people's own funds) totaled 8 billion lei or approximately $667 million in U.S. tourist dollars. The planned average yearly housing investment over the period 1976-80 is 20 billion lei or roughly an additional billion dollars.[32] A change in housing strategy is that since January 1975, families with monthly incomes of over 1,100 lei per member have been required to purchase their present apartment from the state using state credit facilities provided for this purpose. Failure to buy means that the state will increase rents from 50 to 100 percent.[33]

If this interfunctional approach to housing construction, funding, economic development targets and productivity requirements actually works and results in sizable additions to the housing stock and increased productivity, possible adaptation and experimentation in mixed and free enterprise systems should be considered.

NOTES

1. "Romania, Bulgaria, Albania—Annual Supplement 1974," Quarterly Economic Review, Economist Intelligence Unit (London).

2. Draft Directives of the Eleventh Congress of the Romanian Communist Party Concerning the 1976-1980 Five Year Plan and the Guidelines for the Economic and Social Development of Romania in the 1981-1990 Period (Bucharest: Romanian News Agency, 1974), p. 15.

3. Ibid., pp. 15, 16, 17, 19, 20, 21, 23, 24.

4. Ibid., p. 81.

5. Ibid.

6. Ibid., p. 25.

7. Ibid., pp. 8, 9.

8. Conversations, Bucharest, June 1974 with chairman, vice-chairman, and other key executives of the Committee for the Peoples Councils Problems, which plays a key role in housing policy and its implementation, and the Rutgers University Graduate School of Business Administration Interfunctional team (Professors S. George Walters, David W. Blakeslee, Hal P. Eastman, and Jack A. Lucken.)

9. S. George Walters, "Recent Economic Developments and Trends in Romania," paper presented at Romanian Conference, Institute of Soviet and Eastern Studies, University of Michigan, Ann Arbor, Michigan, December 17, 1974, p. 5.

10. U.S. Congress, Joint Economic Committee, Reorientation and Commercial Relations of the Economies of Eastern Europe, 93d

Cong., 2d sess. (Washington, D.C.: Government Printing Office, August 16, 1974), p. 55.

11. Romanian Territorial Social-Economic Development Study 1976-1990 (Bucharest, 1974), pp. 6, 7.

12. Hugh P. Donaghue, "Romania Today—Opportunities for U.S. Products and Technology," Address at World Trade Institute, New York, November 21, 1974, pp. 14, 15.

13. Collection of Legal Decrees, January 1-March 31, 1973, Counsel of Statutes, Romanian Socialist Republic, Bucharest, p. 54.

14. Michai Ionescu, "Incentives to Assist Home Buyers," Scinteia, November 1, 1974, p. 3.

15. Nicolae Ceausescu, "Closing Speech at June 27-28, 1966 Plenum of the Central Committee of the Romanian Communist Party," in Romania Achievements and Prospects, 1965-1969 (Bucharest: Meridiane Publishing House, 1969), p. 280.

16. Nicolae Ceausescu, "Report Concerning the Measures for Perfecting the Management and Planning of the National Economy and for Improving the Territorial-Administrative Organization of Romania," in ibid., pp. 471-72.

17. Ibid., p. 478.

18. Ibid., p. 616.

19. Nicolae Ceausescu, "Executive Committee of the Central Committee of the Romanian Communist Party and Government Meeting," in Romania on the Way of Building Up the Multi-laterally Developed Socialist Society (Bucharest: Meridiane Publishing House, 1971), 5: 279, 280.

20. Ibid., pp. 294-95.

21. Ceausescu, Romania Achievements and Prospects, 1965-1969, p. 777.

22. Ibid., p. 800.

23. Ibid., pp. 812 and 813.

24. Ceausescu, Romania on the Way of Building Up the Multi-laterally Developed Socialist Society, 5: 267, 268.

25. Ibid., pp. 274-75.

26. Ibid.

27. Mircea Dima, "Modern Homes for All," Romania Today, no. 10 (1974), pp. 19, 20.

28. Paul Lendvai, "The Romanian Economy—It's Always Riches Tomorrow," The Financial Times, January 10, 1975, p. 6.

29. Ibid.

30. Ibid.

31. Ibid.

32. Information developed by Romanian Library, New York, July 1975.

33. "Living Standards," Doing Business with Eastern Europe (Geneva: Business International S.A. Corporation, 1975), p. 7.

9

JAPAN:
FUNDS FOR HOUSING
TO EMPLOYERS

The housing programs in the countries heretofore discussed have, for the most part, been financed by nonpublic funds. In Japan, however, the reverse situation exists, that is, the government furnishes funds or facilities to private companies for employee housing. Prior to examining these programs, the conditions leading to so different an approach should be cited and recognition given to the dissimilar cultural and economic background. Also, it should be noted that, as contrasted with the United States, the government housing programs in Japan are closely and interfunctionally coordinated with national employment, manpower, and labor market policies. Thus, a prerequisite to a discussion of the housing programs is an understanding of industrial relations in Japan.

INDUSTRIAL RELATIONS

Prior to 1940, the major industrial relations problems evolved around recruitment, the development of skilled workers, and the growth of the labor movement. In terms of recruiting, the concept of an open labor market with extensive career and employer mobility was not the general practice. After World War II, employer and employee looked to the well-being of the enterprise as the first priority. Workers did not look to the market for job security and wage improvements. New unions were largely enterprise based, that is, organized into autonomous units by companies or enterprises instead of plant or craft locals. The professional staff and the lower echelon managerial staff were eligible for membership.

Before World War II, white collar employees and only a small percentage of blue collar workers received nenko jorestu (age- and

seniority-based wage system) and <u>sushin koyo</u> (permanent employment);
after the war, it was expanded to all union members, including blue
collar workers. The system is noticeably absent in small firms and
generally applies to regular employees in large-scale enterprises in
both the private and public sector. The feasibility for large firms is
enhanced because the system does not apply to large numbers of temporary and subcontracted workers.

<u>Nenko</u> is least applicable to small firms in the private sector or
where working conditions are poor, bankruptcy rates are high, product demand unstable, and capital funds usually in short supply. In the
private sector, about 37 percent of all employees work for establishments of some 100 or more employees. This would be a minimum estimate of the influence of <u>nenko</u>.[1]

<u>Nenko</u>'s underlying assumption is that, with increasing age and
length of service, the worker's value to the firm grows and that over-
payment of older workers is compensated by the low wages paid to
young workers.[2] The Japanese employee voluntarily obliges to provide lifetime service (contrary to his or her American counterpart).
Also, the company's honor in maintaining lifetime employment is much
more an issue of pride than in the United States.[3]

The difference in employment practices is highlighted by the
varied separation rates for Japan and the United States. The United
States rate has, at times, been double the Japanese rate (see Table
9.1).

Personnel practices of large companies usually follow the same
pattern. Recruitment is made immediately after the completion of
education. Employees who are then permanently retained are not subject to layoffs or discharge. Beginning compensation is low and is
based on the level of education and, then, the length of service subsequently attained. The paternalistic fringe benefits encompass housing
and family allowances. Except for top management, there is compulsory retirement at a relatively early age, usually 55 years of age,
with a lump sum retirement allowance.

A dominant factor in determining the character of Japanese labor
relations has been the surplus of labor. The likelihood of increased
interfirm mobility and a labor market organized along Western lines
may be in the offing with an expanded economy, demographic changes
due to birth control, rapid technological changes, the rise of mass
production industries, and signs of increased mobility among younger
workers.

Large firms still view the hiring of new permanent employees
with previous job experience as a last resort, to be undertaken only
during periods of severe labor shortages.

Though increased interfirm mobility was anticipated, permanent
employment, prior to the economic crisis of 1974-75, was expected to

TABLE 9.1

Annual Average Monthly Separation Rates for Wage and
Salaried Employees in the Manufacturing Sector, Japan, 1959-67

Year	Japan	United States
1967	2.4	4.6*
1966	2.2	4.6*
1965	2.3	4.1
1964	2.6	3.9
1963	2.3	3.9
1962	2.4	4.1
1961	2.5	4.0
1960	2.1	4.3
1959	2.0	4.1

*High rate due to huge economic growth and inflation created by
Vietnam involvement—highest rate since 1953.

Source: Robert E. Cole, Japanese Blue Collar: The Changing
Tradition (Berkeley: University of California Press, 1971), p. 127.

continue in some form, and there were no portents evident of its even-
tual disappearance.

> That the permanent employment practice has not
> withered away under "modern" pressure is not sur-
> prising. We know the factors that bring about a
> structural pattern are now always those that maintain
> it. Although the initial resources that crystallized
> the permanent employment practice are being di-
> verted, it is not conclusive evidence that the practice
> will disappear. The Japanese may yet develop new
> equivalent resources to support permanent employ-
> ment. The move of Japanese business into the labor
> surplus area of Southeast Asia represents just this
> search for alternative resources.
> The resilience of Japanese tradition insures the
> traditional elements will be represented in the emer-
> gent new pattern. [4]

In early 1975, the system of lifetime employment was at a critical juncture and in danger of crumbling under the pressure of adverse business conditions, inflation, and the oil shortage. Should economic recovery come within a fairly reasonable time, as has been forecast,[5] the lifetime employment system should survive. But in the face of the crisis, many companies have been desperately attempting to maintain the system through furloughs or similar cutbacks.[6]

Paradoxically, the United States could be moving to a modified version of permanent employment under the same economic pressures. As a result of the 1975 recession and employees being faced with layoffs or dismissals, the conflict arose between those last hired, minorities and women, versus those with seniority rights. Employers found themselves in the midst of the controversy, with labor unions stressing seniority based on contractual obligations and minority, feminist, and civil rights groups asserting that they were entitled to preference for retention, regardless of seniority.

Pending a definitive resolution by the Supreme Court, firms could attempt to avoid conflict by dividing the reduced workload, instead of firing employees. With a business recovery, this policy could be continued, even though more of the formerly excluded groups could gain sufficient seniority to eliminate the problem.

Westerners have looked critically upon the Japanese employment system as a source of competitive weakness and inefficiency.

> Countering this view, it can be noted that this approach to social organization, which is generally less individualistic, more personalized, and more group centered than Western societies. Loyalty to and identification with the work group and company seem to substitute well in Japan for compensation techniques as a motivational base. And it is not at all self-evident that Japan's lifetime employment system is more costly than the costs and losses involved in the high rates of job mobility in United States organizations.[7]

In addition to affirming that long-lasting ties of culture and history tied to positive economic factors will hold firm, one viewpoint is that the expectation should really be that American practices will move in the direction of the Japanese pattern rather than the other way.[8] An indication of the likely transferability of the Japanese employment practices would be how they actually do work in the United States. A study of plants in America under Japanese management approvingly finds that "by studying how the Japanese manage a network of complex relationships we can learn a good deal about how to live and work as a collectivity."[9]

The concern for the whole employee, not just his job performance, is vital to the success of the enterprise, and there is much merit to the adoption of these practices in the United States.

> When we think of how the Japanese treat their employ-
> ees, the word paternalism may come to mind. It is
> well known that the Japanese organization traditionally
> offers its workers housing, extensive on-site recrea-
> tion facilities, and lifetime employment. The Japanese
> operating in the United States have not come to that
> point yet; [emphasis added] nevertheless, on both sides
> of the Pacific, concern for the whole employee—not
> for just his work performance—is a characteristic of
> the Japanese company. This concern, the Japanese
> are convinced, is essential to attaining productivity
> and high standards. It is, however, more than a mat-
> ter of policy; it is a philosophy.[10]

Following this broad-gauged review of Japanese industrial rela-
tions, with its emphasis on permanent employment, the subsequent discussion of employer-provided housing should be more readily un-
derstood. As has been indicated, the Japanese labor relations system should not be considered purely indigenous and thus susceptible to transferability to the West; therefore, the Japanese experience with employer-related housing should be viewed in this context.

HOUSING IN JAPAN

Japan still lags behind other developed countries in respect to an adequate supply of housing. The need for housing was intensified by the loss of over 2 million units in World War II through bombing; Tokyo lost 40 percent of its housing stock.[11] Besides the loss of housing during World War II, another cause of the deficiency was that families had consciously given housing a lower order of priority than the accumulation of savings and expenditures for the education of children. Furthermore, housing credit by Western standards was prac-
tically unavailable. Only recently have banks begun to provide mort-
gage loans with repayment periods longer than 15 years and interest rates under 9.5 percent.[12]

> It has to be remembered that the housing stock of
> any community at any moment is the result of the
> conditions of some 30 years past, and in that period
> Japan could not have afforded better housing, although

she now can, it will take some time before she catches
up to her present and future income status in the
world.[13]

In 1966, as a means of alleviating the housing shortage, the government initiated a five-year program, "One house for one family,"
aimed at the construction of 6.7 million dwellings or housing units,
40 percent government-sponsored and 60 percent privately financed.
The plan's objectives were not only attained but were slightly exceed-
ed.[14] At the conclusion of the period, 1970, housing activity in Japan
was the highest of the major developed countries (see Table 9.2).

The second five-year program started in 1971, with the goal of
"one room for each person" and the construction of 9.5 million dwelling units, with the same proportions as in the first five-year program:
40 percent publicly aided, or 3.85 million units, and 60 percent privately financed, or 5.65 million units. Based on economic conditions
as early as mid-1974, there was doubt as to the likelihood of the 3.85
million publicly sponsored units being completed.[15] The proportion
of publicly aided housing in the Japanese plan is much higher than was
contained in the 10-year housing goals for the United States beginning
in 1968. In terms of new units only, the goals were for 24.2 million
units, of which 4 million, or 16.5 percent, were to be publicly assisted
and 20.2 million, or 83.5 percent, unassisted.[16]

Between 1969 and 1971, new housing starts in the United States
were 4.758 million units, of which 899,000, or 18.9 percent, were
subsidized and 3.859 million, or 81.1 percent, were unsubsidized.[17]
The proportion of dwelling units actually built in Japan between 1960
and 1968 was 23.7 percent with public aid and 76.3 percent with private funds.[18]

In recent years, housing investment in Japan has been increasing at a rate exceeding the country's economic growth. The percentage of housing investment in the GNP increased from 4.3 percent in
1960 to 7.2 percent in 1968.[19] Even with the additional housing expenditures, former Prime Minister Kakeui Tanaka stated that "in spite
of this quantitative increase in housing facilities the housing shortage
in urban centers is far from solved. Especially in big cities and suburbs, the inflow of population surpasses the speed of construction making the housing problem still more acute."[20]

The government has attempted to use residential construction as
an antirecession measure, as well as to alleviate the acute housing
shortage. Housing plans of the period were primarily designed to be
labor force acquiring measures in order to aid the main features of
the national government policy, the National Income Doubling Plan of
1961 and the Nationwide Development Plan of 1961.[21]

TABLE 9.2

Dwellings Completed per Thousand Inhabitants, Selected
Developed Countries, 1965-70

Country	1965	1966	1967	1968	1969	1970
France	8.4	8.4	8.5	8.4	8.7	9.3
Germany: Federal Republic	10.1	10.1	9.6	8.6	8.2	7.8
Italy	7.5	5.6	5.2	5.3	5.5	7.0
Japan[a]	8.6	8.7	9.9	11.9	13.2	14.3
Romania	6.4	6.1	6.3	5.8	7.2	8.0
Spain	9.0	8.4	6.3	7.6	8.2	9.3
United Kingdom: England and Wales	7.4	7.4	7.6	7.7	6.8	6.4
Union of Soviet Socialist Republics	9.6	9.8	9.8	9.4	9.3	9.4
Yugoslavia	6.3	6.5	6.4	6.4	5.9	6.2
United States[b]	7.8	6.1	6.6	7.7	7.4	7.1

[a]Dwellings started.

[b]Dwellings constructed by the private sector based on permits issued; dwellings constructed by the public sector based on work
started.

Source: UN Committee on Housing, Building and Planning,
World Housing Survey: Report of the Secretary General (E/C.6/CRP/
No. 1), January 31, 1974, pp. 84-87.

The Japanese economy was fairly stagnant between 1962 and
1965. The depression that arose in 1965 from overproduction could
not be resolved by new investment in industrial equipment, since it
would only result in further overproduction. "So housing investment,
which would not enter that vicious circle, but would instead bring demands on industries related to housing, came to be regarded as an effective means of stimulating recovery."[22] Notwithstanding, the government's economic policy still was inclined to stress increased productivity of goods.

Japanese housing policy has allocated a minor role to public
housing, relying instead on private individual houses and employer-
provided housing.[23] As employer-provided housing is a key component
of the housing programs under review in this study, the examination
of Japanese housing policy next turns to this subject.

HOUSING FROM EMPLOYERS

In contrast to the industrialized countries of the West, employer-provided housing has not declined as sharply in importance. Japanese employees receive a variety of fringe benefits and perquisites; however, the increment to their income from these benefits is minor, except for housing. Employer-provided housing is not a recent development; it was started as a means of carrying out forced labor for profit. In 1900, when the textile industry began to cultivate overseas markets, imported spinning machines were kept in operation for long hours by a vast army of low-wage factory girls from poor families in remote farming villages, who were forced to live in dormitories similar to detention houses from which they were unable to escape. Dwelling facilities for mine workers were also like detention houses and were called naya (barn) or hanba (meal shed).[24]

Slums remaining from feudal days were in use until recently and were used as quarters for those engaged in domestic industry, as well as for "low-class" laborers, such as rickshawmen and cart pullers.

The procurement of labor for the war economy became difficult without government assistance, and, in 1938, boarding houses for single laborers were built in Osaka and five other cities. A three-year plan for laborers' housing, started in 1939, was aimed at building 30,000 dwelling units for families, as well as 200 boarding houses. The government enterprise that undertook to finance construction of these houses had 30 million of the 100 million yen necessary to cover building costs.

A system of compensation for losses incurred in building laborers' houses was instituted in April 1940; it required local authorities of Tokyo and several other prefectures and cities to supply houses for laborers working in war industries, assuring them that the government would pay half the building costs.

In May 1941, the central government formed the Japan Housing Corporation, the public authority for wartime laborers' housing, with a government investment of 100 million yen and an authorization of 1 billion yen for housing bonds. Following the war, construction work was suspended.[25]

Only during periods of housing shortages in relation to wartime activities has the U.S. government become extensively engaged in programs for providing housing to civilian workers. The background of these programs is given in Appendix to Chapter 10.

The Japanese government's concern for housing its labor force continued into peacetime. After World War II, housing for industrial rehabilitation rather than for the people was the government's postwar housing policy.[26] To secure the necessary labor force, 52,412 housing units were built and 48,935 housing units repaired for coal miners.

Loans to colliery companies from the Rehabilitation Finance Corporation, amounting to 15.4 billion yen, made this possible. The loans made during the 20 months ending in September 1948 were comparable in monetary terms to five times the housing expenditures in the 1946 national budget. In a similar manner, 30,000 housing units were provided for workers in other major industries.[27]

Especially since World War II have many Japanese companies and government institutions supplied free or low-rent housing to employees. In 1941, in urban districts (shi) with over 150,000 inhabitants, employer-provided housing made up 1.8 percent of occupied units.[28] The 1950 rate was 6.9 percent nationally and 8.6 percent for urban areas; for 1958, the comparable rates were 6.7 percent and 7.6 percent, respectively (see Table 9.3). In 1968, out of 2,967,520 housing units in Tokyo, 203,770, or 6.9 percent, were employer-provided; in Japan out of 24,197,900 units, 1,528,400, or 6.5 percent, were employer-provided.[29] In recent years, the proportion of employer-provided housing has been declining—from 4.2 percent in 1970 to 2.7 percent of new construction (see Table 9.4).

Another benefit available to workers is housing allowances; in 1973, 11.3 percent of workers received the allowances.[30]

During the postwar period, commercial and industrial enterprises began supplying housing to their high-level employees who would otherwise have been precluded from performing their managerial functions in Tokyo. An increase in employer-provided housing played a role in mitigating the shortage of rental housing.[31] The housing for workers in basic industries was supplied within the system of employer-provided housing, and public housing was never seriously considered.

> The large amount of currency in circulation due to the lax loan procedures used to provide funds for workers' houses invited rampant inflation by which heavily indebted enterprises gained large profits. In addition, enterprises were granted cost-adjustment subsidies. So they acquired workers' houses for next to nothing.[32]

A survey of the Ministry of Labor in 1949 revealed that 60 percent of the 25,294 establishments employing more than 30 workers offered dwelling facilities and 42 percent of workers in firms with facilities were covered. Of workers accommodated, 28 percent paid no rent and the remainder an average rent of 196 yen per month. The amount was only 1.6 percent of the average monthly cash income of families of urban workers in 1949. In dormitories, 83 percent of the workers paid no rent.[33]

TABLE 9.3

Tenure Characteristics of Dwelling Units, Japan,
1950, 1955, and 1958
(in percent)

	Owner-Occupied	Rented	Issued*
October 1, 1950			
All areas	69.8	23.2	6.9
Urban	52.6	38.8	8.6
Rural	80.8	13.3	5.9
October 1, 1955			
All areas	71.8	21.6	6.6
Urban	63.0	29.5	7.5
Rural	83.6	10.9	5.5
October 1, 1958			
All areas	71.2	22.1	6.7
Urban	62.9	29.6	7.6
Rural	84.9	9.8	5.2

*Issued units are those supplied to employees; they include both
rental and rent-free housing. No comparable figures are available
for the United States.

Source: Alan H. Gleason, "Postwar Housing in Japan and the
United States," corrected copy, in Studies on Economic Life in Japan,
Richard K. Beardsley, ed., Center for Japanese Studies, Occasional
Papers, no. 8 (Ann Arbor: The University of Michigan Press, 1964),
p. 9.

The proportion of firms with company housing is high in such
industries as electricity, gas, water, mining, finance, and insurance;
73.1 percent of manufacturing firms have company housing. A better
indication is the average percentage of employees per enterprise living in company housing: 77.1 percent in mining; 32.9 percent in electricity, gas, and water; 57.9 percent in textile manufacturing; 35.8
percent in nonferrous metals; and 34.3 percent in steel.[34]
A 1966 survey of 25 large companies on company-owned housing
and housing allowances paid to employees disclosed that those benefits were received by 21 percent of top management personnel, 44
percent of middle management, 34 percent of male employees, and
8 percent of female employees. An average of one-third of the com-

TABLE 9.4

Employer-Provided Housing Units, Japan, 1970-73
(thousands of units)

Items	1970	1971	1972	1973
Employer-provided housing units	61.7	44.5	44.6	50.7
All housing units	1,484.6	1,463.8	1,807.6	1,905.1
Percent	4.2	3.0	2.5	2.7

Source: Ministry of Construction, Planning Bureau, Annual Report of Construction Statistics (Japanese government publication).

pany employees were given housing; the proportion was slightly down from 1956 for all categories. The number of companies paying special worker allowances for housing in 1956 was 8 and, in 1966, 13 out of 25. The survey included companies who were leaders in their fields and represented a broad range of business types—manufacturing, trading, and banking. They accounted for a significant share of national economic activity.[35]

The housing covered in the survey was available at nominal rentals. The quality depended on company rank; as promotions were received, larger and better housing was given.

In housing-short Japan, where high rentals prevail, company housing constitutes a substantial addition to real income. The low proportion of senior executives in company housing does not entirely reflect the real housing benefits; for example, some companies desiring to reduce capital commitments for housing make it possible for executives to purchase company-owned housing at book value, which is likely to be well below the market value, and have it financed through company loans against retirement allowances. The capital gain to the employee can be considerable.

In Tokyo, 30 percent to 50 percent of the occupants of employer-provided housing are in the 40-to-49 and 50-and-over age groups and the over-100,000-yen-income managerial group.

> On the whole, the elite in enterprises have a relatively rosy prospect of moving from tenement houses to employer provided houses and then to their own houses. The elderly and low income classes not among the fortunate remain submerged in tenement houses.[36]

A comparison of time of construction and time of occupancy would indicate that the employer-provided housing in Tokyo consists of units not originally built for this type of occupancy; the dates of construction and occupancy vary considerably (see Table 9.5).

Though figures on the proportion of employer-provided housing in Tokyo vary somewhat, a sizable percentage is employer-provided, that is, 8.6 percent of the ownership in 1969 (see Table 9.6).

The benefits to Tokyo residents of employer-provided housing are illustrated by the statistics, which reveal that the majority of those living in company housing have a rent-income ratio of 9 percent or less, as compared to a citywide average of 34 percent (see Table 9.7).

TABLE 9.5

Relation of Time of Construction and Domiciliation for Tokyo Housing Units, Pre-World War II-1968

	All Housing		Employer-Provided Housing		Per- cent of Total
	Number	Per- cent	Number	Per- cent	
Construction					
Pre-World War II	437,950	14.8	28,110	13.0	6.4
Postwar-1955	629,500	21.3	43,430	20.1	6.9
1956-60	611,040	20.6	45,670	21.1	7.5
1960-65	868,200	29.3	68,280	31.6	7.9
1966-September 1968	417,350	14.1	30,040	13.9	7.2
Occupancy					
Pre-World War II	303,790	10.2	2,500	1.2	0.8
Postwar-1955	494,210	16.7	13,750	6.4	2.8
1956-60	354,660	12.0	20,870	9.7	5.9
1960-65	771,930	26.1	78,130	36.2	10.1
1966-September 1968	1,042,920	35.2	100,790	46.7	9.7
Total*	2,967,520	100.0	216,030	100.0	7.3

*Totals do not agree due to rounding.

Source: Tokyo Metropolitan Government, Municipal Library, Tokyo's Housing Problem, no. 5 (Tokyo, March 1972), p. 105.

TABLE 9.6

Ownership of Housing in Tokyo, 1969
(percent)

Items	Households on Welfare[a]	General Households[b]
Private houses	11.0	43.3
Private rental housing	21.0	15.1
Apartments	46.6	28.5
Public housing	18.5	3.1
Japan and Tokyo housing corporations	0.5	1.4
Employer-provided housing	0.8	8.6
Other	0.7	3.4

[a]Households under public livelihood protection.
[b]Total households, including households on welfare.

Source: Tokyo Metropolitan Government, Municipal Library,
Tokyo's Housing Problem, no. 5 (Tokyo, March 1972), p. 44.

A survey of rentals in the Tokyo area of housing occupied between 1966 and 1968 indicates that, on the basis of space received,
the employer-provided housing has the lowest costs. The monthly
house rents per mat ($1.65m^2$) are as follows:[37]

Items	Yen
Average	1,084
Public housing	540
Privately run single houses	1,400
Privately run apartments	1,317
Employer-provided houses	205
Combined houses	1,681
Living with other families	771

On a national (and more recent) basis than the Tokyo survey,
the employer-provided or -issued housing still has the lowest rentals
(see Table 9.8).

The dormitory system, developed in the late nineteenth century
as a hedge against high labor mobility, served to strengthen worker
dependence on company-sponsored leisure activities. An example of
dormitory life is found in an auto parts company with extensive com-

TABLE 9.7

Rent-Income Ratio, Tokyo, 1970
(percent)

Ratio	Average for All Housing	Employees' Housing Units for Families and Official Residences	Single Persons Living in Employers' Houses and Dormitories
Unknown	15.0	13.0	32.0
30 percent and over	3.0	—	—
25-29	3.0	1.0	1.0
20-24	10.0	1.0	1.0
15-19	12.0	2.0	2.0
10-14	23.0	8.0	7.0
9 and below	34.0	75.0	57.0
Total	100.0	100.0	100.0

Source: Tokyo Metropolitan Government, Municipal Library, Tokyo's Housing Problem, no. 5 (Tokyo, March 1972), p. 35.

pany housing. Each year, newly hired workers are recruited from distant prefectures and given housing together, enabling them to build friendships on the basis of a similar year of entry and regional ties. They may live in the company dormitory for as long as 10 years before marrying, since most Japanese workers marry fairly late in life. In some large firms, marriage simply means moving from bachelor dormitories to company houses. While dormitory housing may cement relationships among occupants, it may also serve to divide the labor force—occupants versus fellow workers living outside the dormitories. Such divisions exist within the auto parts firm.[38]

Divergent factors are developing that becloud the future growth of company-owned housing. In the last few years, because of the increasing cost of land, maintenance, and the shortage of suitable craftsmen, large companies have started to curtail their stock of housing facilities in the more heavily populated areas and to provide employees with financial stipends to obtain their own dwellings. The rents only return the company some 15 percent of maintenance and operating costs.[39]

The investment in housing facilities by business firms in 1966 was 5.7 percent of total assets.[40] The housing facilities represented

TABLE 9.8

National Average Rents per Mat, Japan, 1973

Items	Yen
National average	770
Exclusively used for dwellings	750
Rented, publicly owned[a]	446
Rented, privately owned[b]	1,015
Rented, privately owned	1,163
Issued	210
Combined with agriculture and fishery use	273
Combined with store and other use	1,058
Lodging households in dwellings	375
Living in other occupied dwellings	77

[a]Dwellings with cooking and toilet installations for exclusive use.
[b]Dwellings with cooking and toilet installations for shared use.

Source: Office of the Prime Minister, Bureau of Statistics, Housing Survey of Japan, 1973.

an average investment per employee of 70,600 yen; the size of the investment varied from 115,600 yen in firms with 5,000 or more employees to 25,000 yen for firms with 30-99 employees.[41] The average housing allowance in 1966 was 1,701 yen per month, or 3.1 percent of the monthly wage.[42]

As an alternative to company housing, programs have been started to aid employees to purchase or build a home through low-interest, long-term loans and payroll savings programs.[43] Since retired employees cannot remain in company housing, it is more propitious for them to buy a home earlier in their work career and remain there upon retirement.

A mitigating factor in favor of an expansion in employer involvement in housing is the dispersion of industry away from congested and environmentally polluted areas to locations without an adequate stock of housing. To implement the 1962 Act for the Promotion of New Industrial Cities, financial and other assistance is given to private industry for the acquisition of land and for housing estates.[44]

There is an ongoing program for the development of 15 new industrial cities and six special industrial areas. However, the rate of industrial decentralization has been limited by the reluctance of the

government to provide adequate financial support and the apparent
political selection of cities, that is, the degree of local support for
the ruling Liberal Democratic Party.[45] Former Prime Minister
Tanaka proposed that new industrial cities, economically self-sustaining, with populations of 250,000, be created. The core would be an
industrial park stemming from the process of industrial relocation.[46]

Unions have shown little interest in sharing welfare responsibilities with management. Therefore, they are left in the hands of the
employer or, more precisely, are one of the functions of the industrial
family, for which the employer is traditionally held responsible.[47]
Though unions may not be eager to share responsibilities, company
benefits are not always the result of a passive acceptance of benevolent
paternalism, especially since the end of World War II; they are now
the subject of collective bargaining.

Since governmental assistance for employer-provided housing is
based on a formal system or program, the next step is to examine the
legislation under which the assistance is made available.

JHC

The Japan Housing Corporation (JHC), a public corporation set
up in 1955, carries out government housing programs throughout Japan
unhampered by administrative jurisdictions. It develops sites and constructs buildings, then either sells the sites and buildings or retains
ownership and manages them. It constructs housing and supporting
facilities, such as educational and retail facilities. Building sites
may be developed for residential and related activities. It can develop
land for industrial and commercial uses. To maximize the turnover
in funds within the shortest possible time, JHC has given priority to
the sale of housing.[48]

Construction funds for JHC have come from loans by national
and local governments and private financing institutions, such as insurance firms and trust banks, and from the sale of bonds. In 1965,
the government stopped making further loans and, instead, granted
subsidies to JHC out of the General Account to reduce the financial
burden from interest payments to local governments and private financial institutions. In fiscal year 1971, JHC funds consisted of government loans of $750 million and nongovernment loans of $700 million.[49]
From 1955 to 1971, JHC provided some 606,000 housing units and developed 21,000 hectares (51,900 acres) of building sites.[50]

The JHC activity most germane to this study is the construction
of dwellings for specific sale. For individuals or companies wishing
to buy housing for company residences or dormitories for employees,
JHC prepares a building site and constructs the housing. Planning and

design are in accordance with the buyer's preferences. Payments on the principal are made in equal installments over a 15- to 20-year period.[51] JHC has provided 180,000 such dwellings.[52]

EPPC

The Employment Promotion Projects Corporation (EPPC), a semiindependent body under the overall responsibility of the Ministry of Labor, established on July 1, 1961, was given a broad mandate:

> This corporation carries out businesses necessary
> for assistance to acquire and to improve technical
> skills, to move workers smoothly among different
> geographic areas or among different industries and
> to other activities for workers' employment promo-
> tion and, by so doing, to promote employment suit-
> able for workers' ability and further to contribute to
> the welfare of workers and development.[53]

The role planned for EPPC was to carry out operations deemed inadvisable or inconvenient for the government to perform. The line of demarcation between the areas of responsibility for the ministry and the corporation has not been clearly drawn. Yet, the setting up of the EPPC was regarded as one of the creative administrative innovations in Japanese labor policy, which has performed with great success in facilitating the adaptation of workers to ongoing changes in the labor market.[54]

The organization performs such functions complementary to the government's manpower policies as construction and operation of lodging and welfare facilities for workers, extends aid and loans to those seeking employment as part of employment promotion measures, conducts vocational training, assists laborers displaced from the coal mining industry, and coordinates these various operations.

More specifically related to housing are "loans of lodging allowances for assisting workers who change employment and move and . . . loans for employment promotion concerning housing for workers for the sake of securing labor force."[55] The operations are financed by the Unemployment Insurance Special Fund, financial support from the government General Account, loans from the capital operation fund, and income from facilities operated by the EPPC.[56]

Among the special activities of EPPC is the bonus paid to medium- and small-size enterprises to cover expenses resulting from the provision of housing for middle-aged and older persons engaged through the Public Employment Security offices to work away from their permanent residences. This provision is part of a larger program designed to encourage the employment of middle-aged and older persons.[57]

Lodgings and other accommodations managed by EPPC are financed in the main by investments from the Special Account of the Unemployment Insurance Fund. The major share of the investment is used for the construction of lodgings and hour houses for remover workers (floating body of labor between industries and districts). The lending system has two forms: the first is where the houses are lent directly to remover workers, and the second is where the houses are lent to employers in the harbor business, whose employees are permitted to live in these houses.[58]

To provide housing for workers relocating to areas with a shortage of labor under the aegis of the Public Employment Security Office, EPPC has built over 60,000 apartments. Rents are 3,000 yen to 5,200 yen per month, and the rental period is generally one year. If it is difficult for a remover worker to leave the house for other housing managed by public or municipal authorities during the rental period, the term can be extended. Another rental system allows any employer with five or more remover workers to rent a prefabricated house (pipe house) for a year, and if the employer so desires, it can be sold to him.[59]

Lodgings for harbor laborers (longshoremen) are lent to any employer who will hire longshoremen through the Public Employment Security Office as a means of keeping labor in the major harbors. Welfare centers for longshoremen are located in major harbors throughout the country; each center contains accommodations, such as lodging rooms. Simple boarding houses for day laborers with low room charges have been set up and managed by EPPC in each of the main harbors.[60]

There are a variety of funds providing employment promotion loans to employers or their associations wishing to establish boarding or welfare facilities for workers referred by the Public Employment Security Office. The loans have a low rate of interest and a long term for repayment.[61] From 1966 to 1970, EPPC, with the use of public funds, built 125,000 housing units.[62]

HLC

Another public corporation established in 1950, the Housing Loan Corporation (HLC), provides long-term, low-interest loans for housing construction that are available to firms desiring to provide their employees with housing. The original aim, still valid, was to finance homeownership. Sources of funds are government investments and loans, with an interest rate of 6.5 percent, private funds, and loan repayments.[63] The government loans come from the reserve funds of postal savings and postal life insurance premiums. Postal savings are the principal source of government funds for the construction of housing.

The receipts collected by the postal savings bank, the only savings bank in the country, are deposited with the Trust Fund Bureau, through which they are invested in the HLC and the JHC, in accordance with national investment programs. In 1969, postal savings invested in these corporations was 157,100 million yen, or about 37 percent of their total funds. This investment represents a sizable contribution to housing construction.[64]

In 1970 and 1971, 84.4 and 85.5 percent, respectively, of HLC funds came from government loans (see Table 9.9). In contrast, the direct loan programs in the United States have been replaced by interest subsidy programs, which, in turn, the Ford administration has replaced with a revised leasing program; however, proponents of the direct loan programs have sought their reinstatement without success.

To make HLC operational, the government, in 1950, invested $41.7 million. Through fiscal year 1970, the total HLC borrowing from the government reached $3.6 billion.[65]

Through fiscal year 1970, total HLC loans came to some $5 billion for land acquisitions, land development, and housing construction. By the end of fiscal year 1970, HLC was responsible for 2,584,171 units built according to its construction standards.[66]

Originally, loans were limited to the construction of owner-occupied housing and rental apartments operated by juridical persons, nonprofit corporations. In the face of a severe housing shortage, such a policy was inadequate to meet the heavy demand for loans; thus, loan conditions and the scope of loans were eased in 1953 by forming the Industrial Workers Housing Fund and, in 1955, by the Housing Loan Insurance Law.

The Industrial Workers Housing Fund provides financing to employers to build housing for their personnel through long-term, low-interest loans and "where employees can keep a wholesome and cultured living."[67] Financing is obtainable for industrial firms employing five or more permanent workers for the construction or purchase of housing for subsequent sale or rental to employees, to companies or corporations established by investment or finance by industrial companies (apparently subsidiaries) to be sold or rented to employees of the investing or financing companies, and companies or corporations who will construct housing to be sold to industrial companies for subsequent resale or rental to employees.

Loan terms are more favorable for medium and small companies, and the term of redemption depends upon the type of construction (see Table 9.10).

TABLE 9.9

Housing Loan Corporation Source of Funds, Japan, 1970-71
(millions of yen)

Item	1970 Amount	1970 Percent	1971 Amount	1971 Percent
Government investment	—	—	—	—
Government loans	234,800	84.4	282,900	85.5
Bonds	2,500	0.9	2,000	0.6
Recovered loans	33,723	12.1	34,024	10.3
Government subsidy	7,097	2.6	11,500	3.6
Total	278,120	100.0	330,424	100.0

Source: The Housing Loan Corporation, General Information on the Housing Loan Corporation, p. 20 (Japanese government publication).

TABLE 9.10

Industrial Workers' Housing, Loan Conditions, Japan, Fiscal Year, 1971

Size of Company	Annual Interest (percent)	Limit of Loan* (percent)	Term of Redemption (years) Wooden or Prefab (number)	Term of Redemption (years) Semi-fire-proof (number)	Term of Redemption (years) Fire-proof (number)
Medium and small	6.5	75	18	30	35
Other	7.0	50	18	30	35

*Based on percent of construction cost or land cost according to standard construction costs or standard land prices set by HLC.

Source: The Housing Loan Corporation, General Information on the Housing Loan Corporation, p. 14 (Japanese government publication).

TABLE 9.11

Housing Loan Corporation Loans, Japan, 1970–71
(millions of yen)

	All Loans	Industrial Workers Housing	Medium and Small Companies	Other Companies
1970				
Units				
Number	256,000	9,000	5,400	3,600
Percent	100.0	3.5	2.1	1.4
Loans				
Amount	289,721	7,537	5,401	2,136
Percent	100.0	2.6	1.9	0.7
1971				
Units				
Number	262,000	9,000	5,400	3,600
Percent	100.0	3.4	2.1	1.3
Loans				
Amount	344,781	8,300	5,966	2,334
Percent	100.0	2.4	1.7	0.7

Source: The Housing Loan Corporation, General Information on the Housing Loan Corporation, p. 19 (Japanese government publication).

Between 1950 and 1970, of the 2,584,171 housing units built with HLC funds, 184,519, or 7 percent, consisted of housing for industrial workers.[68] However, in 1970 and 1971, the annual rate was about 3.5 percent (see Table 9.11). The decline in the industrial housing fund share of HLC funds is expected to continue.[69]

The 1955 Housing Loan Insurance Law was designed to encourage financing by private banks with private funds. Some 90 percent of the loan balance was insured; the annual premium was 0.3 percent of the balance of the insured amount, 90 percent, or 0.45 percent of the loan amount, 100 percent. When private financial institutions made loans, the annual interest rate was 8 percent to 10 percent, and the terms of repayment were 5 to 20 years, considerably more stringent than the terms for the Industrial Workers Housing Fund.

In the 1960s, private financial institutions made significant inroads into the HLC monopoly. Among the private programs is one whereby private lenders, in agreement with employers, grant loans

to employees to build their own homes. The redemption term is longer
and the interest rate lower than it would be without employer involvement.[70]

PENSION RESERVE FUND, MINISTRY OF
HEALTH AND WELFARE[71]

A large share of the contributions collected under the Employees
Pension Insurance Scheme are used to pay benefits; they are deposited
in the Trust Fund Bureau of the Ministry of Finance on condition that
the term of redemption is seven years and the interest rate is 6.5 percent per annum.

The funds of the Trust Fund Bureau are allocated to various government special accounts, local public bodies, government-affiliated
agencies, for example, HLC, National Railway Corporation, and other
public corporations, such as JHC, Pension Welfare Promotion Public
Corporation, and for activities of other groups complying with the requirements of the government Fiscal Investment and Loan Program.

About 80 percent of the annual net increase in the pension reserve fund deposits is used for financing housing, environmental sanitation facilities, welfare facilities, small enterprises and agricultural
and fishing industries, all of which are necessary to raise the standard
of living for the entire nation. The 20 percent balance serves as financing for fundamental investment in economic development, such as
roads, transportation, communication systems, regional development
works, and where natural disasters occur and relief is needed.

The Pension Welfare Promotion Public Corporation, a legally
defined special juridical person, borrows from the Trust Fund and finances employers and prescribed corporations for the construction of
housing, hospitals, and welfare facilities, such as health resort facilities, gymnasiums, and so forth, for insured persons.

CONCLUSIONS

As indicated by the discussion of the various programs, Japan
has succeeded in relating housing to national economic and manpower
policy and the needs of enterprises, in extreme contrast to the United
States, where there has been practically no comparable activity.
These practices have been seen by Westerners as a source of competitive weakness and inefficiency, since investments in employee housing
are costly and not directly profitable. Yet, while giving these benefits,
Japan has attained a remarkable level of industrialization and productivity.

What is the likelihood of other countries adopting the Japanese housing programs for employees? It is unlikely that there could be direct and immediate transferability.

Once the cultural overlay and special circumstances have been penetrated, a convergence of tendencies at this point in time in Japan and in the other member OECD (Organization for Economic Cooperation and Development) countries becomes evident illustrating common problems and policy options. Japan is clearly moving toward a more Western-type labor market, as Western countries may be moving toward more of the security arrangements that can be seen in the Japanese labor market. Culture and history have been so different, however, that one would expect adaptation and not mere imitations, as Japan and the West draw upon the experience of each other.[72]

The devaluation of the dollar, the opposition to a free flow of manufactured imports into the United States, and the need to move outside of Japan for purposes of industrial expansion, with the encouragement of the Japanese government, have resulted in an increase in manufacturing operations in other countries. The question posed is whether the employee housing programs will also be exported as Japanese companies expand their international operations.

The major obstacles to the expansion of manufacturing investment in the United States by the Japanese have been the high labor costs and the lack of familiarity with the indigenous trade unions, and the ability to manage American workers. Because of this unfamiliarity, the Japanese have preferred highly automated plants with labor-saving technology and minimal industrial relations problems.[73] Thus, for the present, there would appear to be no need to develop a system of employer-provided housing for those plants in the United States; however, the lack of familiarity with U.S. industrial relations would eventually be overcome, and there appears to be a tendency for labor costs among industrialized countries to come closer to the same levels. If proven successful outside of Japan, there could be a growth in importation of the Japanese industrial relations policies, of which housing benefits are an integral part.

The provisions of the Japanese legislation providing financial assistance to employers for housing are not apt to gain immediate acceptance in the United States. The implications of such a program would be to facilitate the establishment or movement of industrial facilities outside of central cities and older urban areas. The political pressures against facilitating or financing industrial mobility would be strong enough to forestall such assistance.

NOTES

1. Robert Evans, Jr., The Labor Economics of Japan and the United States (New York: Praeger Publishers, 1971), p. 39.

2. Robert E. Cole, Japanese Blue Collar: The Changing Tradition (Berkeley: University of California Press, 1971), p. 100. Originally published by University of California Press: reprinted by permission of the Regents of the University of California.

3. Evans, op. cit., p. 47.

4. Cole, op. cit., p. 126.

5. "Japan's Recession Seen Ending Soon," Wall Street Journal, January 6, 1975, p. 6.

6. "Economic Uncertainty—Japan Can Depend on That," New York Times, January 26, 1975, pt. 2, sec. 3, p. 40.

7. James C. Abbeglen, "Organizational Change," in The Japanese Employee, Robert J. Ballon, ed. (Tokyo: Sophia University, in cooperation with Charles E. Tuttle Co., Rutland, Vt., 1969), p. 101.

8. Robert Evans, Jr., "Japan's Labor Economy—Prospects for the Future," Monthly Labor Review 95 (October 1972): 8.

9. Richard Tanner Johnson and William G. Ouchi, "Made in America (under Japanese Management)," Harvard Business Review 52 (September/October 1974): 69.

10. Ibid., p. 66.

11. Ministry of Posts and Telecommunication, "Housing Finance in Japan," World Thrift, no. 4 (July/August 1970), p. 216.

12. Caleb Hathaway, "Construction in Japan," Construction Review 18 (November 1972): 8.

13. K. Beida, The Structure and Operation of the Japanese Economy (Sydney: John Wiley and Sons, Australasai Proprietary Limited, 1970), p. 3.

14. Hathaway, op. cit., p. 7; Tokyo Metropolitan Government, Municipal Library, Tokyo's Housing Problem, no. 5 (Tokyo, March 1972), p. 154; and information provided by Y. Uchida, Deputy Head, Housing Planning Section, Housing Bureau, Ministry of Construction, Tokyo, in letter from Japanese Embassy, Washington, D.C., July 30, 1974.

15. Hathaway, op. cit., p. 7; Tokyo Metropolitan Government, Municipal Library, op. cit., p. 152; and Uchida, letter to authors, July 30, 1974.

16. U.S. Congress, House, Committee on Banking and Currency, First Annual Report on National Housing Goals, 91st Cong., 1st sess., H. Doc. 91-63 (Washington, D.C.: Government Printing Office, 1969), p. 17.

17. U.S. Congress, House, Committee on Banking and Currency, Fourth Annual Report on National Housing Goals, 92d Cong., 2d sess., H. Doc. 92-319 (Washington, D.C.: Government Printing Office, 1972), p. 9.

18. Ministry of Posts and Telecommunication, op. cit., p. 216.

19. Ibid.

20. Kakeui Tanaka, Building a New Japan (Tokyo: The Simul Press, Inc., 1973), pp. 51-52.

21. Tokyo Metropolitan Government, Municipal Library, op. cit., p. 150.

22. Ibid., pp. 146, 150.

23. Ibid., p. 7.

24. Ibid., p. 133.

25. Ibid., p. 135.

26. Ibid., p. 138.

27. Ibid., p. 140.

28. Alan H. Gleason, "Postwar Housing in Japan and the United States," corrected copy, in Studies on Economic Life in Japan, Richard K. Beardsley, ed., Center for Japanese Studies, Occasional Papers, no. 8 (Ann Arbor: The University of Michigan Press, 1964), p. 9.

29. Tokyo Metropolitan Government, Municipal Library, op. cit., pp. 58, 59.

30. Office of the Prime Minister, Bureau of Statistics, Housing Survey of Japan, 1973.

31. Tokyo Metropolitan Government, Municipal Library, op. cit., p. 110.

32. Ibid., p. 140.

33. Gleason, op. cit., p. 9.

34. Tadashi Umezawa and Masahiko Honjo, "Company Housing in Japan," International Labour Review 99 (June 1969): 581.

35. Abbeglen, op. cit., pp. 111, 112.

36. Tokyo Metropolitan Government, Municipal Library, op. cit., p. 111.

37. Ibid., p. 38.

38. Cole, op. cit., p. 151.

39. Umezawa and Honjo, op. cit., p. 584.

40. Abbeglen, op. cit., p. 127.

41. Ibid., p. 128.

42. Ibid.

43. M. Y. Yoshino, Japan's Managerial System—Tradition and Innovation (Cambridge and London: The MIT Press, 1968), p. 242.

44. Organization for Economic Cooperation and Development, Salient Features of Regional Development Policy (OECD, October 1971), p. 69.

45. "Regional Planning," Town and Country Planning 40 (October 1972): 491, 492.

46. Tanaka, op. cit., p. 169.

47. Abbeglen, op. cit., p. 128.

48. Tokyo Metropolitan Government, Municipal Library, op. cit., p. 191.

49. Japan Housing Corporation, 72 The Annual Report of Japan Housing Corp., p. 20; and M. E. Witherick, "The Japan Housing Corporation," Town and Country Planning 40 (November 1972): 521.

50. Japan Housing Corporation, op. cit., p. 17.

51. Ibid., p. 92.

52. Ibid., p. 6.

53. Article I, Law 116, Employment Promotion Projects Corporation, 1961.

54. Organization for Economic Cooperation and Development, Manpower Policy in Japan, Reviews of Manpower and Social Policies, no. 11 (Paris, 1973), pp. 17, 135, 136.

55. Employment Promotion Projects Corporation, n.d., p. 203, provided by Ministry of Construction, Japanese government, letter of December 15, 1972.

56. Ibid.

57. Organization for Economic Cooperation and Development, Manpower Policy in Japan, p. 54.

58. Employment Promotion Projects Corporation, op. cit., p. 206.

59. Ibid., p. 209.

60. Ibid., p. 210.

61. Ibid., p. 213.

62. U.S. Department of Housing and Urban Development, "A Country in Transition," HUD International Brief, no. 6 (June 1971), p. 16.

63. The Housing Loan Corporation, General Information of the Housing Loan Corporation, n.d., p. 16, provided by Ministry of Construction, Japanese government, letter of December 15, 1972.

64. Ministry of Posts and Telecommunication, op. cit., p. 523.

65. The Housing Loan Corporation, op. cit., pp. 2, 3.

66. Ibid., pp. 3, 4.

67. Ibid., p. 10.

68. Teretumo Ozawa, "Japan's New Industrial Offensive in the United States," MSU Business Topics 21 (Autumn 1973): 28.

69. Uchida, letter to authors, July 30, 1974.

70. U.S. Department of Housing and Urban Development, op. cit., p. 6; and Ministry of Posts and Telecommunication, op. cit., p. 216.

71. Material on Pension Reserve Fund provided by Ministry of Construction, Japanese government, letter of December 15, 1972.

72. Organization for Economic Cooperation and Development, Manpower Policy in Japan, pp. 9-10.

73. Johnson and Ouchi, op. cit.

How has the basic housing legislation in the United States developed, and have any deficiencies emerged that call for the consideration of alternatives? The first important step taken by Congress in respect to housing was the resolution passed July 20, 1892, to provide an additional $20,000 to the Secretary of Labor to investigate slums in cities with populations of 200,000 or more. Objections were raised when the resolution was introduced, and to overcome them, the sponsor had to amend the resolution and to compare the slums in the United States with those in Europe. Then, the Commissioner of Labor wrote an extensive legal opinion substantiating the constitutionality of the expenditure and assured Congress that he would draw upon the additional $20,000 only as needed. Thus, the final report, because of the limited funds, was confined only to certain districts of four large cities: Baltimore, Chicago, New York, and Philadelphia.[1]

It was not until the depression of the 1930s that Congress took a strong interest in housing; and, in 1949 and 1968, Congress and the president acknowledged the importance of housing. In 1931, President Hoover's Conference on Home Building and Home Ownership recommended the broadening of homeownership, an adequate system of credit for the benefit of both homeowners and lenders, improved planning and zoning, better homes at lower costs through improved technology, and the rehabilitation of existing homes.

It was during the severe depression of the 1930s that the outlines of existing federal housing legislation were formulated: the FHLB system, the FHA, public housing, and the Federal National Mortgage Association (FNMA). Three factors influenced the role of the federal government: the desire for economic stability, assistance for those unable to afford decent housing, and the desirability of community development.

LEGISLATION OF THE 1930s

On July 1932, the Federal Home Loan Bank Act was enacted; it set up a system of regional home loan banks under the supervision of the FHLB Board. The banks were given authority to make advances secured by first mortgages to its home-financing institutions, made up largely of savings and loan associations. The associations would have an independent source for borrowing funds to meet seasonal and emergency liquidity needs.

The enactment of the National Housing Act in 1934 included the establishment of the FHA. The short-range goals of the act were to increase the supply of funds for new construction and repairs, to revive the homebuilding industry, to get men back to work, to restore confidence, and to improve general economic conditions. The long-range goals were to reform mortgage-lending practices, to expand opportunities for homeownership, and to raise housing standards. The mechanism by which this was to be accomplished was to insure mortgage loans made by private financial institutions for construction, rehabilitation, and purchase.

FHA operations have been self-supporting, with the income emanating from insurance premiums and investments. In addition to the normal or traditional mortgage insurance programs, the FHA has, over a period of years, assumed responsibility for a varied group of special housing programs, devised to provide low- and moderate-income families with decent, safe, and sanitary housing. These later programs have not been self-supporting and have required additional financial assistance from the federal government. They include rent supplements, below market interest rate loans,* and direct loans for senior citizens' housing, ** interest subsidies for homeownership assistance,† and for rental housing assistance. ‡

As part of a broad package of benefits for veterans of World War II, a vast homeownership program to guaranty loans was made part of the GI Bill (Servicemen's Readjustment Act of 1944).

The Housing Act of 1949 created the Farmers Home Administration to make direct loans to farmers to obtain decent, safe, and sanitary dwellings for themselves, their laborers, and tenants. In 1961, the loans were made available to nonfarm residents in rural areas. Until 1965, the source of the funds for the loans came from the U.S. Treasury. In 1965, there was a change from direct to insured loans,

---

*Section 221(d)(3).
**Section 202.
†Section 235.
‡Section 236.

and the outstanding loans no longer had to be included in the budget or national debt.

In 1933, the National Recovery Act had provisions for a program of low-cost housing through federal activity. The housing program culminated in the enactment of the U.S. Housing Act in 1937 to provide loans and annual contributions to local public housing agencies for low-rent housing to be occupied by those unable to afford decent housing without financial aid. The housing was to be owned and managed by local housing authorities set up under state law. Initially, the program was conceived primarily in terms of new construction; however, it now encompasses the use of existing housing by leasing or acquisition with or without rehabilitation. The turnkey method has been adopted, whereby the local housing authority contracts to purchase a newly completed property.

In 1968, the FNMA was formed to make mortgages a liquid investment. FHA insurance did not give the mortgage holder the freedom to shift from one investment to another. FNMA's function was to encourage the flow of capital from areas of surplus funds to areas of short supply by means of a secondary market to purchase mortgages.

In the 1970s, there was widespread criticism of existing housing policies and programs, a reluctance to continue them unchanged, and agreement on the need for basic reforms. The inadequacies were affecting all categories of housing consumers. The assistance programs upon which most criticism was focused in Washington were Sections 235 and 236 of the Housing Act of 1968 for low- and moderate-income households. The severe shortage of housing credit and high interest rates affected all income levels in respect to housing, and questions arose about the capabilities of existing financial institutions to provide the solution.

FINANCIAL INTERMEDIARIES

In the face of the sensitivity of housing production to credit restrictions and rising interest rates and the necessity to correlate the availability of credit with the demand or need for housing, the objective of an analysis of housing finance is to seek avenues whereby adequate funds can be channeled into the housing sector and avoid the cyclical fluctuations.

Credit for mortgages has become the residuary for long-term investment funds; when other credit users are forcefully seeking funds, mortgage credit is in short supply, as in 1955-57, 1959-60, 1966, 1969-70, and 1974. Restrictive money policies hit housing hardest, and, following the 1966 experience, Sherman Maisel of the University of California at Berkeley (formerly a governor of the Federal Reserve

Board) estimated the impact of tight money on the housing sector; it had to absorb between 60 percent to 70 percent of the impact, whereas the housing industry comprised only 3 percent of GNP. "When an industry accounting for only three percent of the economy takes 70 percent of the cutback because of policies that result in tight money the impact is clearly discriminatory and unfair."[2]

> The view that restrictive monetary policy and tight credit markets bear down heavily on housing is not new. What may be new, however, is a rising national commitment to housing. In many quarters this commitment has led to increased concern over housings' fate during periods of tight credit. The cries to "insulate" housing from the more severe impacts of changes in financial markets seem to grow louder and more frequent. But the noisier the cries get, the more they elicit responses from those who would follow a hands-off policy, a policy of allowing the forces of free enterprise to channel the "correct" amount of credit into housing.[3]

Among the various government-sponsored institutions aimed at "facilitating the financing of residential housing, enhance the liquidity of the mortgage market and provide direct support to selected types of mortgages" are the intermediaries, who "provide second layer support to the private mortgage lenders."[4] The major intermediaries are the FNMA, the Government National Mortgage Association (GNMA), and the Federal Home Loan Mortgage Corporation (FHLMC).[5]

FNMA

The FNMA was chartered in 1938 to convert mortgages into a liquid investment, as FHA insurance did not give the mortgage holder the sufficient freedom to shift from one investment to another. Greater liquidity in the mortgage market was to be secured by the availability of a secondary market for new FHA-insured mortgages. In the first 10 years of operation, it bought FHA-insured mortgages when mortgage funds were scarce and sold mortgages when there was a surplus of loanable funds and other investment outlets were limited. In 1948, FNMA was authorized to purchase Veterans Administration (VA) mortgages. Although given the authority to purchase conventional mortgages by the Emergency Home Finance Act of 1970, until 1972, all of its activity was confined to government-insured or -guaranteed mortgages.

The Housing and Urban Development Act of 1968 divided FNMA into two corporate entities: FNMA and GNMA. The recast FNMA became a government-sponsored privately owned, taxpaying corporation subject to a limited degree of government regulation, yet whose expenditures and receipts were not subject to the constraints imposed by the federal budget. It retained the secondary market functions for residential mortgages through buying and selling mortgages. Financing for its operations comes from mortgage repayments, sales of obligations, fees, mortgage sales, and the surplus from the excess of interest income over borrowing costs.

GNMA

In 1968, GNMA was created to assume the special assistance functions and management and liquidation functions of the original FNMA. GNMA became a government-owned corporate body within HUD. The special assistance functions are operated solely for the account of the federal government, with treasury funds as authorized by Congress to buy mortgages for specific government housing programs, for example, Sections 202, 221(d)(3), Below Market Interest Rate (BMIR), 235, and 236. Many of these mortgages are subsequently sold to private parties, under the Tandem Plan. Under certain Tandem plans, GNMA buys insured mortgages at less than the prevailing interest rates (under government-subsidized housing programs) from lenders and resells them to FNMA or other purchasers at a discount to meet the prevailing market interest rate. Congress appropriates funds to cover these losses.

FHLMC

In 1970, FHLMC, a private corporation, was created under the Emergency Home Finance Act, with the objective of serving as central credit reserve facility and secondary market for conventional and government underwritten mortgages. It operates under the jurisdiction of the FHLB system, which supervises the federally chartered savings and loan associations. The lack of a central credit facility for conventional mortgages hampered the capabilities of public agencies to ease fluctuations in housing starts and to give mortgage lenders sufficient funds to maintain liquidity.

FHLMC was initially financed by the sale of $100 million of securities to the Federal Home Loan District banks. Additional funds have been secured from the sale of bonds and participation certificates and by borrowing from FHLB banks or, through these banks, as they,

in turn, sell securities to finance the FHLMC. As with FNMA,
FHLMC is not mandated to seek congressional approval for the issuance
of debt obligations and is not subject to the federal debt limit or the
federal budget.

Effectiveness

There are questions about the effectiveness of the federal intermediaries, based upon their performance. In periods of tight money,
do their combined efforts supply the housing sector with an appreciably
greater amount of funds? When money is in ample supply, under the
present rules of governance, will they minimize their support for private lending, as the basic strategy may demand?[6]

For all their efforts, the three major federal intermediaries
cannot meet more than a fraction of housing credit needs, nor can
they drive down interest rates.[7] Not all of the funds redirected by the
intermediaries into housing represent a net gain. The additional competition for funds engendered by the heavy borrowing of intermediaries
in money markets adds to the pressure on interest rates and leads,
paradoxically, to an exodus of funds from those lending institutions
that invest in mortgages. In turn, the higher interest cost rates raise
the costs of housing. The amount of federal subsidy is increased to
support the same number of units, for example, the higher interest
costs are reflected in the rents for the expanded Section 8 leasing program for new construction and in the FHA interest subsidy programs
(Sections 235 and 236).

> While the programs involving massive borrowing of
> funds in the markets by FNMA and the Federal Home
> Loan Banks succeeded in greatly moderating the im-
> pact of monetary restraint on mortgage financing in
> 1969-1970, there were perverse effects that cannot
> be overlooked. The resulting obligations provided
> additional investment alternatives that stimulated
> disintermediation. Moreover, it is important to rec-
> ognize that these borrowings did not add to the total
> available funds but represented only the ability of
> the agencies to preempt funds from the total savings
> available for investment. Since their borrowings
> are not sensitive to interest rates, they played a
> part in escalating market interest rates.[8]

Undoubtedly, changes in institutional arrangements for mortgages are useful, but "they cannot be expected, and of themselves, to

cushion, but not fully eliminate, the inherent sensitivity of housing to variations in overall credit conditions."[9]

> Their effectiveness during a credit crunch is doubt-
> ful, however, since they do not come to grips with
> the fundamental differences in competitive borrow-
> ing strength between homebuyers (or indirectly, rent-
> ers) and other capital fund borrowers. The differ-
> ences in borrowing strength, i.e. ability to pay
> higher interest rates, lead to credit cycle housing
> downturns. Probably broader economic policies
> which go beyond efforts to improve mortgage finance
> market mechanisms would be required to give hous-
> ing a stronger competitive position in periods of rela-
> tive capital funds shortage.[10]

INTEREST SUBSIDIES

The major accomplishment of the Johnson administration in respect to putting its stamp on housing assistance legislation was the replacement of the direct loan programs by interest subsidy programs.

> Four years after the adoption of the 1968 Housing Act,
> which at that time was heralded as one of the greatest
> housing advances in the history of the U.S., that act
> is in serious trouble. Speculators, "get-rich-quick
> artists," real estate operators, brokers, builders,
> creditors, appraisers, all of them have found the
> act to be a bonanza for their activities; and for the
> thousands of low-to-moderate income families it has
> been a nightmare. I recognize this and this subcom-
> mittee recognizes that to hundreds of thousands of
> others it has been of great benefit.[11]

Section 235 was designed to promote homeownership for low-
and moderate-income families and individuals by reducing monthly
payments on mortgages. The owners pay 20 percent of their income
toward monthly mortgage payments, and the government pays the balance by subsidizing interest payments, the maximum interest subsidy
being the equivalent of the difference between the actual interest rate
and 1 percent.

Section 236 covers rental housing for low- and moderate-income
families and individuals with reduced monthly rentals. The rentals
are cut through a subsidy to lower interest costs; the maximum inter-

est subsidy is the equivalent of the difference between the actual interest rate and 1 percent.

At the time of enactment, these programs were new and untested; insufficient consideration was given to their ultimate costs. They replaced direct loan programs at a below market interest rate of 3 percent (Section 221(d)(3) below market interest rate for rentals and cooperatives for low- or moderate-income families and Section 202 for the elderly). The direct loan programs were dropped because of their high immediate impact on the federal budget. On the other hand, Sections 235 and 236 have a low impact on the budget initially but are costlier over the term of the mortgage.

The federal government is already committed to about $15 billion in future subsidy payments, based on the number of units approved through fiscal year 1975, although the maximum payments legally allowable for Sections 235 and 236 could reach as high as $39 billion (see Table 10.1). Paradoxically, the lowest-income families in the country are not benefited by these massive expenditures. Estimates of the total commitment vary. The Wall Street Journal, in a March 31, 1972 editorial, cited an estimate by federal officials that the long-term commitment could reach $200 billion by 1978.[12]

Other shortcomings of the programs are not entirely the fault of the legislation itself but, in part, due to poor administration by the FHA. There has been shoddy construction, poor site selection, excessive profiteerings, and a lack of concern by owners over the life of the housing beyond the tax benefit period.

> Under the 235 and 236 programs you set up a system which effectively tells everybody not to worry about the fellow down at the end. There are guaranteed mortgages for the mortgagees. The appraiser gets his chunk, the real estate guy gets paid, the developer gets profits. If it is a sponsor, he is entitled to a certain amount of tax shelter. We have a system now where the mortgagee is absolutely guaranteed he is going to be all right. He doesn't have to go a thing. When you set up a system like that it seems to me we are making a mistake. We ought to look at the people who can benefit in the private sector, in this case the mortgage industry, the developers and all the rest of them, to at least find a way to make them share the risk.[13]

REPLACEMENT

The shortcomings, scandals, and abuses in the interest subsidy programs have led to demands ranging from complete replacement to

TABLE 10.1

Maximum and Estimated Federal Assistance Payment Costs for Subsidized Housing Programs, from Inception of Program Through Fiscal Year 1975

Item	Section 235	Section 236	Rent Supplements Market Rate	Rent Supplements "Piggy-Back"	Public Housing Owned	Public Housing Leased	Public Housing Modernization	Section 221(d)(3) Below Market Interest Rate	Section 202	Total
Cumulative Program										
Period covered	1969-74	1969-74	1966-74	1966-74	1937-75	1966-75	1968-75	1966-70	1966-70	n.a.[e]
Contract or loan authority (thousands of dollars)	445,346	640,614[a]	266,136[a]		942,601	1,419,292	127,357	1,607,000	277,000	n.a.[e]
Number of units supported	505,267	627,430	114,017	105,755	1,161,200	587,490	511,000[d]	95,200	19,700	3,216,059
Maximum years commitment	30	40	40	40	40	16.0	20-21	40	50	n.a.[e]
Estimated years subsidy is paid	12-15	21-31	40	9-12	40	16.0	20-21	40	50	n.a.[e]
Maximum contractual payments (thousands of dollars)	13,360,380	25,624,560	10,645,440		37,704,040	22,812,523	2,607,541	425,000	90,000	113,269,484[f]
Estimated contractual payments (thousands of dollars)	3,446,650	12,369,355	9,405,613	427,853	37,704,040	22,812,523	2,607,541	425,000	90,000	89,288,575[f]
Per Unit Basis										
Maximum contractual payments	27,000	38,000	112,200	106,200	32,500[b]	38,900[c]	5,100	4,500	4,600	n.a.[e]
Estimated contractual payments	6,800	19,700	85,100	3,900	32,500[b]	38,900[c]	5,100	4,500	4,600	n.a.[e]

[a] Net of recaptured contract authority in fiscal year 1975.

[b] Does not include operating subsidies for owned public housing that is funded out of separate authority.

[c] Includes adjustments to prior years leasing agreements.

[d] These units are included in the units under owned public housing and thus are not added again to the total number of units supported.

[e] Not applicable.

[f] The totals, excluding Public Housing Modernization, are $110,661,943,000 maximum contractual payments and $86,681,034,000 estimated contractual payments.

Note: Per unit costs may not add to aggregate cost because of rounding.

Source: U.S. Congress, House, Subcommittee of the Committee on Appropriations, Hearings on HUD-Space-Science-Veterans Appropriations for 1975, pt. 6, Department of Housing and Urban Development, 93rd Cong., 1st sess., 1974, p. 575.

retention with improved administration. There were proposals for
a return to the direct loan programs that were dropped during the
Johnson administration.

The Nixon administration's preferred solution was direct cash
assistance. Rather than providing housing, the federal government
would give qualified recipients a realistic housing payment and then
allow them to select their own housing on the private market. Payments would be calculated to make up the differential between what a
family itself could pay and the going rental for housing. It would allow
the poor to make their own decisions on housing and minimize the federal government's participation in the housing area, and the housing
market would respond to the demands of the allowance recipient.

What control mechanisms will be necessary to police the program? How large a bureaucracy and what cost will this entail? Since
the allowances are confined to existing housing, the effect would be in
those areas with low vacancy rates to shift the demand curve and increase rental levels. A basic objection is that there are no additions
to the housing stock, and the special needs of the handicapped, elderly,
and large families are overlooked. Housing is not apt to be forthcoming in better suburban areas or in neighborhoods where little housing
for low- or moderate-income groups is being built or exists. Rather
than eliminate substandard housing, such housing is more likely to be
perpetuated. The assertion has been made that welfare rent payments
are a form of housing allowance, and, based on the results, there is
little justification for continuing or expanding a modified version of
such a program.

The Chairman of the Senate Committee on Banking, Housing
and Urban Affairs, John Sparkman, affirmed that the allowance approach to solving housing problems, as favored by the administration,
had fundamental shortcomings.

> The analysis is simplistic, and its policy is seri-
> ously defective. The low-income housing problem
> of our country is not simply an income problem. It
> is, at this point in our history, a housing problem—
> a problem arising from an insufficient supply of decent
> housing. Direct Federal assistance for the production
> of housing is required to help solve that problem be-
> cause as long as the supply is insufficient, the cost
> of decent housing will remain out of the reach of low-
> income groups. To say that a system of direct cash
> assistance will solve the housing problems of the
> poor while, at the same time, shutting off all Federal
> assistance for the production of housing, is to ignore
> the very real facts that there just is not enough decent

housing in this country now to go around, even if every
family were given enough money to buy it. Nor is it
likely that a program of cash assistance would, in the
absence of a production program, assure an adequate
supply—at the right places and times—for many years
to come.

A system of direct cash assistance may also prove
to be a useful tool in the housing field. In the Housing
Bill of 1970, the committee authorized the housing allowance experiment which has been undertaken by HUD.
In this year's housing bill, a significant expansion of
that program would be authorized. It is, consequently,
the view of the committee that direct cash assistance
should be examined as one of the means for solving
housing problems. But the committee rejects the view
that such a program should replace production programs
at this time.[14]

The first housing allowance experiment was started in 1970 in
Kansas City, Missouri; it was opened to 222 of the city's poorest families. Kansas City had a relatively high vacancy rate of 6 percent, and
although the number of families in the test were only a small proportion of the market, there was a contention that most of the families
were overcharged for their accommodations. Nearly 90 percent of
the families did move from substandard to livable housing, but there
still remained a strong need for tenant counseling.

There were many problems which the tenants were
unable to handle. If you're going to deal with low-
income groups, you have to realize that their problems are multiple. Housing allowances work for
people whose only problem is financial. Usually
these are fairly sophisticated people, upwardly mobile, who have middle-class skills.[15]

The same comment could be made about the public housing program. When admission standards were lowered and problem families
accepted without offering the necessary supportive services, public
housing fell into disrepute.

Proposals for housing allowances in the United States are not of
recent origin. During the 1930s and 1940s, they figured prominently
in the debates on national housing policy. The housing allowance concept in the form of rent certificates, as it was then termed, was reviewed by the Subcommittee on Housing for Low-Income Families of
the President's Advisory Committee on Government Housing Policies

and Programs and, in December 1953, not deemed a suitable alternative to public housing.[16] The 1965 Housing and Development Act did
move in the direction of housing allowances, with the authorization of
rent supplements and the Section 23 leased housing program. Rent
supplements were made available to eligible occupants in privately
owned new or substantially rehabilitated housing. Section 23 leasing
is administered by the local housing authority, who leases the privately owned housing and then subleases it to low-income residents.

The final report in 1963 of the President's Committee on Urban
Problems, better known as "the Kaiser Committee," proposed testing
of the merits of a housing allowance program.[17] Sections 501 and 504
of the 1970 Housing and Development Act mandated a national experiment on national housing allowances. Since then, HUD has proceeded
with contracts for the design and implementation of the experiments.[18]

As expressed earlier, the authors favor reliance upon an examination of a full-scale operational program, where it exists as a model.
However, the Nixon administration appears to have placed greater reliance upon the housing allowance experiments than in an in-depth analysis of the European housing allowance programs (or than at least
giving both approaches coequal weight). Certain problems inherent
in the experimental approach are conceded in the First Annual Report
of the Experimental Housing Allowance Program.[19] These problems
are the significant cost of gaining the information, the lack of labora-
tory-type control over the environment, the necessity to maintain the
confidentiality of the information gathered, the difficulty of foreseeing
and replicating in an experiment of short duration and scope all the
aspects of a nationwide program, plus the time required to secure
sufficient information from the test.

> For questions like those involved here, however,
> there is no alternative other than an experiment,
> which can provide reliable information on important
> policy issues in advance of putting into operation a
> new program. An experiment can be a major source
> of evaluation data as to whether a major shift in
> housing policy is desirable. Moreover, in case of
> such a shift in policy, the potential savings from
> avoiding any wrong initial decisions in establishing
> an allowance program and from establishing a bet-
> ter program based on advance testing of alterna-
> tives justify this type of experimental effort as man-
> dated by Congress.[20]

There are a number of potentially serious weaknesses in the
housing allowance approach. Costs of the allowances have not been

ascertained, and they could be even greater than the programs they
are to supercede.

The General Accounting Office review of the Experimental Housing Allowance Program tentatively concluded that a housing allowance
program would be more costly than the production programs placed in
limbo, that is, Sections 235 and 236, but less costly than the Section
23 leased housing program and that some of the housing allowance
payments would result in higher rents rather than in improved housing
quality; nonrecipients of allowances might have to pay higher rents
without any improved quality due to the tighter housing market.

The annual payments for a national program using 1970 figures
for those with incomes of under $10,000 would range from $7 billion
to $10 billion annually. For a $5,000 income limit, costs would range
from $6.2 billion to $8.8 billion. Administrative costs would be about
15 percent of the payments. On the basis of the experiments, results
cannot be validated with any degree of certainty before 1977.[21]

Section 23 appealed to the Nixon administration as the logical device for extricating it from subsidy expenditures for new construction
housing programs for low- and moderate-income families and shifting
to a type of program considered more desirable and more in accord
with its objectives, that is, to institute a general minimum-income
maintenance program.

In 1965, Congress added Section 23 to the U.S. Housing Act,
permitting local housing authorities (LHA's) to lease apartments in
private structures for occupancy by low-income families. The original intention of Congress was to allow only the leasing of existing units,
but HUD stretched the language of Section 23 to cover the leasing of
new construction. In 1970, Congress ratified HUD's action and allowed
the leasing of newly constructed units for periods up to 20 years.

In January 1973, a moratorium was declared and funding im-
pounded for the basic housing assistance programs. There would be
a thorough reevaluation of all the programs on the basis of a HUD
study. President Richard M. Nixon, in September 1973, lifted the
January suspension with respect to Section 23:

> I am advised by the Secretary for Housing and Urban
> Development that one of the existing construction
> programs—the Section 23 program under which new
> and existing housing is leased for low income fami-
> lies—can be administered in a way which carries out
> some of the principles of direct cash assistance. If
> administered in this way, this program could also
> provide valuable information for us to use in develop-
> ing this new approach.[22]

The efforts to set the foundations for a national housing allowance plan were successfully continued after President Nixon left office, with the passage of the Housing and Community Development Act of 1974, with its emphasis on Housing Assistance Payments (HAP). The HAP, or new leased housing program, modified Section 23 and replaced it with a new Section 8. According to Assistant Secretary for Housing Production and Mortgage Credit, Sheldon B. Lubar, the new leased housing program would make a "natural bridge" toward housing allowances.[23]

Section 8 gives the LHA's a nominal role in acquiring and operating leased units. Previously, they would rent and pay for the units, which, in turn, were rented to the occupants. The new Section 8 could weaken the relationship whereby the LHA protected the low-income tenant in dealing with the landlord, as under Section 23.

> Based on the serious shortcomings of the leased housing program, it seems inevitable that the low-income tenant armed with only his housing allowance will have little protection against landlords who charge excessive rents, fail to make repairs, or otherwise exert the power inherent in a seller's market.[24]

Leasing for new construction or extensive rehabilitation may be directly between HUD and the housing sponsor or to the LHA to the sponsor. For existing housing, the leasing may be from HUD to the LHA or directly to the owner where there is no LHA.

Critics contend there is insufficient incentive to construct new housing due to the low level of permissible rents. Also, the leasing contract is limited to 20 years for new housing or substantial rehabilitation, except for state and local agency financing (40 years), and there is no correlation, in that mortgage terms are in the neighborhood of 40 years, leaving the owner without leasing contracts after only 20 years.

Since the housing allowances appear to perpetuate many of the problems that have plagued the programs they are designed to replace, the search for alternatives should continue. One approach that has not received adequate attention in the United States is one based on mandatory allocation of funds for housing from outside the federal budget; they have been operational in other countries. Prior to an evaluation of the mandatory programs, it would be well to examine various proposals for housing funds in the United States and attempt to gain an understanding of mandatory programs, and their pluses and minuses.

PRESCRIBED HOUSING INVESTMENTS

A proposal to offset the outflow of deposits from the two major
sources of housing credit, savings and loan associations and mutual
savings banks, has been offered in a report by the Subcommittee on
Domestic Finance of the House of Representatives Committee on Banking and Currency.[25] These institutions cannot function effectively as
sources for mortgage funds in the face of rapidly growing demands for
credit. If the national housing needs are to be met by financial institutions in the private sector, all major financial institutions must become
funding sources.

In effect, commercial banks, life insurance companies, and private pension funds and foundations, along with savings and loan associations and mutual savings banks, could be compelled to share equitably
the task of providing residential mortgage investment funds for all
levels of the housing market, including money for low- and moderate-
income occupants.

An ongoing system of determining the country's housing needs
could be conducted by a suitable federal agency, and the aforementioned
institutions could be directed to make the prescribed investment in
residential mortgage loans adequate to meet the housing shortfall. All
major categories of financial institutions would assume a proportionate share of supplying residential mortgage funds.

> Establishing and implementing a policy of requiring
> prescribed housing investments by various types of
> financial institutions carries with it the clear impli-
> cation that the responsibility for providing residen-
> tial mortgage loans should as a matter of equity be
> shared by all major types of financial institutions
> which provide consumer, business and industrial
> loans and which are either supervised, regulated,
> and insured by the Federal Government or which en-
> joy Federal tax advantages applied to income earned
> by such investments. In this way, required levels
> of investment in residential mortgages would be ex-
> tended to privately controlled pension funds, life
> insurance companies and foundations.[26]

There would be no sharp and decisive turn away from traditional
investment patterns to housing, which would be unnecessarily disturb-
ing to financial markets and the economy.

> What is required is a gradual shift toward allocation
> of funds for housing based on the overall asset growth

of financial institutions in relation to housing credit
needs as these are periodically determined by an appropriate Federal department or agency—The Department of Housing and Urban Development for example.[27]

Any required investment in residential mortgage loans should
be based not only on housing credit needs but on the asset growth rate
of the individual financial organizations themselves. For example, a
commercial bank has had an average asset growth rate of 10 percent a
year over the previous three years; assuming a prescribed minimum
mortgage portfolio is held, it would not be required to increase its
volume of residential mortgage loans by more than that percentage
during the current year. Thus, there would be a linkage to both recent
and current performance in terms of residential mortgage investments
and to overall asset growth, thus avoiding both a sharp disruption of
existing flow of credit to other sectors of the economy and unreasonable demands on financial institutions during periods of slow growth.

Required investment in housing could be cut back as national
housing needs, determined by annual surveys, begin to be met. The
amount of required investment by financial institutions could be designated annually by the president. Housing needs could be determined
on a regional basis, and required investments would be first applied
to the region in which they originated; the balance could be applied
elsewhere. In this way, a balance could be achieved among those areas
having a greater number of financial institutions, but smaller housing
needs, than other regions. Institutions not regionally based would
make housing investments anywhere. Surveys would determine housing
needs for low- and moderate-, middle-, and upper-income groups.
Figures for the two categories could then be applied to required housing investments for that region.

Financial institutions failing to comply with required housing investment levels would be required to place a sum equivalent to the
shortfall in noninterest bearing accounts held by the Federal Reserve
Bank. In turn the Federal Reserve Bank would be required to invest
these funds in residential mortgages or residential mortgage-backed
securities. Funds equal to the shortfall would remain on deposit at
the Federal Reserve Banks until the shortfall is eliminated. The risk
to lenders would be covered by FHA-VA insurance. Loans at below
market interest rates could be done through existing federal programs.

A number of questions arise after examining this proposal. The
administration of the system appears to be unduly complex in respect
to determining housing needs by the use of surveys and setting investment levels among various categories of financial institution. What
would be the cost of administering such a system to the government

and the affected institutions? Could there be a lack of flexibility in
adjusting quickly enough to changing housing supply and demand? How
rapidly could the regulatory mechanism, once in motion, be reversed
when the housing supply was deemed adequate, or, conversely, when
there was a sudden slowdown in housing construction, how long would
it take for the definitive data to be gathered and the mechanism set in
motion? Is it equitable to ask depositors, shareholders, policyholders,
and retirees to accept the reduced return that a housing investment
might bring? If these groups were presented with an option, would
they move their holdings into more lucrative bonds? Would mandating
financial institutions in one region or even the same type of institution
in the same city, for example, competing banks, as opposed to no
required housing investment, result in a lower return and cause an
outflow of funds. It may be that the difference in return before and after the prescribed allocation of funds to housing may be insignificant
and have no discernible effect on the movement of funds.

ASSET RESERVE REQUIREMENT

Another proposal to channel funds into designated sectors to
meet social and economic priorities, the asset reserve requirement,
has been outlined by Lester Thurow of the Massachusetts Institute of
Technology.[28] Under this system, the government places a 100 percent reserve requirement of some fraction of each financial institution's assets, unless this fraction is invested in the desired sector.

If national goals call for the investment of 25 percent of national
savings in housing and other preferred categories, each financial institution would have a 100 percent reserve requirement on that part
of its assets. However, as long as it invested 25 percent of its assets
in housing, it would not have to leave any reserves with the government. If it had only invested 20 percent of its assets in housing, 5
percent of its assets would have to be held with the government as required reserves.

If it invested nothing, 25 percent of its assets would be held as
reserves. Thus, financial institutions would be given the option of
making interest-paying loans in the housing field or making an interest-free loan to the government. (Different asset reserve requirements are essentially different tax rates.)

The advantages claimed by Thurow over the present system for
housing assistance are the following:

1. It works in that it insures that housing obtains whatever
fraction of total funds policy makers think housing should receive.
Credit crunches have no impact on its effectiveness. Funds cannot

flow away from housing, since there are no financial institutions that
can avoid investment in housing. Every financial institution is required
to be a source of housing finance to some degree. This does not mean
that every financial institution must operate in the housing field at the
retail level. Specialized housing institutions could issue bonds for
those institutions with no expertise in housing and no desire to get into
this field.

    2. It is a simple, straightforward regulation that does not re-
quire the cumbersome and complex set of regulations needed to maintain the present system.

    3. It does not discriminate between the small and large saver;
each can receive the same interest return.

    4. Institutions are not locked out of other areas; if savings and
loan societies have good industrial lending opportunities, they can
make such loans.

    5. The government does not have to raise taxes demanded by
the need for financing fiscal alternatives and does not need to build a
bureaucracy large enough to manage a huge direct involvement in the
housing field.

    This proposal elicits a number of questions. Is it fair to force
savers to invest part of their funds for national, as opposed to, private goals? Is the asset reserve requirement a better or worse tax
than other taxes that might be used to reach the same goal? Can
existing housing programs be eliminated and budgetary expenditures
be reduced?

        It must be noted that asset reserve requirements
        (formal or informal) are used in many developed
        countries. Based on two studies conducted by my-
        self and some colleagues at M.I.T. for the U.S.
        House Banking and Currency Committee, they seem
        to be the only effective regulatory mechanism for
        moving funds into priority areas. This does not
        eliminate the need to choose between the fiscal and
        regulatory approach, however, since the fiscal
        approach can also work. Nor would adoption of
        the asset reserve requirement allow the elimina-
        tion of all budgetary expenditures for the same
        areas. Asset reserve requirements can move
        funds into particular areas, but they really cannot
        be used to move funds to particular individuals.
        If the goal is low income housing, as opposed to
        just housing, for example, expenditure programs
        and asset reserve requirements would need to be

coordinated. Without programs to move the necessary
funds into the desired areas, however, distributional
policies simply cannot work. If there are no funds to
build houses, new houses cannot be distributed. [29]

In commenting on the asset reserve requirement, Edward J.
Kane of Ohio State University questions the ability of the Federal Reserve, who apparently would be involved, to intervene in specific markets and states where there is an economic case against the asset reserve proposal. [30]

No one knows enough about either social priorities or how credit,
goods, and factor markets interact to use financial markets as an effective vehicle for allocating funds among competing sectors in accord
with social priorities. Besides having a miserable track record in administering selective controls, the Federal Reserve has allocated
precious little research in learning from its past mistakes. Perhaps,
most important, the specific restrictions tied to the amount borrowed
or the size, purpose, or location of the borrower as envisaged in the
asset reserve proposal are based on partial equilibrium thinking; they
can only be justified by ignoring the affected parties' natural inclina-
tion to take action directed at getting around the mandated restrictions.
In particular, such controls can be largely and easily offset by bank
and borrower adjustments in related markets, adjustments that lead
frustrated regulators to extend the range of their controls to more and
more loan instruments and lender activities. Realistic political economists would add that new selective controls inevitably introduced
windfall gains and losses, since they are shaped by legislators and
administrative decisions closely influenced by the unsatisfactory current distribution of political and economic power, whose correction is
being sought. The Federal Reserve should not be given power over the
distributional problems facing society; the problems are political and
should be decided by Congress.

Economists at the Federal Reserve Bank of Philadelphia have
done preliminary theoretical work, developing and manipulating a
small-scale general equilibrium model, in attempting to measure the
potential results of differential asset reserves. The results have been
inconclusive and not overly encouraging. The likelihood of success
would be enhanced if reserve requirements were placed on all intermediaries and not only on banks, if business firms were refused the
option of obtaining funds directly in credit markets, and if households
were permitted to use mortgages just to finance housing. "But even
with all these conditions, it is difficult to rule out the possibility that
the scheme would not work."[31]

Asset reserve requirements will not work according to Eli Shapiro, Chairman of the Finance Committee of the Travelers Corpora-

tion and formerly Professor of Financial Management at Harvard University.

> Savers will still be free to acquire the debts and
> equities of real investors directly as well as to ac-
> quire the financial liabilities of intermediaries.
> Constraining intermediaries to invest a specific
> fraction of their (new?) funds in specific assets
> will not assure any specific dollar flow of finance
> or resources to that activity. Real investors who
> do not receive what they consider to be sufficient
> funds will be induced to attract savings by the is-
> suance of direct securities (debt or equity). House-
> holds will be induced to buy these assets by their
> relatively attractive returns. Since the regulated
> financial institutions do not account for all of house-
> hold financial asset accumulation (even excluding
> corporate retained earnings), controlling them does
> not control the total flow of savings. [32]

Asset reserve requirements would not be easy to administer.
Decisions would have to be made as to what kind of housing was to be
financed, what would financing cover, and what businesses and what
types of financial institution would be subject to the regulation. There
would be no equal treatment of small and large savers. If real asset
acquirers who issue direct securities found that distribution costs required large unit sales, rather than widespread retail distribution,
then savers with large amounts to invest would still have better alternatives than those savers who had to acquire the financial assets created
by the intermediaries subject to the asset reserve requirements.

The Shapiro view is to set only modest objectives for allocating
some expenditures differently from the pattern the income distribution would bring about and to center our attempts in this direction on
tax and expenditure policy rather than on financial regulation.

HOUSING FUND PROPOSALS

A number of differing plans calling for mandatory contributions
to be utilized for housing have been suggested, and the substance of
several of these proposed systems is summarized and reviewed. The
former Mayor of Cleveland, Carl B. Stokes, has offered a national
housing insurance program financed by a national housing insurance
trust fund administered by the federal government. [33] Revenue would
come from a tax on real estate transactions or through other tax mech-

anisms. Based on the experience with highways, health insurance, and social security, an earmarked revenue fund not subject to the vagaries of annual appropriations is considered essential. Under the Stokes plan, the family unit would pay 20 percent of its income as a tax deductible amount, and the national housing insurance trust fund would pay the difference between the 20 percent and the market rental or homeownership costs up to a specified maximum amount. The benefits of the program would be to give every income group an independent choice of housing in any community they wanted and could eliminate segregated public housing and the myriad of confusing subsidy programs and bureaucracies; with a guaranteed market, builders would erase the housing deficit in short order.

Harold Ostroff, Executive Vice-President of the United Housing Foundation, in a statement to the Federal Trade Commission hearings in New York City, recommended a 2 percent sales tax on all construction, with the proceeds to go into a low- and moderate-cost housing fund.[34] He stated that, based on the 1970 figures, such a tax would amount to $83.1 million and, for the period 1965-70, would total $546.9 million in New York State.

Another housing fund variation has been suggested by the Metropolitan Council on Housing in New York City, a militant tenants' group. It calls for a 1 percent tax on the face value of all mortgages, with an additional 1 percent levy on all real estate, with the proceeds to be used for housing construction and rehabilitation.[35]

In 1971, Donald F. Rodgers, then Executive Director of the Board of Urban Affairs of the New York Building and Construction Industry, a labor management group, proposed the establishment of a $50 billion housing trust fund patterned after the highway trust fund and, therefore, not dependent on annual congressional appropriations.[36] The $50 billion was the estimated amount required to rebuild the nation's cities in the next 10 years. A small portion of existing taxes would be diverted to a trust for housing poor and lower- and middle-income families. Each state would get back what it contributed. There were no specific recommendations on taxes to be selected.

In 1971, in testimony before the Federal Trade Commission hearings in New York City, Peter Brennan, then the President of the New York Building and Construction Trades Council of Greater New York and later to become Secretary of Labor, stated:

> Before we undertake the task of writing any more
> housing programs, we should ask ourselves if we
> are really committed to the concept of providing
> a decent home for every American? Are we ready
> to commit $50 billion dollars to an irrevocable
> housing trust fund which must be spent only on hous-

ing? Are we ready to sacrifice our private wants
for public needs in raising the $50 billion dollars
for the housing program? Are we finally ready to
rank housing on an equal footing with some of the
other major programs in the Federal budget?[37]

Andrew J. Biemiller, a Legislative Director for the AFL-CIO,
would "utilize the experience of other nations in directing financial institutions, including life insurance companies, to make available a
certain percentage of their funds in the housing market."[38]

In 1966, W. Willard Wirtz, then Secretary of Labor, and Raymond F. Male, New Jersey's Commissioner of Labor and Industry,
devised a formula for guaranteeing construction workers a specified
period of employment annually.[39] If normal contract construction was
insufficient to meet the guarantee, workers would be employed on public works projects and compensated out of a special fund. The financing would be derived from the 20 cents an hour that would otherwise
represent a pay increase and would guarantee a stabilized annual income. Wirtz and Male foresaw a number of benefits arising out of
the scheme. Year-round employment would cut unemployment insurance benefits to unemployed construction workers by millions of dollars. Slum areas in core cities would benefit from the construction.
Training and job opportunities for minority workers would be provided.
Opposition to the introduction of new technology by union-imposed hold-
backs on housing would be removed. However, New Jersey contractors were hesitant about continuing with the plan because of their concern that the costs would be excessive; instead labor and management
used the fund for supplemental unemployment compensation.

The critical factor in several of these plans is that they are based
on a tax or charge on real estate, construction, or mortgages, and
the imposition could represent a new and significant rise in the cost of
housing, in addition to the already growing costs of labor and materials. Further increases in the price of housing serve to limit the number of families able to afford housing without government subsidies.

The imposition of a mandatory set aside for housing cannot be
analyzed in isolation or as a self-contained package. There are other
proposals for payroll deductions that, if effectuated, could quickly
reach a breaking point in terms of the amounts that could be collected
on the basis of wages and salaries from either employers or employees on top of the existing social security contributions, despite the
discernible benefits that might accrue to the contributors. The issue
of relative priorities thus comes to the forefront, if such levies are to
be considered.

Related to the discussion of housing contributions are the proposals for such areas as health insurance and mass transit. Though

not adopted at present, they do serve to indicate the different approaches
to financing and the possibility of adopting specific aspects for housing
legislation.

The various proposals for health insurance in 1974 relied heavily
on payroll contributions for their financing. [40] The Kennedy-Griffiths
bill (which Senator Kennedy later abandoned) called for a health security trust fund backed by a social security tax of 3.5 percent on employers' payrolls and 1 percent of the workers' revenues, wage and nonwage,
up to $15,000 annually. Federal general revenues were to supplement
the tax. The Kennedy-Mills bill, to which Senator Kennedy shifted,
contained a minimum tax of 3 percent on employers and a maximum tax
on employees of 1 percent. The Long-Ribicoff bill added 0.3 percent
to the social security tax to be shared by employers and employees.
The Nixon administration proposal called for private insurance coverage to be financed by employers and employees. The premiums would
have to be paid just as if they were taxes. The premium contributions
paid by employers would be treated as taxable income by employees
and the employee contribution considered a nondeductible expense.

In the New York metropolitan area, as public transit fares no
longer could be held to existing levels if service were to be continued,
a number of proposals were offered to support mass transit and to mitigate the necessary fare increases by means of payroll taxes on employers and employees.

The governors of Connecticut, New Jersey, and New York appointed a commission to determine how mass transportation service
could be assured at appropriate fare levels for all people on a regional
basis. The commission recommended that each city in the region impose a mass transportation tax on all individuals who live or work in
the respective cities. [41] The imposition of such a tax would be contin-
gent on the federal government granting 100 percent transportation income tax credits to all those paying the tax. With a total tax credit,
there would be no additional financial burden on those paying the tax.
The commission assumed that there would be no cost to the federal
government, since only future tax revenues would have been involved.
An advantage of the tax credit system would have been that no continuing congressional approval for appropriations would be necessary.

At $25 per person, the tax would yield $100 million per year in
New York City alone. If levied on a regional basis, the 8.5 million
employees could generate over $200 million. By 1980, the tax as-
sumedly would rise to $50. There were questions about the tax that
the report did not discuss: the regressive nature of the tax and, as
contrasted to health insurance, the large numbers of people who do
not use mass transit and would have presented heavy opposition to the
mass transit tax.

To keep mass transit solvent, then Mayor John V. Lindsay of
New York City proposed in April 1973 a new regional governmental

body, the New York Regional Transportation District.[42] The new district would have the power to receive state and federal funds and to impose taxes. In the event federal subsidies were not forthcoming, a new payroll tax of 0.5 percent on payrolls in the New York Metropolitan region would be levied. Half the tax would be 0.25 percent to be levied on all employers on the basis of their total payroll; the remaining half would be imposed on employees. Self-employed individuals would be subject only to the employer's share of the tax. The tax would be automatically repealed when equivalent federal subsidies become available. The plan called for a matching share from state revenues in an amount equal to funds provided by the federal government or raised from the payroll tax. It was noted that payroll taxes were then in effect in Philadelphia, Detroit, and 84 other major cities. The plan was not enacted, and the search for solvency turned to the federal government for subsidies to support mass transit.

What is the desirability of the establishment or enactment of legislation calling for a housing fund with employment-related contributions that, to date, has received little attention in the United States as a replacement or supplement to existing housing programs? How feasible an alternative to existing and proposed legislation is such a program?

Among the issues that must be faced in respect to the payroll-based contributions is whether the added costs would be so high as to affect adversely the competitive position of U.S. exports, accelerate automation to avoid the added burden, and create unemployment? Do the benefits from an increased housing supply outweigh the costs? To what extent would additional resources added to the housing sector be inflationary? Is the flow of funds into housing likely to become adequate to negate any need for this type of legislation? How would the legislation react to cyclical changes in funds for housing?

Related to the fund for housing are the proposals for payroll-based taxes for other purposes, such as health insurance and mass transit. The pressures for national health insurance are so strong that enactment of such legislation is likely. If a housing plan were initiated, there could be demands for similar type impositions for other urgent needs. Eventually, there could be such a multitude of levies that it might be administratively feasible to eliminate them and return to the use of general revenues from a broad-based source, for example, income taxes. These questions have been discussed in other chapters, with consideration given to the relative priority housing should receive in the broad spectrum of needs.

A drawback of a payroll-based program is that it can become a drain on the firm. Profit-based, productivity-related programs could minimize these drawbacks. Inherent in any mandatory program is an important prerequisite—productivity increases must occur if the

firm is to be capable of making sustained contributions for housing.
Therefore, it is imperative that any national program be accompanied
by an economy characterized by formal programs jointly supported
by labor and industry, which bring about constantly improving levels
of productivity. Thus, in any consortium, labor and management must
address themselves to the specific ways in which the sales per asset
dollar and per employee will actually be increased.

NOTES

1. U.S. Congress, Senate, Committee on Banking and Currency,
Congress and American Housing—1892-1967, 90th Cong., 2d sess.
(Washington, D.C.: Government Printing Office, February 1968), p. 1.

2. U.S. Congress, Senate, Committee on Banking and Currency,
Expanding the Mortgage Market, 91st Cong., 1st sess. (Washington,
D.C.: Government Printing Office, 1969), p. 3.

3. Ira Kaminow, "Should Housing Be Sheltered from Tight
Credit?" Business Review, Federal Reserve Bank of Philadelphia,
November 1970, p. 24.

4. U.S. Department of Housing and Urban Development, Housing
in the Seventies (Washington, D.C.: Government Printing Office, October 1973), pp. 3-39.

5. Information on financial intermediaries from Committee for
Economic Development, Financing the Nation's Housing Needs (New
York, April 1973), pp. 31-44; "Riding to the Rescue-Fannie, Ginnie
and Freddy Are Providing about the Only Mortgage Funds Available,"
Wall Street Journal, July 1, 1974, p. 22; Henry B. Schechter and
Marion K. Schlefer, "Housing Needs and National Goals," in U.S.
Congress, House, Committee on Banking and Currency, Subcommittee
on Housing Panels, Papers Submitted on Housing Production, Housing
Demand, and Developing a Suitable Living Environment, 92d Cong.,
1st sess., June 1971, pt. 1, pp. 130-35; and U.S. Department of
Housing and Urban Development, op. cit., pp. 3-39 to 3-48.

6. Committee for Economic Development, op. cit., p. 42.

7. "Riding to the Rescue-Fannie, Ginny and Freddy Are Providing about the Only Mortgage Funds Available," op. cit.

8. Report of the President's Commission, Financial Structure
and Regulation (Washington, D.C.: U.S. Government Printing Office,
December 1971), p. 84.

9. U.S. Congress, Senate, Committee on Banking and Currency, Hearings on Mortgage Interest Rate Commission Report, 91st
Cong., 1st sess. (Washington, D.C.: Government Printing Office,
1969), p. 49.

10. Schechter, op. cit., p. 135.

11. U.S. Congress, House, Subcommittee of the Committee on Appropriations, Hearings on HUD-Space-Science-Veterans Appropriations for 1973, pt. 3, Department of Housing and Urban Development, 92d Cong., 2d sess. (Washington, D.C.: Government Printing Office, 1972), p. 2.

12. Editorial, "HUD's Hang-Ups," Wall Street Journal, March 31, 1972, p. 4.

13. U.S. Congress, Subcommittee of the Committee on Appropriations, Joseph M. McDade, member, p. 1694.

14. U.S. Congress, Senate, Committee on Banking, Housing and Urban Affairs, Critique of "Housing in the Seventies," prepared by Congressional Research Service, Library of Congress, 93rd Cong., 2d sess. (Washington, D.C.: Government Printing Office, February 22, 1974), p. ix.

15. Robert Bechtel (Research Director, Environmental Research and Development Foundation, Kansas City), in Scott Jacobs, "The Housing Allowance Program in Kansas City Turns into a Notable Failure," Planning 39 (October 1973): 13.

16. United States, President's Advisory Committee on Government Housing Policies and Programs, A Report—Recommendations on Government Housing Policies and Programs, Appendix 3, Exhibit 21 (Washington, D.C.: Government Printing Office, December 1953), pp. 263 and 323.

17. United States, President's Committee on Urban Housing, A Report—A Decent Home (Washington, D.C.: Government Printing Office, 1968), p. 14.

18. U.S. Department of Housing and Urban Development, Office of Policy Development and Research, First Annual Report of the Experimental Housing Allowance Program (Washington, D.C.: Government Printing Office, May 1973).

19. Ibid., p. 2.

20. Ibid.

21. United States, Comptroller General, General Accounting Office, Observations on Housing Allowances and the Experimental Housing Allowance Program, Report to the Congress, B-171630 (Washington, D.C.: General Accounting Office, March 28, 1974), pp. 2-6.

22. U.S. Congress, Committee on Banking and Currency, Message from the President of the United States, Recommending Improvements in Federal Housing Policy, 93d Cong., 1st sess. (Washington, D.C.: Government Printing Office, September 19, 1973), Doc. 93-152, p. 10.

23. Arthur J. Magida, "Housing Report/Major Programs Revised to Stress Community Control," National Journal 6 (September 14, 1974): 1378.

24. Chester Hartman and Dennis Keating, "The Housing Allowance Delusion," Social Policy 4 (January/February 1974): 32.

25. U.S. Congress, House, Committee on Banking and Currency, Subcommittee on Domestic Finance, Staff Rept., Financial Institutions: Reform and the Public Interest, 93d Cong., 1st sess. (Washington, D.C.: Government Printing Office, August 1973).

26. Ibid., pp. 37-38.

27. Ibid., p. 38.

28. Lester C. Thurow, "Proposals for Rechanneling Funds to Meet Social Priorities," Policies for a More Competitive Financial System, Conference Series, no. 8 (Boston: Federal Reserve Bank of Boston, June 1972), p. 179.

29. Ibid., p. 188.

30. Ibid., pp. 196-98.

31. David P. Eastburn, "Federal Reserve Policy and Social Priorities," Business Review, Federal Reserve Bank of Philadelphia, November 1970, p. 6.

32. Federal Reserve Bank of Boston, op. cit., pp. 199, 202.

33. Carl B. Stokes, Address, International Conference of Mayors, Indianapolis, Indiana, May 26, 1971.

34. U.S. Federal Trade Commission, Hearings in New York City on Expansion of the Building and Construction Industry, October 1971.

35. New York Times, June 13, 1971, p. 45.

36. New York Building and Construction Industry, Board of Urban Affairs Fund, Housing Trust Fund Proposal, April 1971; and "$50 Billion Housing Trust Fund Urged by Construction Executive," Real Estate Weekly 42 (May 13, 1971): 6.

37. Peter Brennan, Testimony, Federal Trade Commission, Hearings in New York City on Expansion of the Building and Construction Industry, October 5, 1971.

38. U.S. Congress, Senate, Committee on Banking and Currency, Hearings on Mortgage Interest Rate Commission, 91st Cong., 1st sess. (Washington, D.C.: Government Printing Office, 1969), p. 219.

39. A. H. Raskin, "Unused Inflation Curb," New York Times, March 1, 1971, p. 29.

40. Richard J. Margolis, "Where Does It Hurt?" The New Leader, vol. 57 (April 15, 1974).

41. The Governors' Special Commission on the Financing of Mass Transportation, Final Rept., Financing Mass Transportation: A Positive Approach, April 1972.

42. New York City, Office of the Mayor, Press Release 267-73, April 30, 1973.

APPENDIX: U.S. GOVERNMENT HOUSING
PROGRAMS FOR CIVILIAN WORKERS

The federal government has, at various times, taken a positive stance with respect to supplying housing for workers. During World War I, an acute housing scarcity existed for employees of shipyards, munitions factories, and other defense-related industries. On March 1, 1918, Congress authorized the U.S. Shipping Board and the Emergency Fleet Corporation to furnish housing for employees in shipyards by means of loans to real estate companies, which were then assumed by the shipbuilding companies.* A total of 9,000 houses, 1,100 apartments, 19 dormitories, and 8 hotels in 24 localities were built under this program.

Public laws 149 and 164 (65th Congress), of May 16 and June 4, 1918, respectively, gave approval to the establishment of a Bureau of Industrial Housing and Transportation in the Department of Labor, which operated through the U.S. Housing Corporation, created by an executive order of the president. Congress, in these acts, authorized and appropriated funds for housing for war workers. The bureau built and managed 25 community projects, consisting of over 5,000 single-family dwellings, plus apartments, dormitories, and hotels. After World War I, except for some dwelling units transferred to other government agencies, all the housing was sold to private owners.[1]

Again during World War II, Congress enacted legislation for defense housing. In 1940, the military appropriation acts included emergency funds for the use of the president; subsequently, an appropriation of these funds was used to purchase capital stock of the Defense Homes Corporation. The corporation was organized to make defense housing available in Washington, D.C. and other defense areas.** On June 30, 1948, Public Law 860 (80th Congress) transferred all assets and liabilities of the corporation to the Reconstruction Finance Corporation for liquidation.

The U.S. Housing Act of 1937, initially enacted to supply public housing, was amended in 1940 by Congress to authorize the use of the loan and subsidy provisions and the projects for low-income occupants to house defense workers during the war emergency.†

Under the president's war powers, the Office of Defense Housing Coordinator was formed on July 21, 1940, with the responsibility for planning a defense housing program through private enterprise in cooperation with the pertinent federal agencies.

---

*Public Law 102, 65th Cong.
**Public Law 588, June 11, 1940, and Public Law 611, June 13, 1940, 76th Cong.
†Public Law 671, June 28, 1940, 76th Cong.

The Second Supplemental National Defense Appropriations Act of 1941 appropriated $100 million for defense housing to be constructed by the War and Navy departments.* Temporary shelter acts also appropriated funds for emergency housing for defense and war workers.**

The basic war housing law was the Lanham Act, passed in 1940 and subsequently amended.† Under this and related laws, 739,704 war and defense housing units were completed.[2]

An amendment to Title VI of the National Housing Act authorized more liberal mortgage insurance to builders constructing new housing in critical defense areas.‡ Under the amended title, 962,000 dwelling units were provided for war workers and for veterans following the war.[3]

In 1950, Public Law 475 (81st Congress) authorized the disposal of all war and veterans' housing. To facilitate the sale of war housing previously built, FHA mortgage insurance was made available.

On September 1, 1951, Congress passed Public Law 139 (82nd Congress) creating the Defense Housing and Community Facilities and Services Act to help in obtaining housing and community facilities needed for national defense purposes.

In 1956, Section 809 was added to the Mortgage Housing Act authorizing mortgage insurance on homes built to be sold to essential civilian employees at research and defense installations of the armed services. Subsequently, the Atomic Energy Commission (AEC) and National Aeronautics and Space Administration (NASA) employees were included. By the end of 1971, some 16,000 homes were insured under this program.[4]

Section 810 was added to the National Housing Act in 1959 authorizing insurance for mortgages on off-base rental housing for the military and essential civilian personnel at armed service installations. The program was expanded in 1963 to cover any research or development installations of AEC and NASA. By the end of 1951, approximately 2,700 units in multifamily housing developments were insured by Section 810.[5]

NOTES TO APPENDIX

1. U.S. Congress, Senate, Committee on Banking and Currency, Congress and American Housing 1892-1967, 90th Cong., 2d sess.

---

*Public Law 781, September 9, 1940, 76th Cong.
**Public laws 9, 73, and 353, of March 1, May 24, and December 17, 1941, respectively, 77th Cong.
†Public Law 849, October 14, 1940, 76th Cong.
‡Public Law 24, March 28, 1941, 77th Cong.

(Washington, D.C.: Government Printing Office, February 1968), pp. 1, 2.

    2. U.S. Congress, Senate, Committee on Banking and Currency, Subcommittee on Housing and Urban Affairs, Progress Report on Federal Housing and Urban Development Programs, 91st Cong., 1st sess. (Washington, D.C.: Government Printing Office, September 1969), p. 134.

    3. Congress and American Housing, p. 46.

    4. U.S. Department of Housing and Urban Development, HUD 1971 Statistical Year Book (Washington, D.C.: Government Printing Office), p. 159.

    5. Ibid.

11

ALTERNATIVES FOR
THE ALLOCATION
OF CONTRIBUTIONS

A positive feature of the mandatory contribution system is the flexibility or choice of alternatives in the disposition of the funds. Although a number of options are examined, other approaches should not be precluded. These choices are reviewed in terms of their optimum utilization in the United States of the proceeds, making allowance for the unique national characteristics.

EMPLOYER-OWNED HOUSING

An option for employers in the disposition of the housing fund could be direct investment and ownership of housing. At first glance, there would be little basis for recommending such an approach. An International Labour Office Recommendation of 1961, on workers' housing asserts:

> It should be recognized that it is generally not desirable that employers should provide housing for their workers directly, with the exception of cases in which circumstances necessitate that employers provide housing for their workers, as, for instance, when an undertaking is located at a long distance from normal centres of population, or where the nature of employment requires that the worker should be available at short notice. [1]

Along the same lines, it has become part of American folklore that employers should not become directly connected with the ownership and management of housing for their personnel; the employer-

employee relationship should not encompass a landlord-tenant relationship. All too often, company-owned housing conjures up the specter
of the company-dominated mill town, with its drab and gloomy housing
and stores. However, a one-dimensional picture is not totally accu-
rate, and the acceptance of a generalization denying any validity to
company-owned housing can be questioned, as will be subsequently
seen.

Housing Assistance by Employers

Large corporations have, for many years, been indirectly involved in providing housing for certain groups of employees. They
have assisted in the financing of home purchases for managerial personnel, as well as the disposal of homes for those transferred to
other locations.[2] In isolated communities or areas, companies have
had to assure the availability of housing.

In at least two countries, the Federal Republic of Germany and
the Netherlands, housing financed and owned by employers or company-owned housing enterprises play an important role.[3] The widespread Japanese programs for providing housing to employees was
reviewed in Chapter 9.

In Italy, industrialists are deemed to have a social responsibility for furnishing housing directly to workers. From 1955 to 1965,
some 60,000 such houses were provided. "Apart from the obvious
benefit to employees it is claimed that the system is advantageous to
employers since it enables them to plan ahead in the definite knowledge
that houses will be provided at the right time."[4]

Housing and Industry

If the housing fund is used to provide housing to employees,
subject to the removal of local ordinances and the exigencies of the
energy shortage, a major exodus of firms from central city locations
could ensue. The local ordinances are concerned with controlling
growth, including zoning, and are now the subject of legal actions.[5]

The issue seems destined for resolution by the U.S. Supreme
Court. Traditionally, courts have favored city growth curbs over developers, based on the 1926 high court decision upholding the constitutionality of zoning in the case of Village of Euclid v. The Ambler
Realty Co.[6] But there no longer is passive acceptance of zoning and
related controls. "The housing industry has found allies among civil
libertarians who argued that deliberate slow-growth policies deny
housing to the less affluent and abridge the constitutional rights to
equal protection, due process and freedom of travel."[7]

The linkage between jobs and housing is illustrated by the obligation of corporations holding major federal contracts to deal with minority housing problems when there is a negative impact on equal employment. The U.S. Department of Labor feels "that an employer cannot excuse a bad hiring or promotion record solely on the basis that discrimination exists in the housing market; this is not always outside the control of the employer and where feasible can and should be changed by affirmative action."[8]

If a firm decides on an inner city location, there is likely to be a smaller need for housing than in an outer city location. Also, there is apt to be greater reluctance to become involved in housing developments in the inner city; although directed toward the entry of large corporations into the housing field on a profit basis, the following comments apply equally to investment in housing for low- and moderate-income employees:

> Thus when all of these problems are added together, it may be somewhat more understandable as to why many of the best and most qualified sponsor-developers do not want to tackle the problem of the inner-city, especially if the project at the end of the rainbow is an FHA low- or moderate income development . . . under present conditions the most respectable sponsor-developers may simply feel the rewards are adequate for the time, money and energy which will be expended in developing a true inner-city FHA project.
>
> Sponsorship-development and ownership management of housing projects simply do not fit within conventional big business guidelines—particularly within the large manufacturing firm.[9]

The manufacturer warrants the basic quality of his product but customarily performs neither ongoing servicing nor normal maintenance. However, sponsorship development and ownership management of housing does not permit this clear-cut fulfillment and subsequent absolution of responsibility.

The need for rezoning and the relocation of on-site residents, added to the concern over aesthetics, ecology, and the environment, are all too frequently highly volatile issues that engender conflict, which a gun-shy corporate management seeks to avert. A continuing and close involvement with activist community and tenant groups is another potential source of conflict and adverse publicity.

The ownership-management of housing is unlikely to increase the firm's earnings. Rents are likely to lag behind increases in costs

or what could be obtained at market levels, but rents below market
levels could also be reflected in softer wage demands, particularly
when housing is in short supply. There could be tax benefits from
company-owned housing, but one view is that "tax savings do not aid
a financial balance sheet. Rather they harm it."[10]

Tied Housing

Attractive housing at moderate rentals can be a strong magnet
for recruiting and retaining workers, but it is questionable that employees should be tied to their jobs by virtue of occupancy of company
housing. On the other hand, should the firm subsidize former employees?

> Indeed in some countries legislation has been
> passed to control housing tenancies tied to particu-
> lar jobs. Where public financial aid is available
> for housing, special provision is made to prevent
> permanent tied tenancies. Thus in the Federal Re-
> public the legislation lays down that "when dwellings
> are to be built by the owner of a commercial enter-
> prise for its employees, public funds are granted
> on the condition that the lease contracts with employ-
> ees of the company stipulate that at the end of five
> years the tenancies shall no longer be dependent
> on the employment relationship."
> Special provision, however, has had to be made
> in relation to housing miners, where labour short-
> ages are frequently acute. Again in the Federal Re-
> public there is a time limit of ten years and the ten-
> ancy is tied to the coal mining industry as a whole
> and not with a specific employer in the industry.[11]

Foreign Workers

There is another body of experience on employer-owned housing
in Western Europe. The influx of large numbers of foreign workers
into the industrial countries of Western Europe has exacerbated the
already acute housing shortage. As new arrivals, with limited funds
and unable to understand the new language, they could only find housing under extremely difficult conditions.[12] To prevent such deplora-
ble conditions, in the case of the nationals of a member country going to another Common Market country, European Economic Commu-

nity (EEC) Regulation no. 15 of 1961 affirms that workers who are nationals of a member state and their families enjoy the same rights and
access to the same facilities as in obtaining accommodations. The
same type of provision has spread by way of bilateral agreements with
other nonmember countries. These rules do not usually apply to workers who do not come through official recruiting channels or are directly
engaged by a firm. When an employer uses the official agency, he
agrees to provide accommodations. In Switzerland, when the housing
fell short of requirements, the alien department could authorize placement of the worker with other employers.[13]

In practice, any preference to foreigners for desirable accommodations arouses resentment among the resident nationals. And
where there are priorities for those longest on waiting lists for housing, foreigners, by virtue of their more recent arrival, are effectively
excluded. Thus, assistance by employers to new workers can lead to
dissension, as those members of the existing labor force in inferior
housing become resentful. This is not only true for foreign workers
but with nationals of the same country, for example, workers from
southern Italy brought to northern Italy.

To provide housing for foreign workers in Germany, the unemployment insurance fund made DM 200 million ($50 million) available
in loans for the construction of housing in 1960-61, and an additional
DM 191.5 million ($47.9 million) up to the end of 1964. While DM 50
million ($12.5 million) were designated especially for housing for mar-
ried workers, for the most part loans were to construct housing for
single workers; in this way more workers per deutschemark spent
could be accommodated.[14]

Port Sunlight Village

Not all company-owned housing falls into the undesirable category; and bearing in mind its unique characteristics, the case of Port
Sunlight Village can be presented as an example of how company-owned
housing can have a positive image. Company housing built by Unilever
in 1888 in the village of Port Sunlight in Merseyside, England (opposite
Liverpool) for its workers in the adjacent soapworks are today considered so desirable that there is a waiting list of 800 for the 900
houses.[15]

How has the village managed to overcome the problems of obsolescence and decay and to accommodate to the emergence of new
housing standards and new life styles, while, during the same period,
so many other housing developments, both public and private, have
failed. An examination of Port Sunlight reveals guidelines for housing
policy with broader applicability than merely the subject of company-
owned housing.

William Lever, when he founded Port Sunlight in 1888, stated
he did not intend to build for posterity: "Dwellings for the masses of
the people need not be monumental. If they can be inexpensively built
to stand absolutely sound, weatherproof and sanitary for say 50 to 60
years, they will better supply the present day requirements than if by
increased cost they were built to last 300 years."[16] But the village
was meant to be a showplace and was not inexpensively built by the
standards then prevalent for artisans' dwellings. At a time when or-
dinary industrial cottages could be constructed for some £100, the
average cost of a Port Sunlight cottage was £385.[17] Features of the
estate were spaciousness, variety, use of natural landscape features,
and good internal design. Thus, a sound basis was laid for the long
life of the housing, extending over more than three-quarters of a century and with many more years to come.

From the beginning, the village has been under the same ownership and management, which has always been proud of the village's
fine reputation. The costs of repairs and improvements have always
enjoyed a degree of immunity to external circumstances, such as political factors, to which publicly aided housing is susceptible. In the
United States, cost ceilings for the construction of subsidized housing
have contributed to premature obsolescence and decay due to political
considerations that too high construction costs and standards would
lead to charges of coddling the poor and low-income occupants. Sunlight was not designed to extract in the shortest possible period the
maximum benefit from a minimal cost outlay, and its history indicates
how difficult the cost benefit equation is to calculate over the long run.

As publicly subsidized housing is dependent upon budgetary and
political considerations and unsubsidized housing upon prevailing rent
levels, both often unrelated to meeting the costs of adequate housing
standards and maintenance, so is employer-owned housing, if not com-
pletely self-sustaining, dependent upon the parent company's financial
condition and management policies. But with Sunlight,

> There seemed to be some chance that the amount ac-
> tually spent on repair and maintenance very closely
> approached what was necessary, at the time it was
> necessary, to keep the houses in good condition, of-
> fering for a low price a quality of accommodation
> high enough to ensure that a tenancy on the estate
> remained a privilege of which employees of the Com-
> pany were very much aware.[18]

Because of the careful maintenance policy, the village was able
to withstand normal physical deterioration. An aspect of the present
desirability of the housing is that in the depression years, the price

of building materials was low, and there were a number of surplus
workers at the Unilever factories who management wanted to avoid
having to lay off, and they were utilized on the estate.

At the close of the 1950s, a major decision had to be made about
the future of the housing. On purely economic grounds, it would have
been more attractive to demolish the housing rather than to initiate a
new program of major improvements. But it was decided to retain
and improve the village; "perhaps the most significant argument was
that the initial layout of the estate had built into it the degree of flexibility in the use of space and that the environmental and density standards set by Lever were so high that they were still not only adequate
but good."[19] Another factor in the 1960 decision was the improvement
expenditures of the 1930s, or else obsolescence would have been too
far advanced.

> Whatever the crucial factors were in the final decision
> to go ahead with the improvement scheme, it is quite
> clear that they had little to do with a fine calculation
> of cost and benefit of the sort implied by accepted de-
> cision models. Cost estimates were of course made
> in some detail and expected revenues were calculated
> but, retrospectively at least these seem to have been
> post hoc justifications of a scheme whose desirability
> was accepted on other grounds—or perhaps demonstra-
> tions for the commercial management that the inevita-
> ble loss on the estate was not likely to be unmanagea-
> ble.[20]

Today, it is considered economically feasible to have the firm's
large staff of building craftsmen and gardeners work in the village,
as well as on the maintenance of the nine major Unilever enterprises
in the area. The village is an officially designated conservation area.
"And hard headed as the company likes to be, it does derive a lot of
satisfaction from being the owner of a village that people come from
all over the world to admire. So the current policy is a compromise
between head and heart."[21]

Steinway

Another case that belies the stereotype of company-owned housing as depressing and forbidding is the November 26, 1974 proposed
designation of the Steinway Historic District in Long Island City by
the New York City Landmarks Preservation Commission.[22] Founded
in 1853, the Steinway firm, manufacturers of pianos, was one of the

leading cultural forces in the nation, and the company town it started
in 1870 reflects the company's high-mindedness.

Since the municipality of Long Island City offered little or no
services, the Steinway family assumed these responsibilities through
the construction of a company town. In addition to building housing for
the workers, the company furnished a library, public bathhouse, and
park; established a kindergarten; and subsidized the teaching of music
and German in the public school.

The attractive two-story attached houses have been well maintained and still remain, though now individually owned. These modest
well-built dwellings, enlivened by Italianate and neo-Grec detail, give
the district distinction as a well-defined urban area and, in turn, the
district has played an important role in the social development of the
city.

The chairwoman of the commission, Beverly Moss Spatt, stated
that the designation honored an historical social experiment to give
the original Steinway workers decent housing, and that "it was a success in terms of the well being of the employees as well as enhancing
the interrelationship between the employees and employer."[23] The
Landmark Designation would, thus, ensure the continuity of the high
environmental quality.

A Policy of Company-Owned Housing

Over the long term, the Unilever policy on company-owned housing has proven beneficial to the firm, the occupants, and the public.
The crucial question is whether other firms can also successfully
adopt such a policy. If management is willing to make the necessary
commitment, company-owned housing can be a viable proposition.
However, today's corporate environment mitigates against such a commitment.

Corporations are more prone to change plant locations; and, in
the face of increased mobility, there is less incentive to think of construction and then have to consider disposition. The energy shortage
can have an impact, as plants would be moved less frequently into
sparsely populated and isolated areas, where management has to
consider the supply of housing.

It is questionable that too many corporations are willing to think
in terms of the long-range effects of company-owned housing in the
face of more immediate financial pressures and the desire to have
current financial statements put forth the best picture (whereas the
benefits from a Port Sunlight cannot be measured in precise dollar
terms in a specific time frame). As the turnover of corporate management accelerates, survival may depend upon their demonstrating

quick dollar returns. With mergers and conglomerate takeovers, corporate identities fade, and the long-range view on such issues as company housing becomes secondary.

Another factor is the amount collected for housing under a mandatory plan. Would it be substantial enough to cover an appreciable share of the costs of the housing? Would supplemental financing be necessary? If the funds collected were insignificant and the major financing had to be sought elsewhere, then it would be more practical for the firm not to think in terms of direct investment. A possible means of handling the funds could be the financing of construction, followed by quick sale to employees close to cost. Direct construction by the firm, if on a fairly large scale, could appreciably lower housing prices and also provide for a high level of community planning. There also could be a favorable impact on collective bargaining in respect to wage demands. Workers might consider the value of fringe benefits in respect to housing services, which are not subject to income taxes, as are direct salary increases. Corporations are under pressure to demonstrate positive actions in terms of their reputed public responsibilities, and a program that produces well-designed and constructed housing could be a means of community service.

On balance, although direct investment in housing can be a viable option and provide the firm with a capital asset, as well as the potential for an improved public image, there is little basis for assuming that corporate management under existing conditions can, or is, willing to make an adequate commitment. Therefore, a more indirect role has to be sought and alternative options are presented.

A NEW ENTITY FOR THE ALLOCATION
OF CONTRIBUTIONS

As already discussed, the desire of business management to avoid any direct involvement in providing housing for their employees is traditional. In France, the firm, if it so wishes, can meet its responsibility under the mandatory requirement by drawing upon the services of CIL. If the concept of a housing fund in the United States is to be workable, a domestic counterpart to CIL must be developed.

The shortage of housing in such suburbs as Westchester County (in New York) would be resolved, according to the chairman of the board of one of the country's major banks, by businesses sponsoring nonprofit development corporations to build housing.

> I know there is a great deal of concern . . . over
> certain types of housing, proposed locations, the
> absence of mortgage funds—and the usual housing

related problems. At the same time, there are certain needs for skilled employees, the very persons
who would live in such housing. It would seem the
two needs are very related, and it does not seem at
all unrealistic for major business and financial institutions to sponsor non-profit development corporations that would build such properties in cooperation
with local governments.[24]

A proposed organization, though not intended to serve as an
American equivalent of the French CIL, could be possibly adapted to
serve as a conduit for the use of the mandated housing contribution;
this is the broad-range plan developed by Sherman Maisel, a well-
known housing economist.[25] His emphasis in his plan is on homeownership and existing housing, whereas the bulk of the mandated funds
would probably be absorbed by new multifamily construction; however,
the organizational structure he proposes is the key aspect.

HOPE's

The program is based on the establishment of entities, homeownership promotion enterprises, or HOPE's, one or more in each standard metropolitan statistical area (SMSA). Their primary task would
be to assist low- and medium-income families to buy or rent the most
suitable housing, preferably existing rather than new housing; there
is little discussion of the absentee owner. HOPE's would conform to
government housing policies and would administer existing and proposed housing subsidy programs.

They would be nonprofit, limited dividend, or cooperatives, approved as contractors by HUD; recognition would be dependent on approval of a table of organization and a plan of operation. A HOPE
would be organized by such groups as financial institutions, municipalities, planning and housing councils, trade unions and churches,
housing cooperatives, and community groups. Staffing would be by
high-caliber professionals, assisted by volunteers drawn from community organizations. It would be monitored by a board of directors
drawn from a wide spectrum of civic groups and private groups, with
knowledge and experience in housing. There would be geographical
duplication, with a variety of organizational forms leading to competition among HOPE's.

Operations

The costs of operating HOPE's would come from servicing fees, counseling fees, and grants and loans. Maisel anticipates congressional appropriations as the ultimate source of their receipts. However, they could be self-sustaining, with fees charged borrowers, as with FHA and housing finance agencies.

> It would basically be funded on contracts with HUD of the type that HUD now has. In other words, it would be a channel or a funnel—not it, but they, since I would hope that there would be many of them. It would exist as mortgage bankers or others do through the servicing fees, through counseling fees, and through grants and loans. I do recognize one problem; how to make it a fully accountable unit. This is what I suggested one way; if you had quite a few of these you would hope that better ones would grow, and the poorer ones would die. I think it would be wrong to set up a monopoly for a HOPE in each city. I would hope that one of the objectives would be to have several that would compete with each other. But I think the answer on the funding is that since they would be service units, servicing mortgages and doing counselling service, they would be paid in accordance with the normal way that such servicing units are paid, which ultimately comes from congressional appropriations.[26]

The HOPE's are given a number of functions; however, our main interest is in the disposition and administration of the housing contribution, and HOPE could be one of the alternatives open to the firm. Maisel suggests that the HOPE's in direct lending programs retain title to the housing as fiduciaries for individual owners.

The HOPE concept provides an opportunity to distribute the housing funds in a manner that reflects local conditions. The federal government role is basically supervisory and with very limited participation in the operational details. HOPE's could be self-supporting.

A possible benefit for donors to HOPE's, if deemed eligible, could be the tax exemption under IRS-501-C-3 for grants and loans from individuals, foundations, churches, and private corporations.[27] Furthermore, they might be considered tax exempt on any revenues received as earnings on investments used in furtherance of the tax exempt status.[28]

As contrasted to the state and local housing finance programs, where a good number are already fully operational and provide a body of experience for new programs, there is the time factor with HOPE's. How long before the first ones can be established and begin to function successfully? Who would serve on the boards, and how would the selection be made? How can the multiplicity of differing interests and viewpoints in a community be reconciled? The conflicts within the Model Cities and poverty programs among special interest groups should serve as a warning for the tremendous potential for conflict in seeking the power to handle the housing funds; yet, they do provide a body of experience that can be useful in gaining an understanding of how to avoid such conflict.

The potential for success of this program would be enhanced if the interfunctional concept were applied at the grass roots level. For instance, the firm is a major source of funds and unless operating benefits accrue to the firm, for example, increases in productivity, their enthusiastic involvement is questionable.

PURCHASE OF STATE AND LOCAL GOVERNMENT DEBT OBLIGATIONS

Another feasible alternative for the distribution of the housing funds is the option of allowing firms to purchase securities issued by state and local housing finance and development agencies. The primary function of these agencies is to provide financing for the construction of housing for low- and moderate-income persons for whom conventional unsubsidized housing is out of reach. * The proceeds from the sale of securities, bonds, and notes to private investors through private underwriters are lent to housing sponsors or developers, either nonprofit or limited dividend, as mortgage loans. ** The actual construction is done privately. Due to the questionable constitutionality of loans to individual homeowners as a public purpose, 72 percent of the structures have been high rise or multifamily.[29]

---

*Rising interest and construction costs have placed much of the recently completed housing into a price category more suitable for higher-income occupants than was the original intention of the programs.

**Firms could also act as sponsors of developers of housing by securing mortgage loans.

Growth of Programs

There has been a sizable growth in these programs. Originations of mortgage loans on new properties in these programs rose
from $400 million in 1969 to an estimated $2.6 billion in 1973, or from
2.3 percent of all originations to an estimated 7.6 percent in 1973, or,
in absolute terms, an estimated growth of 650 percent (see Table 11.1).

As of August 1973, 242,419 housing units had been financed or
developed. Some $4.7 billion of tax-exempt debt obligations had been
issued. [30] With the tax exemption, the interest rate is some 2 percent
to 2.5 percent less than would be otherwise; there is a higher loan to
value ratio (up to 100 percent) and longer terms (up to 50 years) than
for conventional financing. The savings are reflected in reduced rents
or carrying charges. With the use of federal housing subsidies and
other state subsidies, it has been possible to serve even lower-income
groups. Also, the assurance of federal subsidies adds another layer
of security to the debt obligations. Section 8, Title II, of the Housing
and Community Development Act of 1974 granted state and local agencies a 40-year subsidy commitment, as contrasted to a 20-year commitment for other sponsors.

The origins of the state housing financing programs, other than
public housing, took place in 1955 with the enactment of legislation
by the state of New York for the sale of general obligation bonds; in
1960, another innovation was the issuance of revenue bonds by the
newly formed New York State Housing Finance Agency, with a moral
commitment or obligation by the legislature to assure repayment.
Subsequently, some 30 states have set up housing and development
agencies. In addition, the cities of New York and Denver have their
own programs (see Table 11.2).

Operating or administrative costs for the agencies are obtained
from fees imposed on the housing developments, with the purpose of
making the agencies self-supporting. The location of the developments
may vary, depending on the initiative of the applicant-sponsor who has
the site, or the agency may take the initiative in finding sites and
sponsors, for example, in an urban renewal area. Not all of the agencies have the power of eminent domain.

The more experienced agencies have achieved occupancy for
their developments much quicker than has HUD for its projects:
12 months to 16 months versus 34 months for HUD projects. They
have also promoted and achieved a substantial degree of racial inte-
gration; nonwhites make up some 21 percent of occupants. The elderly
and handicapped make up 12 percent. [31]

Though their major activity is to make mortgage loans, various
agencies perform other activities. To encourage liquidity in the mortgage market, several states have established mortgage agencies to

TABLE 11.1

Originations of Long-Term Mortgage Loans on New Housing
Properties, State and Local Government Credit Programs,
United States, 1969-73[a]
(billions of dollars)

Item	1969	1970	1971	1972[b]	1973[b]
Amount					
One-to-four-family homes, state and local programs	0.2	0.2	0.5	0.6	1.0
All one-to-four-family originations	12.3	13.0	19.5	23.1	22.6
Multifamily properties, state and local programs	0.2	0.5	1.0	1.2	1.6
All multifamily originations	5.0	6.4	7.4	10.0	11.6
All state and local originations, one-to-four and multifamily	0.4	0.7	1.5	1.8	2.6
Total originations, one-to-four and multifamily	17.3	19.4	26.9	33.1	34.2
Percent					
State and local one-to-four-family homes as percent of total one-to-four originations	1.6	1.5	2.6	2.6	4.4
State and local multifamilies as percent of total multifamilies	4.0	7.8	13.5	12.0	13.8
All state and local originations, one-to-four and multifamily as percent of total one-to-four and multifamily originations	2.3	3.6	5.6	5.4	7.6

[a]Originations pertain to the volume of funds available for direct
lender-borrower transactions, plus the reuse of mortgage loan repayments and use of selected other funds.
[b]Estimated

Sources: U.S. Congress, House, Third Annual Report on National Housing Goals, 92d Cong., 1st sess. (Washington, D.C.: Government Printing Office, June 29, 1971), H. Doc. 92-136, pp. 68
and 80; and U.S. Congress, House, Fourth Annual Report on National
Housing Goals, 92d Cong., 2d sess. (Washington, D.C.: Government Printing Office, June 29, 1972), H. Doc. 92-319, p. 13.

TABLE 11.2

State and Local Housing Finance Programs, Funding Authorized, United States
(millions of dollars)

Governmental Entity	Date Authorized	Funding Authorized[a]
Alaska	1971	Unlimited
Colorado	1973	50
Connecticut	1969	Unlimited
Delaware	1968	Unlimited
Denver	1972	10[b]
Georgia	1972	Unlimited
Hawaii	1970	Unlimited[b]
Idaho	1972	Unlimited
Illinois	1967	500
Kentucky	1972	200
Louisiana	1972	30
Maine	1969	20
Maryland	1970	Unlimited
Massachusetts	1966	1,000
Michigan	1966	600
Minnesota	1971	150
Missouri	1969	100
New Jersey	1967	Unlimited
New York City	1955	[c]
New York City Housing and Development Corporation	1971	800[d]
New York State	1955	5,150[e]
New York State Urban Development Corporation	1968	1,500[f]
North Carolina	1969	200
Ohio	1970	None
Oregon	1971	200
Pennsylvania	1972	Unlimited
Rhode Island	1973	Unlimited
South Carolina	1973	Unlimited
South Dakota	1973	Unlimited
Tennessee	1973	150
Vermont	1968	20
Virginia	1972	Unlimited
West Virginia	1968	130
Wisconsin	1972	150

[a]Revenue bonds, unless otherwise indicated.

[b]General obligation bonds.

[c]General obligation bonds based on housing debt limit of 2 percent of the latest five-year average of assessed valuation of taxable realty. With the 2 percent debt limit encumbered, the city can use general debt limit of 10 percent of latest five-year average of full valuation of taxable realty. According to the state constitution, debt-incurring power is renewed as housing companies become self-supporting.

[d]If capital reserve fund is insufficient and the city does not appropriate necessary amount, the state can withhold aid to the city until reserve fund is replenished.

[e]$150 million of general obligation bonds previously issued.

[f]May be backed by debt reserve funds; if funds fall below minimum, amount has to be appropriated by state legislature.

Sources: U.S. Department of Housing and Urban Development, Housing in the Seventies (Washington, D.C.: Government Printing Office, October 1973), p. 5-6; and various issues, HUD Newsletter and Journal of Housing (National Association of Housing and Redevelopment Officials).

operate in the secondary mortgage market. As a means of obtaining
greater flexibility than is permitted by FHA mortgage insurance, there
are agencies with authority to insure designated types of mortgage.

In the absence of the full faith and credit pledges in such states
as Michigan, New Jersey, Illinois, and New York, their enabling legislation contains specific capital reserve requirements to secure the
bonds and provide for sufficient state appropriations to secure an initial issue of agency obligations. Even more significant, the statutes
contain moral obligation clauses, which are nothing more than legislative commitments to consider replenishing capital reserve accounts
if they fall below minimum levels. North Carolina and Minnesota
have no moral obligation or reserve funds. They limit their lending
to mortgages insured by the federal government.

A Typical Agency

Many of the aforementioned features are common to most state
agencies, for example, the New Jersey State Housing Finance Agency,
created in 1967 as a quasi-independent agency in the State's Department of Community Affairs. The agency's powers are limited to the
mortgage financing of multifamily housing for low- and moderate-income groups. Schools, stores, community meeting facilities, and
day care centers also qualify for financing. The enabling legislation
contained provisions for capital reserve requirements to secure the
bonds and for sufficient state appropriations to secure the initial bond
issue and for a moral obligation commitment. There is no limit on
the amount the agency can borrow; it has the power of eminent domain.

Sponsors are limited to nonprofit and limited dividend groups,
including private developers and builders, church organizations, civic
associations, and labor unions. Nonprofit sponsors can borrow up to
100 percent of project costs; limited dividend sponsors, up to 90 percent, with an 8 percent return on equity permitted. The maximum
loan term is 50 years.

To make the agency self-supporting and, thus, gain acceptance,
project sponsors are charged site evaluation and appraisal fees, are
levied a nonrecurring fee of 2.5 percent of the mortgage loan and a
recurring service fee of 0.25 percent of the full mortgage amount.[32]

As of August 1973, there were $160 million in outstanding bonds,
and 9,338 housing units had been financed or developed. The statutory
authority to purchase existing mortgages or to give tax abatement had
not been implemented.[33]

A unique feature of the New Jersey Housing Finance Agency (by
virtue of the Housing Assistance Bond Act of 1968) is the availability
of general obligation financing as an adjunct to the revenue bond pro-

gram. A $125 million bond issue was intended to permit the state to take advantage of programs in the Federal Housing Act of 1968. Loans from this fund were to be made in the form of interest-free deferred-payment second mortgages, with repayment not to begin until the first mortgages were retired.

Federal Support

State and local housing finance and development agencies received strong federal support under Title VIII of the Housing and Community Development Act of 1974, to encourage their formation and effective operation, to provide housing for low- and moderate-income families, and to revitalize blighted areas, to improve employment opportunities, and to implement the development aspects of state land use and preservation policies.

The Secretary of HUD is authorized to guarantee the obligations of these agencies issued to finance development activities in furtherance of revitalization of slum and blighted areas or to provide housing for low- and moderate-income persons in connection with such revitalization. The secretary is authorized to make grants to cover one-third of interest costs on such obligations. Guarantee and assistance, which need not be together, are available only if there is no tax exemption. The amount of annual interest subsidy is limited to $110 million, beginning in fiscal 1976, and the total amount of guarantees for outstanding bonds is limited to $500 million.

The Moral Obligation

What was once considered the prototype, or model, for state development agencies has become a bellwether for other reasons. At the beginning of 1975, the New York State Urban Development Corporation (UDC) found itself in severe financial straits, unable to meet obligations that were maturing and to cover operating expenses; as a result of these difficulties, there ensued a drastic reappraisal of the moral commitment bonds issued by UDC. Following UDC's misfortunes, the continued issuance of moral commitment bonds by other authorities nationally has been cast in doubt. "Because of [UDC's] size, and the amount of funds involved, the case is the most important test of a state's 'moral obligation' to date. While most observers believe New York will meet its obligation, the case raises many [constitutional] questions."[34]

New York State pioneered in 1960 with the formation of the State Housing Finance Agency in the creation of a new type of public debt,

technically called "the legislative make-up" and popularly known as
the "moral obligation" or "moral commitment," which lacked the support of the state's full faith and credit. General obligation bonds, as
contrasted to these revenue bonds, are backed by the full faith and
credit of a state or city. In New York State, they have to be approved
by the voters, and repayment is guaranteed by the state constitution.
Bondholders have first priority on all state revenues for the amortization of the bonds. This guarantee enables such obligations to be sold
at a reduced interest rate. New York State's Comptroller, Arthur
Levitt, a long-time critic of moral commitment obligations affirms
that "there is also no doubt that the experience of the UDC demon-
strates a basic fault in the way the public authority has been authorized
to finance its program. There must be an end to such financing so far
as new projects by public authorities are concerned."[35]

The legislature that gave the moral obligation cannot bind future
legislatures: "Future legislatures are not bound to make the necessary
appropriations which must preceed any payment of State monies."[36]
This technique has been utilized in a number of other New York State
programs and by approximately 30 other states for their housing programs.

There had already been concern expressed about the legality and
soundness of moral obligation issues. In 1973, Moody's Investor's
Service, a major bond-rating service, announced its intention to re-
evaluate the ratings of all moral obligation bond issues due to their
proliferation. [37]

Would the moral obligation hold up under a constitutional test?
According to Jackson Phillips, Senior Vice President of Moody's:
"Without a legal commitment, what right does the legislature have to
pay an agency deficiency with taxpayers' funds? A taxpayers' suit is
always a possibility." He cited the Calumet Skyway, a toll road that
borrowed $2 million from the city of Chicago some 10 years ago to
cover a deficit. The loans to Calumet stopped with the threat of a law-
suit. [38]

Criticism and Problems

According to HUD, a major criticism of the state and local finance and development agencies is the stress on new housing construction, as opposed to utilization of the existing housing stock, and the
use of costly direct and indirect federal subsidies, that is, tax-exempt
securities and the Section 236 interest subsidy. Yet there is no unanimity outside of HUD in being critical of the stress on new housing.
With respect to tax exemption, the Housing and Community Development Act of 1974 provides an alternative through interest subsidies

and guarantees. The Section 236 subsidy has been replaced by the
new Section 8 leasing program, which is also costly but is also available for new construction.

The 1973 preliminary estimate for wage and salary disburse-
ments in the private sector was $546.0 billion; applying a hypothetical
1 percent mandatory rate would generate proceeds of $5.5 billion,
more than double the state and local mortgage originations of $2.6
billion for 1973 (see Table 11.1). The question arises as to whether
an additional influx of funds could be absorbed. With options for alternative uses of the funds, a lesser amount would be allocated to the
state and local agencies. There are the considerations of the existence
of debt instruments in adequate quantities and suitable maturities and
—basic—the capability of the funds being absorbed in relation to housing needs. Are there qualified sponsors or developers, sufficient labor and material, and an efficient government agency?

The influx of funds for the housing finance programs should be
considered in the light of the concept of supply leading "the creation
of financial institutions and the growth of their assets, liabilities and
ancillary services, prior to the demand for them."[39] Modifying this
concept in accordance with this discussion of housing funds, the implications are that the supply of new funds could force the housing
finance agencies to restructure themselves in such a way that the
funds could be absorbed without undue strain. Also, the availability
of the new funds could stimulate the client groups (housing industry,
tenants) to pressure the governmental agencies to remove restraints
and obstacles. The housing industry should be sufficiently flexible
enough to develop the capacity to absorb the additional funds; the
need for housing still exists.

To summarize, the option of purchasing bonds of state and local
finance and development agencies would be an excellent means for a
firm to fulfill its requirements. The involvement is minimal. The
firm's duties need go no further than purchasing securities and liqui-
dating them at the close of the prescribed period. There could be an
attractive tax-free return, particularly in states with high corporate
taxes. They represent a balance sheet asset.

The issue of the legality and risk for the moral obligation securities has to be resolved, but the risk factor could be negligible with
federal interest subsidies and guarantees. There is also the issue
of the availability of securities in the right denomination, in adequate
quantities and suitable maturities. There could be problems if they
have to be liquidated in the open market prior to maturity at a loss,
when the price would depend on prevailing interest rates. A further
consideration is the potential impact on the bond market of the new demand and, subsequently, should the firm decide to liquidate. A solution could be a new type of security in special denominations and maturities designed to fit the mandatory contribution.

The three options outlined in this chapter indicate the extent to which business firms can be involved. The extent of the involvement ranges as follows:

1. The most direct involvement is with employer-owned housing.

2. The development corporation or HOPE allows less involvement.

3. The purchase of state and local debt obligations could give the firm complete detachment from implementation and administration.

These options are among the innovative tactical approaches that could be implementing mechanisms tied to any U.S. mandatory programs.

NOTES

1. International Labour Office, Workers' Housing—A Selection of Provisions Adopted under the Auspices of the I.L.O., D/21/1962 (Geneva: International Labour Office, 1962), p. 49.

2. "Easier Moves: Housing Worries Spur Companies to Increase Relocation Benefits," Wall Street Journal, November 12, 1974, p. 1.

3. Organization for Economic Cooperation and Development, The Role of Trade Unions in Housing (Paris: Organization for Economic Cooperation and Development, 1968), p. 104.

4. J. P. Cullingworth, Housing and Labour Mobility (Paris: Organization for Economic Cooperation and Development, 1969), p. 61.

5. Chris Kristensen, John Levy, and Tamar Savir, The Suburban Lock-Out Effect, Research Dept., no. 1 (White Plains, N.Y.: Suburban Action Institute, March 1971); and The Potomac Institute, Controlling Urban Growth—But for Whom? (Washington, D.C.: The Potomac Institute, March 1973).

6. 272 U.S. 365, 71 L. Ed. 303 (1926).

7. "No Vacancy: Civil Libertarians Join Developers to Oppose Cities' Growth Curbs," Wall Street Journal, January 31, 1975, p. 1.

8. U.S. Department of Housing and Urban Development, Equal Opportunity in Housing: A Manual for Corporate Employers, prepared by Westchester Residential Opportunities, Inc. (Washington, D.C.: Government Printing Office, November 1973), pp. 3-4.

9. Myron P. Curzon, "Housing and the Role of the Large Corporate Enterprise," in U.S. Congress, House, Committee on Banking and Currency, Papers Submitted to Subcommittee on Housing Panels on Housing Production, Housing Demand and Developing a Suitable Living Environment, 92d Cong., 1st sess., 1971, pt. 1, pp. 186 and 190.

10. Ibid.

11. Cullingworth, op. cit., p. 60.

12. R. Descloitres, The Foreign Worker—Adaptation to Industrial Work and Urban Life (Paris: Organization for Economic Cooperation and Development, 1967), p. 130.

13. Ibid., p. 132.

14. Charles P. Kindleberger, Europe's Postwar Growth—The Role of Labor Supply (Cambridge, Mass.: Harvard University Press, 1967), p. 183.

15. Jane Morton, "Sober Sunlight," New Society 17 (May 6, 1971): 757.

16. W. H. Lever, The Buildings Erected at Port Sunlight (Liverpool: Liverpool University Press, 1902), quoted in R. R. Morton, "Housing Renewal at Port Sunlight," Town Planning Review 44 (October 1973): 319.

17. Jane Morton, op. cit., p. 757.

18. R. R. Morton, op. cit., p. 330.

19. Ibid.

20. Ibid.

21. Jane Morton, op. cit., p. 758.

22. New York City, Landmarks Preservation Commission, Steinway Historic District Designation Report, no. 1, LP-0873, November 26, 1974.

23. New York City, Landmarks Preservation Commission, "Landmarks Commission Designates 2 Historic Districts," Press Release, November 26, 1974.

24. Donald C. Platten (Chairman of the Board, Chemical Bank, New York, N.Y.), "Utopia, Reality and Change: Mistakes We Must Not Make," Remarks to the Westchester County Association, Rye, New York, November 15, 1973, p. 14.

25. U.S. Congress, House, Committee on Banking and Currency, Subcommittee on Housing, Hearings, pt. 2, Housing and Urban Development Legislation—1971, 92d Cong., 1st sess. (Washington, D.C.: Government Printing Office, September 1971), pp. 865-900.

26. Ibid., p. 892.

27. U.S. Department of the Treasury, Internal Revenue Service, How to Apply for Recognition of Exemption for an Organization, Publication 557 (Washington, D.C.: Government Printing Office, Revised October 1974).

28. Brady J. Deaton, "CDCs a Development Alternative for Rural America," Growth and Change 6 (January 1975): 36, fn. 6.

29. U.S. Department of Housing and Urban Development, Housing in the Seventies (Washington, D.C.: Government Printing Office, 1973), pp. 5-12.

30. Ibid., pp. 5-6 and 5-7.

31. Ibid., pp. 5-13 and 5-14.

32. Michael A. Stegman, "Housing Finance Agencies: Are They Crucial Instruments of State Government?" Journal of the American Institute of Planners 40 (September 1974): 331.

33. Housing in the Seventies, p. 5-6.

34. "New York State Mulls 'Moral Obligation' of Helping Ailing Agency Avoid Default," Wall Street Journal, January 20, 1975, p. 15.

35. State of New York, Office of the State Comptroller, Division of Audits and Accounts, Public Authorities in New York State, December 31, 1974, p. 1.

36. Ibid., p. 23.

37. Stegman, op. cit., p. 313.

38. "New York State Mulls 'Moral Obligation' of Helping Ailing Agency Avoid Default," p. 15.

39. Hugh T. Patrick, Financial Development and Economic Growth in Underdeveloped Countries, Center Paper, no. 75 (New Haven, Conn.: Yale University Center for Economic Growth, 1966), p. 175.

CHAPTER

12

ADOPTION OR ADAPTATION
OF A MANDATORY
CONTRIBUTION SYSTEM IN
THE UNITED STATES

Having analyzed the various national systems, examined the development of housing legislation in the United States—the alternatives and options for the allocation of funds and the desirability of assigning a high national priority to housing—the final phase, or epilogue, is to assess and summarize the desirability and impact of enacting legislation for an employment-related contribution system for housing in the United States.

The preferred housing policy of the Nixon and Ford administrations has been to move in the direction of housing or rent allowances for tenants and away from production-oriented programs. There has been no desire to reverse the declining national priority of the 1960s for housing.[1] The leasing provisions of Section 8 of the Housing and Community Development Act of 1974 for housing assistance payments are a step in the direction of housing allowances. Early indications are that the program is extremely complicated to start, will be difficult to manage, and has, in its beginning stage, been deemed "unworkable."[2] The regulations for Section 8 are considered so restrictive that "they virtually preclude the possibility of any large volume of any type of financing for new development."[3] As with the continuing changes in federal housing legislation, the question arises as to how long before a frantic and hurried search for a replacement ensues.

The likelihood of a reversal in this policy is conditioned upon the extent to which the economy declines or remains stagnant. If it continues to decline or remains stagnant, increasing attention will again be focused on the construction of housing as a means of stimulating economic activity, with a concurrent deemphasis of no growth policies restricting construction.[4]

218

HOUSING NEEDS IN THE 1980s

In view of the critical housing needs of the country, the construction of housing does not represent "make work." Housing requirements in the 1980s range from an estimated 27.6 million to 30.1 million units.

> For the decade of the 1980's, projected housing requirements total over 30 million units for the first time in the nation's history, fully reflective of the strength and unique character of the many and varied new trends that surround it. Average housing demand will total just over 3 million units yearly during the 80's, including 610,000 units of mobile homes. Throughout the 1970's and the 1980's the nation will have housing needs the strength of which it has never known before.[5]

Will there be sufficient dollars to match the projected housing requirements? The level will depend on such diverse factors as the state of the economy, competing credit demands, inflation, rate of savings, costs of land, labor materials, money, and environmental and energy controls. The National Planning Association estimates (based on current trends) $83.1 billion in 1969 dollars as the 1980 costs of meeting housing goal requirements, with a shortfall of 32.5 percent, or $27.0 billion, in housing expenditures.[6]

What role would a payroll-related housing contribution plan play in alleviating this shortfall? Private wages and salaries in 1969 were $405.6 billion and 1973 preliminary figures were $546.0 billion; applying a rate of 1 percent, tentatively, could produce proceeds of $4.1 billion and $5.5 billion. By 1980, there should be an increase in the amount of wages and salaries, thus providing an even higher amount; but even at the present unadjusted figures, a sizable portion of the 1980 gap would be filled by the contribution or a higher rate could be set to diminish the gap.

There is the question of whether the new funds brought into the housing sector by the mandatory contribution are replacing or are adding to aggregate outlays for housing. If previously allocated funds are released, they might be directed to aiding or giving housing assistance to the low-income, aged, and other special groups. The degree of substitution partially depends upon the degree of public support, which is reflected in the level of legislative appropriations. The payroll program, although it may affect housing appropriations, avoids the uncertainties and political conflict associated with annual legislative authorizations and appropriations.

The recipients of those programs, for example in France, are primarily blue and white collar workers rather than the low-income, nonworking poor. The opportunity to benefit from improved housing could enhance the work ethic.

Depending upon how utilized, the housing fund could have strong leverage on the demand for housing. An analysis of factors affecting the demand for lower-middle-income owner-occupied housing indicates that elimination of the down payment requirement would be the most effective single action to stimulate potential housing demand.[7] This sensitivity grows as interest rates are lowered and mortgage maturity periods are lengthened. Based on economic studies, a 10 percent change in down payment requirements would have an effect on housing starts three times greater than a 10 percent change in interest rates.[8] The housing fund could be allocated so as to give more liberal terms than conventional financing.

What are the benefits and costs that come from the institution of a payroll contribution plan, modeled largely on the French system? A quantitative benefit-cost study cannot furnish a clearly defined answer, so diverse and resistant to quantification are the factors. Instead, more qualitative measurements have to be relied upon.

ECONOMIC STABILIZATION

There would be a steadier flow of funds than under present programs into the housing sector, with no competition for these funds from other borrowers better able to pay higher interest rates. Financing could be obtained, therefore, at a lower cost, since the funds would have to be invested in housing. There would be less dependence upon the ability of savings institutions to attract deposits. Producers of housing, suppliers, and labor would gain from stabilization, and a more efficient industry would result. With larger expenditures on housing, unutilized or underutilized land would be absorbed, deteriorated housing replaced, and blighted areas redeveloped.

New housing properly sited would enable the distance traveled to work to be reduced gradually, cutting air pollution and fuel consumption—a gain to the economy, as well as to the employee. New housing could incorporate energy-saving materials, lowering heating costs of owners and rents to tenants. By lowering energy usage and reducing imports, the balance of trade could be improved.

The payroll plan enables employees to receive housing benefits (not as taxable income, as with direct money wage increases); there is a loss to the government through the tax revenues not received. This loss should be balanced against the nation's gains from the housing. But does the worker welcome this benefit, or does he prefer to

receive a monetary increase, particularly if the worker has no need
for housing assistance? This element of compulsion is generally accepted in other areas, for example, social security and education.

In addition to basing the mandatory housing contributions on payrolls, a number of other countries such as Chile, Romania, and Yugoslavia have various types of interfunctional mandatory systems tied to
worker productivity and enterprise profits. Japan's interfunctional
but nonmandatory system also depends on the ability of the firm to increase productivity and generate profits.

As with the payroll-based contributions, there are drawbacks in
the profit-based approach. One such weakness comes from those
firms and industries that pass through stages of economic development:
growth, top-out, and possible resurgence or decay. During these
stages and varying phases of the business cycle, the capability of firms
and industries to generate profits and assign significant amounts to
housing may be severely restricted.

Thus, these mandatory programs in and of themselves are generally insufficient to constitute a total housing program and there must
be standby supplemental housing programs, particularly in periods of
top-out and depression when funds from payrolls and profits are not
adequate.

LACK OF MANAGEMENT

A critical failure of the government housing programs has been
their management:

> As much as any other single factor, the nation's
> housing direction suffers from an acute lack of
> management. No one is managing the effort and
> apparently no one is responsible for it. This lack
> of management makes it especially difficult to im-
> plement coordinated housing program activities
> designed to accomplish specified target goals.[9]

The proposed program calls for no large governmental organization or staff to operate the program, other than to assure compliance
with the regulations. Centralized decision making would be supplanted
by the greater flexibility in matching regional and local conditions.
The firm has the discretion and ability to take local conditions into account but could be constrained until such time as there is a local dis-
tributive mechanism, such as the French CIL. The apparent success
of these programs is due to the availability of dispersed operational
controls which are sensitive enough to quickly indicate unevenness of

performance. Thus, management is provided with an option to change
tactical decisions or strategic policies, for example, to shift from
involvement in construction of housing for employees to loans, as in
Spain and Chile. The effectiveness of the control systems emanates
from the employment of managers versed in control and performance
management.

The contribution by the firm does not necessarily represent a
cost; depending upon how it is utilized, it could, if loaned or invested,
be an asset. However, the firm may have to borrow the equivalent
of the housing contribution externally at a high rate of interest. The
firm with high labor costs, which has a stronger incentive to automate,
bears a great burden than does the firm with a small workforce.

PROCEEDS AND HOUSING NEED

The utilization of the proceeds in the geographic area, where
collected, might not match the extent of housing need. The area with
the greatest industrial activity and number of employees would receive the largest benefits, whereas other areas with less industrial
activity, but possibly with greater housing needs, might not receive as
great benefits. If there is too much distortion in the distribution of
the proceeds, as with the legal controversy in the financing of education, changes might be mandated, so that communities receive equal
shares, regardless of the origin of the funds.

In the United States the creation of new industrial and energy-re-
lated communities provides an instrument for establishing on a gradual
scale, the mandatory programs of an interfunctional nature examined
in this volume. A likely vehicle for a phased introduction is a consortium such as was formed in the Roubaix-Tourcoing region. In this
mature French industrial center, a geographically concentrated industry with the cooperation of labor successfully introduced the payroll
based plan, which was then made mandatory by the government as part
of its national housing policy. Because of the diverse and conflicting
interests of industry, labor, and government, the interfunctional solution of relating productivity, funding, and construction can best be effectuated through the joint participation in a consortium of these interest groups.

This program combines the best of public and private action by
directing funds into what is an area of high priority, yet requiring no
close or detailed controls, and can be performed within a framework
of broad guidelines. On balance, a fairly consistent flow of funds
will come into the housing sector and allow for a degree of flexibility
not contained in present housing programs.

This study should not be deemed the final step in evaluating the
effectiveness of these mandatory programs. It should serve as a plat-

form for further examination of their achievements in sustaining continued increases in productivity and the quality and quantity of the
housing stock. Thus, the ensuing examination should encompass
changes in the structure and performance of the programs, following
the analytical framework of this book.

Action is possible and necessary now. The action for initiating
a mandatory program should come from the component units of the
AFL-CIO at the time of their next negotiations. Or it could come from
management. A first step is the creation of a joint task force that
sets up a mechanism to relate and resolve the differing interests of
each group. Present programs are not working, yet needs are com-
pelling. The mining industry is a case in point.[10] Conventional mortgages are unavailable for miners; banks consider such employment
not sufficiently permanent. The energy boom, including mining, is
generating enormous profits, a portion of which should be channeled
into new communities of quality and permanence. Such a program
would require participation of government in the consortium. Appa-
lachia and the Western coal lands are geographic areas of application.
The coal companies and the unions should adapt the French, Japanese,
Romanian, Yugoslavian, and other related foreign experiences and
carefully relate wages, productivity, technology, profits, and funds
for the housing program. Another immediate application should be
the new boom towns, which will be triggered along the East Coast by
off-shore drilling in the Baltimore Canyon. Once again the goal is
the development of communities of quality and permanence, which
will survive with a changed economic base. In a period of governmental budget crises, especially at the state and local levels, a favorable climate for the application of mandatory programs should be fostered at all levels of government, industry, and labor.

NOTES

1. Leonard A. Lecht, National Planning Association, Dollars
for National Goals: Looking Ahead to 1980 (New York: John Wiley
& Sons, 1974), pp. 14-14.

2. "Builders Glum on U.S. Subsidy Plan," New York Times,
March 2, 1975, sec. 8, p. 1.

3. "NAHRO Submits Testimony to Congress Calling for Housing Changes," NAHRO Letter 9 (February 24, 1975): 5.

4. "No Growth Movement Blocks Building of 45,000 Units in
U.S.," Apartment Construction News 9 (December 1974): 1.

5. John Kokus, Jr., Housing Requirements in the 1970s and
1980s, prepared for the Financial and Economic Studies Task Force,
the National Association of Home Builders (Washington, D.C., January 1974), p. 44.

6. National Planning Association, Changes in National Priorities During the 1960's: Their Implications for 1980, prepared by Leonard A. Lecht, Rept. No. 132 (Washington, D.C.: National Planning Association, September 1972), p. 34.

7. Jack E. Gelfand, "Mortgage Credit and Lower Middle Income Housing Demand," Land Economics 46 (May 1970): 163.

8. Kenneth F. Rosen, statement in U.S. Congress, Senate Committee on Banking, Housing and Urban Affairs, Hearings on Emergency Housing and Housing/Energy, 94th Cong., 1st sess. (Washington, D.C.: Government Printing Office, February/March 1975), p. 221.

9. Kokus, op. cit., p. 73.

10. Rick Banks, United Mine Workers, in U.S. Congress, Senate Committee on the Budget, Hearings, The 1976 First Concurrent Resolution on the Budget, 94th Cong., 1st sess. (Washington, D.C.: Government Printing Office, 1975), pp. 568-72.

Allen, G. C. "Why Japan's Economy Has Prospered." Lloyds Bank Review, no. 3 (January 1974), p. 29.

Amsden, Jon. Collective Bargaining and Class Conflict in Spain. London: Weidenfeld and Nicolson, 1972.

Anderson, Charles W. The Political Economy of Modern Spain. Madison: University of Wisconsin Press, 1970.

Balaj, Teofil. Romania: The Land and the People. Bucharest: Meridiane Publishing House, 1972.

Banz, George. "The World-Wide Housing Shortage—Can It Be Overcome?" Cooperation Canada 16 (September/October 1974), p. 12.

Bardach, Eugene. "Gathering Data for Policy Research." Journal of Urban Analysis 2 (1974): 117.

Barrett, M. Edgar, and Judith Ann Gehrke. "Significant Differences Between Japanese and American Business." MSU Business Topics 22 (Winter 1974): 41.

Beckman, Robert. "The Experimental Housing Allowance Program." Journal of Housing 30 (January 1973): 12.

Blaga, Ion. Romania's Population: A Demographic Economic and Socio-Political Essay. Bucharest: Meridiane Publishing House, 1972.

Bogdan, Cornieliu, Ambassador to the United States from Romania. "Prospects of Trade and Economic Cooperation Between the U.S.A. and Romania." Speech at Romanian Conference, Institute of Soviet and Eastern Studies, University of Michigan, Ann Arbor, Michigan, December 17, 1974.

Bryant, John. "Housing and Housing Policies in Western Europe." Carnegie Mellon University Graduate School of Industrial Administration Report, no. 636 (Pittsburgh: Carnegie Mellon, 1973).

Carlson, Eric. "Housing and Urban Development in Spain." Unpublished draft, no. SM/A8. New York, United Nations, August 25, 1961.

Ceausescu, Nicolae. La Roumanie sur la Voie du Parachevement de l'Edification Socialiste. Vols. 1 and 2. Bucharest: Editions Meridiane, 1969.

_____. Romania on the Way of Building Up the Multi-Laterally Developed Socialist Society May 1971-February 1972. Vol. 6. Bucharest: Meridiane Publishing House, 1972.

_____. Romania on the Way of Building Up the Multi-Laterally Developed Socialist Society. Vol. 7, March 1972-December 1972. Vol. 8, January 1973-July 1973. Bucharest: Meridiane Publishing House, 1973.

Center for Economic and Social Studies. "Economic Reforms in Eastern Europe: Industrial Prices." Proceedings of Venice Seminar, August 21-September 2, 1972. Thomas Jefferson Center, University of Virginia and CESES, Milan, Italy.

Centre d'Information et d'Etude du Credit. Housing Finance in France, the United States of America, the Federal Republic of Germany, the United Kingdom and Italy. Paris, 1966. Translated into English and distributed by the International Union of Building Societies and Savings Associations, Washington, D.C.

Chamber of Commerce of the Socialist Republic of Romania. Romania's Development over 1971-1975. Bucharest, n.d.

_____. Romania Pocket Commercial Guide, 2d issue. Bucharest, 1971.

Chamber of Commerce of the United States. Papers of the First Plenum, Romanian, U.S. Economic Council, Bucharest, May 31, 1974-June 1, 1974. Washington, D.C., 1974.

Confederacion Espanola de Cajas de Ahorros, Madrid. "The Housing Sector in Spain." World Thrift, no. 3 (May/June 1970), p. 139.

Constantinescu, G. Romania's Economy. Bucharest: Meridiane Publishing House, 1970.

Constantinescu, Miron, Ovidiu Badina, and Erno Gall. Sociological Thought in Romania. Bucharest, Editura Politica, 1973.

Cooper, James R. Can the 1968-1978 National Housing Goals Be Achieved? Urbana-Champaign: University of Illinois Committee on Housing Research and Development, 1971.

Council of Planning Librarians. A Selected Bibliography on Urban Housing in Latin America. Prepared by Leopoldo Porzecanski. Exchange Bibliography, no. 412. Monticello, Ill., June 1973.

_____. Urbanization in France and Italy. Prepared by Raffaella Nannetti. Exchange Bibliography, no. 340. Monticello, Ill., November 1972.

Demetrescu, Mihai C. Marketing. Bucharest: Editura Politica, 1973.

Di Carlo, Gaetano. "Housing Credit in Italy." World Thrift, no. 3 (May/June 1970), p. 119.

Directives of the Tenth Congress of the Romanian Communist Party Concerning the Plan of Romania's Economic and Social Development in the 1971-1975 Period and the Guidelines for this Development in the 1976-1980 Period. Bucharest: Meridiane Publishing House, 1969.

Dobrescu, Emilian, and Ion Blaga. Structural Patterns of Romanian Economy. Bucharest: Meridiane Publishing House, 1973.

Downs, Anthony. Federal Housing Subsidies: How Are They Working? Lexington, Mass.: Lexington Books, 1973.

_____. "The Successes and Failures of Federal Housing Policy." Public Interest, no. 34 (Winter 1974), p. 124.

Draft Programme of the Romanian Communist Party for the Building of the Multi-Laterally Developed Socialist Society and Romania's Advance Toward Communism. Bucharest: Romanian News Agency, 1974.

Drucker, Mark L. "Relocation to the Suburbs: Can Employees Find a New Home Too?" Business and Society Review/Innovation, no. 9 (Spring 1974), p. 40.

Drucker, Peter F. Management: Tasks, Responsibilities, Practices. New York: Harper & Row, 1974.

Eckstein, Otto. "Health and Competing Claims for the Nation's Resources in the 1970's." Milbank Memorial Fund Quarterly 47 (July 1969): 319.

Edwards, Thomas L. Economic Development and Reform in Chile: Progress under Frei, 1964-1970. Michigan State University, Latin American Studies Center, Monograph Series, no. 8. East Lansing, March 1972.

Elliott, Sean W. Financing Latin American Housing. New York: Praeger Publishers, 1968.

Federal Institute for Statistics. Statistical Calendar for Yugoslavia 1974. 20th Issue. Belgrade: Federal Institute for Statistics, April 1974.

Feteanu, Gheorge. Consumers' Cooperation in Romania. Bucharest: Central Union of Consumer Cooperatives, 1971.

Fisher, Jack C. Yugoslavia—Multinational State. San Francisco: Chandler Publishing Company, 1966.

Fonseca, Jose. Housing Finance in Developing Countries. The Hague: International Federation of Housing and Planning, 1971.

Ford Foundation. Community Development Corporations: A Strategy for Depressed Urban and Rural Areas. New York, May 1973.

Goldberg, Arthur Abba. "State Agencies: Housing Assistance at the Grass Roots." Real Estate Review 1 (Winter 1972): 14.

Gordon, Jack D., Bernardo Benes, and Francisco Basterrechea. A Survey of New Home Financing Institutions in Latin America, pt. 2. Prepared for Center for Housing, Building and Planning, Department of Economic and Social Affairs, United Nations, by Washington Federal Savings and Loan Associations, Miami Beach, April 1969.

Grebler, Leo. Housing Issues in Economic Stabilization Policy. National Bureau of Economic Research Occasional Paper, no. 72. New York: National Bureau of Economic Research, 1960.

Hanke, Byron R. "Urban Densities in the U.S. and Japan." HUD International, Special Supplement, no. 7. U.S. Department of Housing and Urban Development, July 1972.

Harpman, G. Donald. "Spain's Housing Policy." Town and Country Planning 25 (September 1959): 389.

Heller, Walter H. "Has the Time Come for Indexing?" Wall Street Journal, June 20, 1974, p. 12.

Hoos, Ida R. "Can Systems Analysis Solve Social Problems?" Datamation 20 (June 1974): 82.

"Hospital to Sick Companies." New York Times, July 18, 1971, sec. 3, p. 1.

"Housing and Education." Special Center for Urban Education Report. Occasional paper. New York: Center for Urban Education, April 1971.

"Housing and Urban Development in Japan." HUD International Brief, no. 6. U.S. Department of Housing and Urban Development, Office of International Affairs, June 1971.

Howenstine, E. Jay. "Compensatory Public Works Programmes and Full Employment." International Labour Review 73 (February 1956): 107.

"Inflation Is Turning Japan from Affluence to Economic Gloom." New York Times, October 18, 1974, p. 3.

Inter-American Development Bank. Socio-Economic Progress in Latin America—Social Progress Trust Fund. Ninth Annual Report, 1969. Washington, D.C., March 6, 1970.

_____. The Mobilization of Internal Financial Resources in Latin America. Round Table held in conjunction with Twelfth Annual Meeting, Board of Governors, Lima, Peru, May 11-12, 1971.

International Labour Conference, Fifty-Fourth Session. Health, Welfare and Housing of Workers, pt. 2, Summary of Reports on Selected Recommendations. Geneva: International Labour Office: 1970.

International Labour Office. Housing and Employment. Geneva: In-
    ternational Labour Office, 1948.

_____. Manpower Aspects of Recent Economic Developments in Eur-
    ope. Geneva: International Labour Office, 1969, pp. 84-88.

Keating, William D. Emerging Patterns of Corporate Entry into
    Housing. Center for Real Estate and Urban Economics, Special
    Report, no. 18. Berkeley: University of California, Institute
    of Urban and Regional Development, 1973.

Keefe, Eugene W., et al. Area Handbook for Romania. Foreign Area
    Studies, American University, DA Pamphlet 550-160. Washing-
    ton, D.C.: U.S. Government Printing Office, 1972.

Keyserling, Leon H. The Coming Crisis in Housing. Washington,
    D.C.: Conference on Economic Progress, December 1972.

King, John C. "Housing in Spain." Town Planning Review 42 (Octo-
    ber 1971): 381.

Kinzie, George R. "Construction's Input-Output Profile." Construc-
    tion Review 16 (August 1970): 4.

Kristof, Frank S. "Federal Housing Policies—Subsidized Production,
    Filtration and Objectives." Land Economics 48 (November 1972)
    309; and 49 (May 1973): 163.

La Palombara, Joseph. Italy: The Politics of Planning. Syracuse:
    Syracuse University Press, 1966.

Laquian, Aprodicio A. "Slums of Hope . . . Slums of Despair."
    Cooperation Canada 16 (September/October 1974), p. 3.

"Last Hired and Usually the First Let Go." New York Times, Janu-
    ary 29, 1975, p. 17.

League of Communists of Yugoslavia Tenth Congress. Basic Results
    of Economic and Social Development in Yugoslavia 1947-1972.

"Logue Blames Bankers for UDC Flight; Smeal Offers Defense at
    Senate Hearing." Weekly Bond Buyer 198 (January 27, 1975):
    14.

Logue, Edward J., President and Chief Executive Officer of New York
     State Urban Development Corporation. Statement before New
     York State Senate Committee on Housing and Urban Development.
     New York City, January 16, 1975.

Lustig, Morton, and Janet Rothenberg Pack. "A Standard for Resi-
     dential Zoning Based upon the Location of Jobs." Journal of
     the American Institute of Planners 40 (September 1974): 333.

Mann, William, Jr. "Housing and Urbanism in Marxist Chile."
     HUD International Brief, no. 12. U.S. Department of Housing
     and Urban Development, Office of International Affairs, March
     1972.

"Manpower Policy in Japan." Commerce in Germany (June 1973) :
     18.

Maravall, J. M. "Modernization, Authoritarianism and the Growth
     of Working Class Dissent: The Case of Spain." Government
     and Opposition 8 (Autumn 1973): 432.

Marshall, Richard D. "The Flight of the Thrift Institutions: One
     More Invitation to Inner City Disaster." Rutgers Law Review
     28 (Fall 1974): 113.

McDowell, Edwin. "The Formula for Success in Japan." Wall Street
     Journal, January 9, 1974, p. 16.

"Miki Gov't Eyes $982-Mil. Housing Budget." Japan Real Estate
     News 2 (February 15, 1975): 1.

Mills, Rodney H. "Monetary Restraint and Housing in Italy." Mone-
     tary Restraint and Housing in Selected Foreign Industrial Coun-
     tries. Federal Reserve System, Board of Governors, Division
     of International Finance Review of Foreign Developments, Paper
     V, L.5.2. RFD 669. Washington, D.C.: Federal Reserve,
     May 24, 1971.

Mitufusi, Tadashi, and Kiyohiko Hagisawa. "Recent Trends in Collec-
     tive Bargaining in Japan." International Labour Review 105
     (February 1972): 135.

Montia, John Michael. Economic Development in Communist Roman-
     ia. Cambridge: The Massachusetts Institute of Technology
     Press, 1967.

National Realty Committee, Inc. Real Estate in the U.S. Economy.
    Prepared by Norman B. Ture, Inc., n.d.

Nenno, Mary K. "The Housing and Community Development Act of
    1974: An Interpretation, Its History." Journal of Housing 31
    (August/September 1974): 345.

Nevitt, A. A., ed. The Economic Problems of Housing. New York:
    St. Martins Press, 1967.

Organization for Economic Cooperation and Development, Committee
    on Financial Markets. Housing Finance: Present Problems.
    Paris: Organization for Economic Cooperation and Development,
    1974.

"Origins of HUD-FHA." Challenge 2 (July 1971): 4.

Peabody, Jr., Malcolm E. "Housing Allowances—A New Way to
    House the Poor." New Republic 170 (March 9, 1974): 20.

Perceval, Michael. The Spaniards: How They Live. New York:
    Praeger Publishers, 1969.

Petkovic, Svetomir. "The Housing System in Yugoslavia." Interna-
    tional Review of Administrative Sciences 36 (1970): 310.

Phillips, James G. "Housing Report of HUD Proposes Cash Allowance
    System as Link to Broad Plan for Welfare Reform." National
    Journal Reports 5 (August 25, 1973): 1255.

Popisteanu, Cristian, and Petre Panzaru. Romania Historical Itiner-
    ary 1944-1974. Bucharest: Editura Enciclopedica Romana, 1974.

Puiu, Alexandre. Comertul Exterior Si Rolul Lui In Realizarea Pro-
    gramului De Dezvoltare Economica A Romaniei. Bucharest:
    Editura Politica, 1974.

"Recession Layoffs and the Civil Rights of Minorities." New York
    Times, January 29, 1975, p. 17.

Reishchauer, Robert D., and Robert W. Hartman. Reforming School
    Finance. Washington, D.C.: The Brookings Institution, 1973.

Ricks, R. Bruce. Sources of Housing Funds in the 1970's. Washing-
    ton, D.C.: Federal Home Loan Bank Board, February 17, 1970.

"Ripple Effect: Home Building Slump Is Bringing Problems to Supplier Industries." Wall Street Journal, September 12, 1974,
p. 1.

Ritter, Lawrence S. "The Political Arithmetic of Reordered National
Priorities." Morgan Guaranty Survey, July 1971, p. 3.

Romania, Socialist Republic. Central Statistical Board. Statistical
Pocket Book of the Socialist Republic of Romania. Bucharest,
1970.

_____. Embassy. Doing Business with Romania: New Opportunities for U.S. Businessmen. Washington, D.C., 1971.

_____. Embassy. Office of the Economic Counselor. Trading with
Romania: A Guide for Businessmen. New York, n.d.

_____. Anaural Statistic. 2 vols. 1972, 1973.

Romania, Socialist Republic, and U.S. Government. Joint Statement,
Nicolae Ceausescu and Richard Nixon on Economic, Industrial
and Technological Cooperation Between the Socialist Republic
of Romania and the U.S. of America. Bucharest: Official Bulletin, Socialist Republic of Romania, December 1973.

"Romanian Bilateral Agreement." East West Markets—Chase World
Information, January 27, 1975, p. 3.

Romanian News Agency. Romania Documents-Events, no. 44. Bucharest, November 1972.

_____. Romania Documents-Events, no. 5. Bucharest, January
1974.

Rudley, F. W., and F. G. S. Chisholm. "Romania." Europe. Edited by Andrew C. Ramsay. London: Edward Stanford, 1885,
p. 522.

Sfintesco, Cincinat. "Roumania," in Bruno Schwan. Stadtebau und
Wohnungswesen der Welt—Town Planning and Housing Throughout the World—L'Urbanisme et L'Habitation dans Tous les Pays.
Berlin: Verlag Ernst Wasmuth G.M.B.H., 1935, p. 350.

234 MANDATORY HOUSING FINANCE PROGRAMS

Sheehan, Edward R. G. "Europe's Hired Poor: The Immigres Do What the French Won't." New York Times Magazine, December 9, 1973, p. 36.

Smith, Wallace F. "How to Stretch a Tatami." Journal of the American Institute of Planners 34 (November 1968): 389.

Starr, Roger. "America's Housing Challenge." New Leader, vol. 57 (September 30, 1974).

"State Housing Finance Agencies in the United States: A Comparative Analysis." Rutgers University Seminar in Urban Planning, January 1972.

State of New Jersey, Department of Community Affairs. Fifth Annual Report Fiscal Year 1972.

Strassmann, W. Paul. "The Construction Sector in Economic Development." Scottish Journal of Political Economy 17 (November 1970), p. 391.

Sweet, Morris L. Industrial Development in New York City. New York City Housing and Redevelopment Board, Bureau of Planning and Program Research Report No. 10, May 1964.

_____. "The Role of Tax Exemption in Industrial Development." Area Development 14 (February 1967), p. 36.

_____. "State and Local Government Loans for Industrial Development." The Journal of Business (Seton Hall University) 6 (December 1967): 13.

_____, and Finn B. Jensen. "The Planned Community." National Civic Review 51 (May 1962), in S. George Walters, Morris L. Sweet, and Max D. Snider. Marketing Management Viewpoints: Commentary and Readings. 2d ed. Cincinnati: South-Western Publishing Company, 1970, p. 71.

Taggart III, Robert. Low Income Housing: A Critique of Federal Aid. Baltimore: The Johns Hopkins Press, 1970.

"Tax Exempts: Missouri Agency's Bond Offer Spotlights States' Efforts to Bolster Housing Market." Wall Street Journal, October 28, 1974, p. 15.

"The Ripple Effect: When Housing Booms, So Do Grass Seed, Art, Toilets, Rugs and Frit." Wall Street Journal, May 25, 1972, p. 1.

The Tenth Congress of the League of Communists of Yugoslavia. Basic Results of Economic and Social Development in Yugoslavia 1947-1972.

UN Department of Economic and Social Affairs. Compendium of Housing Statistics—1971 (ST/STAT/SER. N/1), 1974.

UN Economic and Social Council, Commission for Social Development. World Social Situation, 1974 Report, pt. 2, Sectoral Developments, Housing, September 24, 1974.

U.S. Congress, House, Committee on Banking and Currency. Sixth Annual Report on Housing Goals. 94th Cong., 1st sess., January 14, 1975, H. Doc. 94-18.

_____, Subcommittee on Housing. Compilation of the Housing and Community Development Act of 1974. 93rd Cong., 2d sess. Washington, D.C.: Government Printing Office, October 1974.

U.S. Congress, Joint Economic Committee. Housing Subsidies. Compendium of Papers. 92d Cong., 2d sess. Washington, D.C.: Government Printing Office, October 9, 1972.

_____. Soviet Economic Prospects for the Seventies. 93rd Cong., 1st sess. Washington, D.C.: Government Printing Office, June 27, 1973.

_____, Subcommittee on Inter-American Relationships. Thrift Institution Development in Latin America. Staff Study. 91st Cong., 2d sess. Washington, D.C.: Government Printing Office, June 4, 1970.

_____, Subcommittee on Priorities and Economy in Government. Benefit-Cost Analysis of Federal Programs. Compendium of Papers. 92d Cong., 2d sess. Washington, D.C.: Government Printing Office, October 9, 1972.

U.S. Congress, Senate, Committee on Banking, Housing and Urban Affairs. An Analysis of the Section 235 and 236 Programs. Prepared by Congressional Research Service, Library of Congress. 93rd Cong., 1st sess. Washington, D.C.: Government Printing Office, May 24, 1973.

U.S. Council on Environmental Quality, Department of Housing and Urban Development and Environmental Protection Agency. The Costs of Sprawl. Prepared by Real Estate Research Corporation. Washington, D.C.: Government Printing Office, April 1974.

U.S. Department of the Army. USSR: Strategic Survey. DA Pamphlet 550-6. Washington, D.C.: Government Printing Office, 1969.

U.S. Department of Commerce, Bureau of International Commerce, Overseas Business Report. "Brazilian Income Tax Legislation." OBR-67-26. Washington, D.C.: Government Printing Office, May 1967.

U.S. Department of Health, Education and Welfare, Social Security Administration. Slums and Social Insecurity. Prepared by Alvin Schorr. Research Report, no. 1. Washington, D.C.: Government Printing Office, 1963.

U.S. Department of Housing and Urban Development. "Housing in Spain." HUD International Brief, no. 19. Prepublication draft. Washington, D.C., 1973.

_____. Legislative History of Urban Renewal. Prepared by Real Estate Research Corporation. Springfield, Va.: Department of Commerce, National Technical Information Service, January 1974.

_____. Low-Rent Housing—Guide-Orientation to the Program. HM G 7401.3. Washington, D.C., April 1971.

Wachtel, Howard. Workers' Management and Workers' Wages in Yugoslavia. Ithaca, N.Y.: Cornell University Press, 1973.

Walters, S. George. "Impact of East-West Trade on U.S. Business." Address, Joint Meeting, American Chemical Society and Industrial Engineers, Seton Hall University, East Orange, New Jersey, April 28, 1975.

_____. "Industry Investments and Raw Materials—A New Consumption Pattern." Paper presented at International Marketing Federation, Academy of Economic Studies, Bucharest, June 1974.

_____. "Institutional Constraints to U.S.-Romanian Trade and Invest-
ment." Briefing Paper prepared for U.S. Section, Romania-
U.S. Economic Council, Center for International Affairs, Washington, D.C., 1975.

_____. "Interfunctional Management: A New Dimension of Manage-
ment Education." In Middle Atlantic Association of Colleges of
Business Administration, Proceedings—New York University
Graduate School of Business Administration, Annual Meeting,
October 11 and 12, 1973. New York: New York University
Press, pp. 64-79.

_____. "Marketing Structure and Economic Development in Brazil."
Ph.D. dissertation, New York University, 1960.

_____. Planifigarea in Activitatea de Marketing. Bucharest: Acad-
emy of Economic Studies, 2d ed., 1974.

_____, and Eli Schwartz, directors. Economic Base Studies, Summit,
Medina, Portage Counties, Ohio. Tri-County Regional Planning
Commission, Akron, Ohio, 1960.

_____, and Morris L. Sweet, with the assistance of Robert J. Cork-
hill. "A New Technique for Determining the Relationship Between Consumer Expenditure Patterns and Land Values." Prepared for Testimony of H. S. Campbell Associates, Bethlehem,
Pa., 1960.

_____, Morris L. Sweet, and Max D. Snider. Marketing Management
Viewpoints: Commentary and Readings. 2d ed. Cincinnati:
South-Western Publishing Co., 1970, pp. iii-iv.

_____. "When Industry Moves to Interurbia." Sales Management,
vol. 82 (February 20, 1959), in S. George Walters, Morris L.
Sweet, and Max D. Snider. Marketing Management Viewpoints:
Commentary and Readings. 2d ed. Cincinnati: South-Western
Publishing Company, 1970, p. 89.

Walters, S. Z. "Is There Any Benefit in Cost-Benefit Analysis?"
Greater London Council. GLC Intelligence Unit Quarterly Bulletin, no. 21 (December 1972), p. 5.

Waterston, Albert. Planning in Yugoslavia: Organization and Implementation. Baltimore: The Johns Hopkins Press, 1961.

Wendt, Paul F. "The Determination of National Housing Policies."
    Land Economics 45 (August 1969): 323.

_____, and Eric Carlson. "Spain's Housing Policy: An Evaluation of
    the National Housing Plan, 1961-1976." Land Economics 39
    (February 1963): 62.

Wool, Harold. "What's Wrong with Work in America?—A Review Es-
    say." Reprint 2868. U.S. Department of Labor, Bureau of
    Labor Statistics. Monthly Labor Review, March 1973, p. 38.

"Yugoslavia." Pratt Planning Papers (March 1972).

Zamfir, Alexander, and Dan Floru. Elemente de Marketing Interna-
    tional. Bucharest: Editura Academiei Republicii Socialiste
    Romania, 1974.

22, 71, 72, 165, 170, 176, 177,
178, 179, 181, 190, 195, 205,
206, 208, 212, 213, 215, 216;
Housing and Urban Development
Act (1968), 170; Housing Bill of
1970, 176; Housing Corporation,
193; housing fund proposals, 185-
87, 189-90; housing in, 3, 5, 11-
12, 71; housing investment, need
for more in, 12-14, 18-28, 177-
79, 219; housing program incon-
sistent, 97; housing rehabilitation, 41; industry purchase of
public agency housing securities,
207-08, 214; insufficiency of decent housing, 175-76; interest
subsidy programs, 172-73; lack
of housing data in, 5-6, 10-11,
16-17; Lanham Act (1940), 194;
management, need of, in housing
programs, 221-22; mandatory financing in, 10; mandatory programs, possible approaches to,
196-215; mandatory programs,
pros and cons, 218-23; modified
permanent employment, 143;
Mortgage Housing Act, 194; national economy, effects of residential construction on, 19-22, 218;
National Housing Act (1934), 167,
194; National Recovery Act, 168;
President's Committee on Urban
Housing, 29; President's Conference on Inflation, 31; programs
for civilian war and defense workers, 193-94; public versus private
housing, 145; ratio of fringe to
payroll costs, 74; required investment in housing, 180-82; social
security, acceptance of, 79; social security funds for housing,
89; subsidized housing, cost ceilings for, 201; subsidized housing,
moratorium on, 20-21; Tandem
Plan, 170; U.S. Housing Act
(1937), 168, 193; Veterans Administration (VA), 169, 181

urban sprawl, 27
Urquidi, Victor L., 105
"useful housing solution," 12

Veterans Administration (VA),
169, 181
Vienna, Austria, 128
Village of Euclid v. The Ambler
Realty Co., 197
Vittorini, Marcello, 80, 81
Von de Muhll, Celia, 59

Walkley, Rosabelle P., 31
Wall Street Journal, 173
Walters, S. George, 29, 82, 138
Warsaw, Poland, 30
Warsaw Pact, 114
Washington, D.C., 127, 193
Watson, Cicely, 59
Welfeld, Irving H., 60
Wendt, Paul F., 64-65, 80
West German Federal Holding Com-
pany, 76
Westchester County, N.Y., 204
Westchester Residential Opportu-
nities, Inc., 215
Wilner, Daniel M., 31
Wirtz, W. Willard, 187
Witherick, M. E., 165
Witney, Fred, 88
Wood, Courtney B., 31
Wood, Ramsay, 30
World Bank, 8
World Housing Survey: Report of
the Secretary General, 8, 11, 12,
28, 29
World Trade Institute Conference,
126
World War I, 193; II, 193

Yoshino, M. Y., 164
Yugoslavia, 106-112, 211, 223;
communes, 108; Economic Reform Act (1965), 111; Federal
Executive Council, 110; Federal
Social Plan (1955), 110; government assistance declining, 112;

ABOUT THE AUTHORS

MORRIS L. SWEET has been affiliated as a senior staff member with the New York City Housing and Development Administration and its predecessor agency since 1962 in a research and analysis capacity and is now a principal planner. Previously, he was connected with Lehigh University as a research assistant professor of business. He has been a consultant to public and private organizations and has completed studies on industrial, commercial, and residential development. His published work has appeared in books, monographs, and articles in professional and technical journals. His undergraduate work in economics was done at Rutgers University, and he received an M.B.A. from New York University. He has done additional graduate work in economics, public administration, and urban planning. He is a member of professional societies in the fields of economics, public administration, urban planning, housing, and international development.

S. GEORGE WALTERS is a Professor of the Graduate School of Business Administration and of the Graduate Faculty, Rutgers University. He holds a B.A. degree cum laude from Western Maryland College, a Master's Degree in International Economics, and an M.B.A. degree with distinction from Columbia University. His Ph.D. degree was awarded by the Institute of International Affairs and Area Studies, New York University, where he was a University Honors scholar. Professor Walters taught at Lehigh University for 10 years, and then entered the business world, doing project management work for the General Tire & Rubber Company and the Mobil Oil Corporation. His project management work included land development. He served as Chairman of the Plans Board, Chemical-Plastics Division at General Tire & Rubber, and Executive Vice-President and Director of Mobil Centers, a subsidiary of Mobil Oil. He is the author or coauthor of seven books, and 123 of his researches have been published. At Rutgers he is the Director of the Interfunctional Management Program and Director of the Romanian Program. He is President of S. G. Walters Associates, and serves as an adviser to federal and state agencies and business firms.

PUBLIC HOUSING AND URBAN RENEWAL: An Analysis of Federal-Local Relations
                    Richard D. Bingham

SOVIET URBAN HOUSING: Problems and Policies
                    Alfred John DiMaio, Jr.

HOUSING COSTS AND HOUSING NEEDS
                    edited by Alexander Greendale
                    Stanley F. Knock, Jr.

HOUSING MARKET PERFORMANCE IN THE UNITED STATES
                    Charles J. Stokes
                    Ernest M. Fisher

THE POLITICS OF HOUSING IN OLDER URBAN AREAS
                    edited by Robert E. Mendelson
                    Michael A. Quinn

HOUSING MARKETS AND CONGRESSIONAL GOALS
                    Ernest M. Fisher